INTERNATIONAL DISPUTE RESOLUTION
Volume 3

INTERNATIONAL DISPUTE RESOLUTION
Volume 3

The Role of Precedent

CARL BAUDENBACHER
SIMON PLANZER (Eds.)

www.germanlawpublishers.com
International Law Edition

ISBN 978-3-941389-08-3

The Deutsche Nationalbibliothek lists this publication in the Deutsche Nationalbibliografie; detailed bibliographic data are available on the Internet at http://dnb.d-nb.de.

© 2011 German Law Publishers, Stuttgart

All rights reserved. No part of this publication may be reproduced, translated, stored in a retrieval system or transmitted, in any form or by any means, electronic, mechanical, photocopying, recording or otherwise, without prior permission of the publisher.

Typesetting: GreenTomato GmbH, Stuttgart
Printing and binding: Beltz Bad Langensalza GmbH, Neustädter Straße 1–4, 99947 Bad Langensalza

Table of Contents

Preface	IX
Authors	XI
Moderators	XIII
Welcome CARL BAUDENBACHER	1
1st Panel **Precedent in Common and Civil Law**	7
Introduction FRANZ WERRO	9
Precedent in Switzerland MARKUS MÜLLER-CHEN	13
Precedent in Common and Civil Law RICHARD PLENDER	19
Cross-border Commitment to Precedents in European Civil Courts ILKA KLÖCKNER	27
Discussion	35
Keynote	37
The Doctrinal Paradox without Doctrine LAWRENCE SAGER	39
Discussion	47

2nd Panel
Precedent in Arbitration 51

Introduction 53
DANIEL HOCHSTRASSER

Precedent in International Arbitration 57
ALAN RAU

Costs in Investment Arbitration 65
SUSAN FRANCK

Discussion 73

Keynote 83

Precedent in International Trade Negotiations 85
CHRISTIAN ETTER

Discussion 93

3rd Panel
Precedent in European High Courts 101

Introduction 103
PAUL MAHONEY

Precedent in the Practice of the European Court of Human Rights 113
LUCIUS CAFLISCH

The Significance of "Precedent" in the Bilateral Agreements between Switzerland and the European Union 125
CHRISTINE KADDOUS

Precedents and Judicial Dialogue in European Union Law, Present and Future 141
JOHN TEMPLE LANG

Discussion 175

4th Panel
Precedent in WTO Law — 185

Introduction — 187
MICHAEL WAIBEL

The System of Precedent (or the Lack Thereof) at the WTO — 191
RACHEL BREWSTER

Introduction to Treaty Interpretation by the WTO Panels and Appelate Body — 199
AKIO SHIMIZU

Precedent in WTO – Zeroing Cases — 203
EDWIN VERMULST AND JUHI SUD

Discussion — 227

Closing Remarks — 231
CARL BAUDENBACHER

Preface

In October 2010, renowned authorities in the field of international dispute resolution from Europe, North America and Asia gathered in the beautiful, historic Parliament of the Canton of St.Gallen to discuss "The Role of Precedent in Dispute Resolution". While most observers associate precedent with common law and the *stare decisis* doctrine, some forms of precedent are nevertheless practiced in civil law jurisdictions and in international or supranational legal orders. It is a rather undefined role that precedent plays in international law and it may strongly vary from one legal order to another. The 3rd St.Gallen International Dispute Resolution Conference approached this subject in four panels: 1) "Common law and civil law", 2) "Arbitration", 3) "European High Courts" and 4) "The World Trade Organization". In addition, Dean SAGER and Ambassador ETTER offered keynote speeches dealing with the topic. The conference was chaired by the President of the EFTA Court, Professor Dr. CARL BAUDENBACHER, and was held in cooperation with the University of Texas School of Law.

After President BAUDENBACHER's welcoming speech, the first panel on the principles of precedent in both common and civil law was chaired by FRANZ WERRO. MARKUS MÜLLER-CHEN then dealt with the practice of precedent in Switzerland while ILKA KLÖCKNER discussed the cross-border implications in European civil courts. Finally, RICHARD PLENDER commented on precedent in both common and civil law. Dean LAWRENCE SAGER from the University of Texas School of Law then delivered the first keynote speech on the subject of the doctrinal paradox. DANIEL HOCHSTRASSER chaired the second panel in which SUSAN FRANCK and ALAN RAU offered an insight into the role of precedent in arbitration. Finally, CHRISTIAN ETTER, the Swiss government's delegate for trade agreements, held the second keynote speech of the day on the role of precedent in international trade negotiations.

The second day of the conference was opened by President PAUL MAHONEY from the European Union Civil Service Tribunal with introductory remarks to the panel on precedent in European High Courts. Former Judge LUCIUS CAFLISCH gave an insight into the case law of the European Court of Human Rights and JOHN TEMPLE LANG commented on the case law of the Court of Justice of the European Union. Finally, CHRISTINE KADDOUS spoke about the significance of precedent under the bilateral agreements between Switzerland and the European Union. After the break, MICHAEL WAIBEL presented the fourth panel on the role of precedent in WTO law where RACHEL BREWSTER gave an introduction to the system of precedent at the WTO. AKIO SHIMIZU followed with his speech about the treaty interpretation by the WTO panels and the Appellate Body. JUHI SUD concluded the fourth panel with her contribution about WTO precedent in zeroing cases. A roundup of the contributions and the final remarks of President BAUDENBACHER then closed the 3rd St.Gallen International Dispute Resolution Conference.

St.Gallen/Luxembourg, September 2011   *Carl Baudenbacher*
                                              Simon Planzer

Authors

PROF. RACHEL BREWSTER, PHD, Assistant Professor at Harvard Law School, Cambridge MA

PROF. LUCIUS CAFLISCH, Honorary Professor at the Graduate Institute of International and Development Studies, Geneva; Member of the United Nations International Law Commission, Geneva; Former Judge of the European Court of Human Rights, Strasbourg

AMBASSADOR DR. CHRISTIAN ETTER, Federal Council Delegate for Trade Agreements, Swiss State Secretariat for Economic Affairs (SECO), Berne

PROF. SUSAN FRANCK, LL.M., Associate Professor at the Washington and Lee University School of Law, Lexington VA

PROF. DR. CHRISTINE KADDOUS, LL.M., Professor and Jean Monnet Chair at the University of Geneva, Geneva; Director of the Centre for European Legal Studies, Geneva

DR. ILKA KLÖCKNER, Lecturer (Maître de conférences associé) at the University of Paris 1 Panthéon-Sorbonne, Paris

JAMES LOFTIS, Partner at Vinson & Elkins, London/Houston; Adjunct Professor at the University of Texas at Austin School of Law, Austin TX

PROF. DR. MARKUS MÜLLER-CHEN, Professor at the University of St.Gallen, St.Gallen; Attorney-at-law, St.Gallen/Zurich

PROF. SIR RICHARD PLENDER, Professor at the Royal University of Groningen, Groningen; Former Justice of the High Court of England and Wales

PROF. ALAN RAU, Burg Family Professor at the University of Texas at Austin School of Law, Austin TX

DEAN LAWRENCE SAGER, Dean of the University of Texas at Austin School of Law and Dean John Jeffers Research Chair in Law, Austin TX

PROF. AKIO SHIMIZU, LL.M., Professor at Waseda Law School, Tokyo; WTO Panelist

JUHI SUD, LL.M., Vermulst Verhaeghe Graafsma & Bronckers, Brussels

PROF. DR. JOHN TEMPLE LANG, Cleary Gottlieb Steen & Hamilton, Brussels; Professor at Trinity College, Dublin; Senior Visiting Research Fellow at the University of Oxford, Oxford; Former Director in DG Competition of the European Commission

PROF. DR. FRANZ WERRO, LL.M., Professor at the University of Fribourg, Fribourg; Professor at the Georgetown University, Washington D.C.; Faculty Director of the Centre for Transnational Legal Studies, London

Moderators

PROF. DR. CARL BAUDENBACHER, President of the EFTA Court, Luxembourg; Professor at the University of St.Gallen, St.Gallen; Director of the Institute of European and International Business Law, St.Gallen

DANIEL HOCHSTRASSER, LL.M., Partner at Bär & Karrer, Zurich

PAUL MAHONEY, President of the European Union Civil Service Tribunal, Luxembourg; Former Registrar of the European Court of Human Rights

DR. MICHAEL WAIBEL, LL.M., Postdoctoral Fellow at the University of Cambridge Lauterpacht Centre for International Law, Cambridge

Welcome

CARL BAUDENBACHER

I. General

The notion of precedent stems from the common law. One may even say that it is one of its cornerstones. I am not a representative of the common law tradition, but rather an interested observer. According to my observations, precedent can be described as a decision of a court (of law) which establishes a rule that another court may or must use when deciding subsequent cases involving the same or similar facts or issues.

In a system which is essentially based on case law the doctrine of precedent is a priori of higher relevance than in a system based on codification. Many people, therefore, think that there is a clear boundary between civil and common law systems. I am not sure whether that is true. The starting points certainly differ, but in times of globalization the problems of life, which the law must resolve, become more and more similar. Examples would be the protection of human rights, the protection of the environment and of the climate, but also certain fields of economic law such as antitrust, corporate governance, accounting standards or intellectual property law. Moreover, it seems that there is convergence between the two systems with regard to the significance of codification on the one hand and of judicial lawmaking on the other. Common law systems do not rely solely on case law anymore, they increasingly rely on statutory law whereas in civil law systems case law is gaining ground as an important source of law.

II. Common Law

American and British lawyers will think of the *stare decisis* doctrine when speaking about precedent. Under this doctrine, a *lower court* must follow the findings made by a higher court which has jurisdiction in the respective territory. However, the binding force of precedent only extends to the ratio decidendi, not to the obiter dicta. The notion of ratio decidendi describes the reason for the decision of the case whereas obiter dicta are peripheral statements. By definition, rulings of lower courts are not binding on higher courts. Higher court rulings are on the other hand not binding on lower courts in a different territory, but may constitute persuasive authority.

It is said that courts must also follow their *own precedents*. However, this is not an absolute obligation. Own findings made earlier in other cases must be honored unless there is a strong reason to change the respective rulings. As US Supreme Court Justice Anthony Kennedy put it:

> "Our precedents are not sacrosanct, for we have overruled prior decisions where the necessity and propriety of doing so has been established ... Nonetheless, we have held that any departure from the doctrine of stare decisis demands special justification" (majority opinion in Patterson vs. McLean Credit Union, 491 U.S. 164).

It is the court itself which decides on whether the requirements of necessity and propriety are fulfilled in a given case. As experience shows, that decision may be taken by a slim majority. In the UK, the House of Lords (now: Supreme Court) declared in 1966 in the so-called Practice Statement that it would henceforth be free, in some circumstances, to overrule its own decisions. It thereby departed from its 1898 London Tramways judgement where Lord Halsbury stated:

> "I am prepared to say that I adhere in terms to what has been said [by other Law Lords] that a decision of this House once given upon a point of law is conclusive upon this House afterwards, and that it is impossible to raise that question again as if it [had never been decided] and could be reargued, and so the House be asked to reverse its own decision. That is a principle which has been, I believe, without any real decision to the contrary, established now for some centuries, and I am therefore of opinion that in this case it is not competent for us to rehear and for counsel to reargue a question which has been recently decided." ([1989] AC 375)

It cannot really surprise that before 1966 the House of Lords had used the technique of distinguishing in order to overrule previous decisions on a couple of occasions.

III. Civil Law

Whether a doctrine of precedent also exists in continental Europe may be debated. It seems that for instance German legal theory assumes that the decisions of the highest courts are not binding on the lower courts. In practice, however, precedents of higher courts will be respected by lower courts. They are deemed to be *de facto* binding, but the system is not as sophisticated as in the common law countries. It appears to be based in particular on the extrajudicial framework conditions of judging. To give an example: A judge's career may depend on his or her compliance with precedent; a judge who is up in arms against the higher courts too often may not be promoted.

The system, therefore, is, on its face, conservative. If taken strictly, it could lead to the judge being the slave to the past and the despot of the future, bound by the rulings of his dead predecessors and binding the rulings of his successors (A.L. Goodhart). At the same time, adherence to precedent is said to serve goals such as clarity, stability and predictability of the law, efficiency, legitimacy, fairness and impartiality.

In reality, progressive and inventive judges may sit on the bench of the lower courts. They are, at least on the European continent, in most cases younger than their colleagues from the higher courts. The question, therefore, arises what a lower court judge should do if he or she disagrees with a higher court precedent on a certain issue. Under the national rules of probably every country, the lower court judge must rule according to precedent. Until the higher court or the legislature changes the rule, the precedent remains authoritative.

IV. EU and EEA Courts

A. ECJ

1. Acte Éclairé

That there is a system of precedent in EU law follows from the case law of the ECJ concerning the obligation of national courts of last resort to refer cases involving questions of the interpretation of EU law.

According to Article 267 (3) TFEU, national courts against whose decision there is no judicial remedy are legally obliged to make a reference to the ECJ. According to the ECJ's *CILFIT* judgement (Case C-283/81), a national court within the meaning of that provision must not seek a preliminary ruling if

(a) the question of EU law is irrelevant;

(b) the EU law provision at stake has already been interpreted by the ECJ; and

(c) the correct application of EU law is so obvious as to leave no scope for any reasonable doubt.

One will not overlook that, as early as 1963, the ECJ held in *Da Costa* (Cases 28-30/62) that

> "[t]he questions of interpretation posed in this case are identical with those settled ... [in Case 26/62 van Gend en Loos] and no new factor has been presented to the Court. In these circumstances, the ... [national court] must be referred to the previous judgement."

With this, a system of precedent has been established. The ECJ has made its judgements similar to precedents in federal systems.

2. ECJ's Own Precedents

The ECJ has been making reference to its own precedents since 1973 when the common law countries United Kingdom and Ireland became Member States. Before, no such references were made. It seems, however, that the ECJ does not first and foremost rely on its previous decisions because it feels bound by them. One has the feeling that citing existing case law rather serves to show continuity and consistency. Moreover, reference to previous rulings may allow the Court to shorten its (already scant) reasons. In any case, the ECJ would never accept a formal doctrine of precedent as a basis for its work. Its approach resembles the one used in many civil law countries.

A number of observers believe that the distinction between ratio decidendi and obiter dictum is unknown to the ECJ. I am not sure whether this is correct. The ECJ (as well as the EFTA Court) may address issues which are not strictly necessary in order to buttress a judgement and national courts will feel bound by such considerations to a lesser extent.

There is no technique of distinguishing and of *overruling* in the ECJ's jurisprudence that could be compared to what happens in common law systems. There are only few cases in which the ECJ openly overruled a precedent. Examples are the *Hag II* case in trademark law (Case C-10/89) and the *Keck and Mithouard* judgement concerning the law of free movement of goods (Joined Cases C-267/91 and C-268/91). In most cases, overruling occurs in a covert way and commentators may even disagree on whether it has actually taken place or not. An example would be the case law on the succession of functions and the succession of contracts under the Transfer of Undertakings Directive.

3. Lower Courts Challenging Supreme Courts' Case Law by Way of Making a Reference to the ECJ

As mentioned, lower courts in the EU and in the EEA/EFTA Member States are *de facto* bound by the proclamations of the highest courts. In the UK and in Ireland, there is even a system of precedent stricto sensu. The Article 267 TFEU preliminary ruling procedure allows, however, for an important exception to that rule. Article 267 gives any court or tribunal of a Member State the right to request the ECJ to render a preliminary ruling on a question of EU law. Article 34 of the Agreement of the EFTA states on the Establishment of a Surveillance Authority and a Court of Justice (SCA) contains a similar rule. These provisions give lower courts the possibility to challenge their own supreme courts' case law which they deem not to be in conformity with EU or EEA law by way of seizing to the ECJ or the EFTA Court. Once the ECJ or the EFTA Court have rendered the judgement, the referring court is bound to follow it. Example: The Liechtenstein security of cost saga.

4. General Court Deviating from ECJ Precedent

With the establishment of the General Court in 1989 (formerly Court of First Instance), an appeal system has been introduced in the EU. As in every appeal system, the lower court is supposed to follow the precedents set by the upper court.

In an important case, the General Court has not lived up to this expectation. In case T-177/01 *Jégo-Quéré*, the General Court, referring to the Opinion of AG Jacobs in case C-50/00 P *Pequeños Agricultores*, defined locus standi in nullity actions in a much broader way than what the ECJ had done in the past. The ECJ rejected AG Jacob's proposal and stuck to its previous case law. The Lisbon Treaty has at least partly amended the provision in question (Article 263 (3) TFEU).

B. Homogeneity Rules in Agreements with Third Countries

The EU has concluded many treaties with third countries which may be characterized as extension agreements. EU law is made part of the agreements themselves and in certain cases of the domestic law of the partnering countries. The law of the EU and the law of the agreements is, therefore, identical in substance. The most important of these contracts is the Agreement on the European Economic Area (EEA), the only extension agreement which has allowed the associated states to have their own court, the EFTA Court.

Although the EEA legal order is a separate legal order, the EFTA Court is under Article 6 EEA Agreement and Article 3 (2) of the SCA bound to follow or to take into account ECJ case law. The EFTA Court has always complied with these obligations. It has, however, in a number of high-profile cases, given reasons that differ from those used by the ECJ. Former ECJ judge and chamber president *Christiaan Timmermans* has aptly called that "creative homogeneity".

The ECJ, for its part, has in certain cases followed EFTA Court case law which addressed a fresh legal question. That case law constitutes some sort of persuasive authority.

C. EFTA Court

EFTA Court decisions in preliminary reference cases are, according to the wording of Article 34 SCA, not binding on the referring court. They are nevertheless indirectly binding because if a national court were to refuse compliance, it would bring its own Member State into a state of violation of the EEA Agreement which could lead to the EFTA Surveillance Authority bringing an infringement action to the EFTA Court.

In the early years of the Court's existence, the judges decided to make systematic reference to own precedent.

V. European Court Of Human Rights

National courts are deemed to be bound to follow the rulings of the European Court of Human Rights. However, compliance has sometimes been a problem.

The European Court of Human Rights will not easily deviate from its own precedents. It has been said that the Court will embed judgements in existing case law in particular in politically sensitive cases.

VI. WTO Panels and Appellate Body

According to widespread belief, there is no precedent system in the WTO Dispute Settlement Mechanism. It seems, however, that in reality precedent plays an important role. It cannot be overlooked in this context that the drafters wanted to set up a system which would provide certainty and predictability.

VII. International Arbitration Tribunals

Commercial arbitrators are said to work without the stare decisis doctrine. I am not sure whether this is true. In my experience, German or Swiss arbitrators would carefully observe the case law of their Supreme Courts. In international investment arbitration, a system of precedent seems to be emerging.

1st Panel
Precedent in Common and Civil Law

Introduction

FRANZ WERRO

Our panel certainly deals with one of the most interesting topics in jurisprudence. This is the case because it addresses fundamental questions about the essence of law and lawmaking. It also seems to be at the heart of a fundamental difference between the common law and the civil law systems. I will not question this difference, but I would like to take the opportunity of chairing this panel to nuance it in some ways. While judges of both systems clearly do not relate to precedents in the same manner, one can show some convergence between the two approaches. My overall claim is that it is not conceivable to imagine the rule of law in a place where courts would not adhere to their precedents.

Let me begin by some references to the differences. One thing one can say is that the French Revolution did not happen in England. The idea that law should be codified and stated in abstract and general propositions that would help judges to find appropriate rules in concrete cases found its legitimacy in the enlightenment philosophy and in the enterprise of rationalisation of the law that took place at the time of the French Revolution and then grew throughout the 19th century. Things were definitely different in England. Now, whether that process of rationalisation of the law, linked to the hope that the parliament would ultimately control the content of the law, and whether that enterprise took place in the same way throughout the continent, is, of course, a subject in its own right. Without going into details, I think it is safe to say that German lawyers do not deal with written law and precedents in the same way as the French do. The relation that lawyers do have to written law differs from one place to the other, just as much as the relation to precedents changes from one common law jurisdiction to the other. The doctrine of stare decisis in the United States is different from what it is in the United Kingdom. Even lawyers within the same country often have a different understanding of the role of precedents. I do not think that Professor Meier-Hayoz understood the role of written statutes as Eugen Huber did. Still today, you will find lawyers who think, like Portalis did, that a civil code merely contains principles that should enable the judge to find concrete rules, and others who think that written law should be as precise as possible, and restrict the law making power of the judge.

Be that as it may, it is quite true that common law lawyers do take precedents more seriously than their civil law colleagues. In the same vein, judges in the civil law tradition operate or at least do as if they operated in the shadow of statutes and of legislative propositions in a way that does not resemble the way in which the common lawyers operate. I am tempted to add that this is one reason why a common law judgement is infinitely more interesting to read than a civil law judgement. Common law judgements cut in the flesh of things with little respect for the law as a "system" that is so worshiped in the civil law tradition. As a consequence, judgements do not have the same soporific effect that civilian law judgements have. It remains part of the civil law lawyers' genes to believe in doctrinal truth and in a system of law that would exist independently of what judges have to say in applying it. The importance of "Professorenrecht" in the civil law system is certainly unique. The idea that what professors have to say about a judgement ends up being more important than what the judgement actually says is also quite foreign to the spirit of the common law. As a result, a common law judgement is, in comparison to a civil law judgement, often refreshingly close to life and more interesting, as it actually copes with the facts and the dispute without pretending to match an abstract notion with a conceptual truth.

Let me come to some converging aspects between the two systems. First of all, while it certainly took time until the common law world accepted the notion that law could be taught at a university, it seems to me that by now lawyers in both systems accept the notion or believe in the fact that lawyers must be trained; if not scholarly, at least in some kind of academic way. On both sides of the Channel and of the Atlantic, they are governed by the notion that lawyers are professionals. Lawyers are not just politicians and they are not priests either. Lawyers are trained professionally and they operate according to certain rules and to certain ways of reasoning that are distinctive of a certain discipline. It seems to me that in both traditions, lawyers are extremely interested in making distinctions, in adopting reasoning that is verifiable and reproducible. In both traditions lawyers are interested in some legal certainty and predictability. Lawyers want to know the cost of a given transaction and they will be able to make a judgement about that if they know what the law is. So, coming back to the first point I was making, I think that lawyers are equally interested in both systems, in what they call the rule of law. The rule of law cannot operate in a system where courts would be free to decide what they want. How could a lower court successfully decide something without being challenged by the losing party who will appeal the decision because it is not in line with the precedent that has been set forth by the Supreme Court? Likewise, highest courts will also feel that they are responsible for what they have decided, and they will most often not change their minds without having an important reason to do so and without wanting to explain it. Now, probably there are various ways of openly recognising that one is changing one's mind; it is true that the civilian courts are not good at doing that very clearly. They often pretend to stick to the law as it was decided before, even if, in fact, they are changing it. It is interesting to count those decisions that are labelled as changes of precedents, compared to those that actually are such changes, but that are not signalled as such.

As already mentioned, civilians are much less sophisticated than their common law colleagues when it comes to deal with precedents. Civilians do not know, for instance, what a prospective overruling is. Civilians do not have such doctrinal techniques for distinguishing precedents. However, and this is the second point that I want to make, I wonder if the difference between the two legal traditions is not ultimately a question of rhetoric and ideology, rather than one of substance. At the time of the French Revolution, the judges were puppets in the hands of the king and they had acquired an awful reputation. The rule of law had to find tools in France to keep them in line and to make sure that the people's will would ultimately be respected. But just as it is a slogan to say that a statute is written in a style that the people understand, the proclaimed subordination of judges to written law is an instrument of propaganda and of rhetoric.

Professor Ehrenzweig was onto something important when he wrote in "Psychoanalytic Jurisprudence" that a civilian believes in a judgement if it refers to a statute, whereas the common law lawyer considers the existence of a statute when a judge applies it. This opposition should not hide the fact that both are seeking justice in a given situation. Accordingly, it could be that, despite differences in style and rhetoric in the civil law and the common law traditions, litigating lawyers end up doing much of the same work when they try to give meaning to precedents.

I would like to say a few words about my distinguished speakers. I will start with Dr. Klöckner who seems to me, as I read her biography, is a true European: After having received her entire education in Germany, she now teaches in France at Paris 1. She has written extensively about the subject that she is going to deal with today, the binding effect of precedents in cross-border settings. Professor Müller-Chen, who practices law as an attorney, is also a full professor at the University of St.Gallen, where he teaches private and commercial law as well as comparative law. I know him from many of his writings, e.g. his interesting case book on comparative law. I finally have the pleasure of introducing you to Professor Richard Plender, who is a former Justice of the High Court of England and Wales and currently a professor of European and Business Law at the Royal University of Groningen. He is going to talk to us about "Precedent in Common and Civil Law".

Precedent in Switzerland

MARKUS MÜLLER-CHEN

Introduction

I was asked to speak about the role of precedents in the area of private and commercial law in Swiss Courts. This means that I will not talk about precedents in criminal or public law cases.

We need to have a basic knowledge of the judicial system of Switzerland to understand the role that precedents play. After reviewing the judicial system we will look into the role, significance, effects and limits of precedents and end with the question of a court's right to depart from its own precedents.

Swiss Judicial System

Switzerland is a federal state with 26 cantons. However, unlike the US, we do not have a federal and a state court system. The courts of first and second instance are cantonal and there is only one Supreme Court, the Federal Supreme Court. Currently civil procedure is mainly cantonal law. This means that Switzerland has 26 procedural statutes plus one for the Federal Supreme Court. This will change as of 1 January 2011 when the Federal Civil Procedure Act (FCPA) will come into force. For practical purposes I will only consider the new FCPA.

Cases concerning private law must, as a general rule, first go through a conciliation proceeding (Art. 197 FCPA). There are exceptions, notably for commercial cases (Art. 199 FCPA). If the parties do not settle their case at that stage (Art. 209 FCPA), the claim will be adjudicated by a court of first instance (Art. 219 ff. FCPA), which is called differently in different cantons (district courts, civil courts etc.). Four cantons (AG, ZH, SG, BE) have specialised courts for commercial cases as the only instance.

The decisions of the civil or commercial courts can be appealed if the litigious amount is at least CHF 10.000 (Art. 308 (2) FCPA). The organisation of the appeal courts is a matter of cantonal law.

Lastly civil and commercial cases can be appealed to the Federal Supreme Court, if the litigious amount is not less than CHF 30.000 (Art. 72 (1) Federal Law on the Supreme Court, FLSC). If the litigious amount is less than that, the federal appeal is only admissable if the case poses a question of law of fundamental significance ("Rechtsfrage von grundsätzlicher Bedeutung", Art. 72 (2a) FLSC). The Supreme Court only examines questions of law.

The Swiss Supreme Court has seven chambers: two dealing with private and commercial cases, two for public and administrative law cases, one criminal chamber and two chambers dealing with social insurance cases. It has two seats: one in Lausanne and one in Lucerne. There are currently 38 Supreme Court Judges, 127 clerks that draft and write most of the decisions and also 19 judges that sit in addition to other day time jobs (professors, attorneys, judges from cantonal appeal courts etc.). This poses special problems in relation to precedents. We will come back to that.

The organisation of the judicial system influences and limits the use of precedents in Switzerland. The lower courts can relatively safely deviate from precedents if the litiguous amount is less than CHF 10.000, because in these cases there is in principle no appeal to the cantonal appeal courts. If the amount is between CHF 10.000 and 30.000 there is no appeal to the Federal Supreme Court save the case of a fundamental question of law.

Let me give you a recent example to illustrate this: The Swiss Code of Obligations (CO) states that a mandate, i.e. the contract between an attorney and his client, can be terminated at any time (Art. 404 CO). According to a long established, but disputed line of cases of the Federal Supreme Court this Art. 404 CO is mandatory: The parties are not allowed to contractually derogate from it. The rationale behind this is that a special relationship is the foundation of a typical mandate contract. The problem is that Art. 404 CO is also applied to atypical mandate contracts, e.g. outsourcing contracts, where the parties make large investments and no special trust is involved; they are purely commercial. Many lower courts oppose the interpretation of the Supreme Court that Art. 404 CO is mandatory. So one court decided the question differently and ruled that in atypical mandates the parties are not free to "hire and fire". Since the litiguous amount was less than CHF 30.000 there was no regular appeal. The only possibility was to argue that a fundamental question of law was involved. What happened? The Supreme Court did not accept the case with the somehow strange reasoning that it is not a fundamental question of law since its own case law is clear and unambiguous – so there is no reason to review the case. This, of course, produced the curious effect that the ruling of the lower court, which is in contradiction to the Supreme Court case law, was indirectly confirmed.

Role, Significance and Effects of Precedents in Switzerland

I like to point out that Swiss Law contains a classic and classy, but sometimes overlooked, provision which addresses the issue of precedents. Art. 1 of the Civil Code (CC) is a provision that is directed towards the courts and tells them how to decide cases. It states that *"the law applies according to its wording or interpretation to all legal questions in respect of which it contains a provision. In the absence of a provision, the court decides in accordance with customary law, in absence of customary law, in accordance with the rule which it would make as a legislator"*. In other words: The courts are first and foremost bound by the statutes, codes etc. Only if there is no answer found therein, the court is advised to turn to customary law and is in the last resort allowed to formulate a general rule modo legislatoris. Art. 1 CC furthermore instructs the courts to *"follow established doctrine and case law"* when interpreting the statutes and finding the right rule.

What does that mean?

- Firstly, it seems from the wording that established doctrine and case law are put on the same level – but this is deceiving. It is recognised that the established doctrine is, compared to precedents, a source of minor importance.

- Secondly, the legal doctrine and the judicial precedents are established if they are materially convincing, reasonable and practicable.

- It is thirdly undisputed that a lower court is at least factually bound by precedents if they are convincing and reasonable (majority opinion in Germany: see Sebastian Schalk, Deutsche Präjudizien und spanische "Jurisprudencia" des Zivilrechts (Frankfurt a. M., 2009), p. 251 ff. w.f.r.; Alexy/Dreier, Precedent in the Federal Republic of Germany, in: Interpreting Precedents, A comparative Study, MacCormick/Summers (ed.), Darthmouth 1997, p. 17, at p. 26 ff.; Ernst Kramer, Juristische Methodenlehre, 2nd ed. (Bern, 2005), p. 210). Thus, a lower court judge will in practice rarely deviate from established case law – or even from a singular decision. Additionally, courts use precedents in their reasoning the same way they use statutes.

However, the question remains if precedents are sources of law like statutes, thus having the same binding force. If that is the case, it would, of course, be mandatory for the lower courts to adhere to precedents. It would also have the effect that attorneys who advise their clients in contradiction of precedents would be liable for damages. A few authors indeed argue that precedents can be viewed as a source of law (Kramer, op. zit., p. 214 f.). But it seems to be the minority opinion (opposing view e.g. BK/Meier-Hayoz, Art. 1 recital 475). Be that as it may: It is a fact that Swiss Civil and Commercial Law is substantially made of case law which interprets, complements and even changes statutory laws and sometimes creates new rules (Hans Peter Walter, Die Sicht des Schweizerischen Bundesgerichts, in: Ehrenzeller/Gomez et al. (ed.), Präjudiz und Sprache (Zürich/St.Gallen, 2008), p. 127, at p. 134).

A Swiss judge is, therefore, called to take precedents into account. We see this also to a certain extent e.g. in Italy (Italian Supreme Court, Nr. 10741, 11. 5. 2009). On the other hand it goes without saying that a decision is not void if it does not follow a precedent of a higher court. Sometimes even the opposite effect can be observed: The Supreme Court is quite willing to take dissenting decisions of lower courts into consideration (Franz Hasenböhler, Richter und Gesetzgeber in der Schweiz, in: Frank Richard (ed.), Unabhängigkeit und Bindung des Richters in der Bundesrepublik Deutschland, in Österreich und in der Schweiz, ZSR Beiheft, 2nd ed. (Basel, 1997), p. 99, at p. 112).

Limits of the Doctrine of Precedents

We have already talked about some limits of the doctrine of precedents in Switzerland due to the organisation of the judiciary system and due to the fact that precedents are not sources of law in the formal sense. There are more factors that constrain precedents.

- Firstly, decisions of the Supreme Court do not contain a great deal of facts. They are mostly focused on the doctrine and application of the law. Often the facts and the law are not properly separated; they are mixed together which makes it hard to recognise if the respective fact is a given or if it is part of the legal argumentation (Heinz Aemisegger, Länderbericht Schweiz: Gedanken aus der Sicht eines Praktikers, in: Ehrenzeller/Gomez et al. (ed.), Präjudiz und Sprache (Zürich/St.Gallen, 2008), p. 171, at p. 173). This is important when we speak about precedents because it is often difficult to decide whether the rule contained in a certain Supreme Court decision fits the particular set of facts of another case. Additionally there is a certain danger resulting from the so called "Leitsatz", a sort of head note that is added to the Swiss Supreme Court decisions that are published in the official journal. Even though they are merely attempts to summarize the main points of the case in a few words, legal practice has a tendency to turn them into rules that seemingly have to be applied to other cases irrespective of the facts at hand. Thus the danger is that lower courts take the head notes and treat them as precedents irrespective of the concrete facts underlying the reasoning.

- Secondly, the frequent use of obiter dicta obscures the reasoning and distracts from the core of the decision, the ratio decidendi. There is a notable tendency in Supreme Court decisions to not only concisely answer the relevant and litiguous questions of the case but to elaborate over many, many pages on general doctrinal questions of law.

- Thirdly, the Supreme Court decisions are mostly written by the clerks which often use text blocks that are not uniform across the different chambers. This creates problems if a lower court is supposed to follow the "established" case law.

- Fourthly, the Supreme Court has two ways of publishing its decisions: A certain number, supposedly the "important" ones are published in the Official Supreme Court Series. The rest – which constitutes the vast number of decisions – are only published on the internet. It is not always clear why a decision is published in the official journal or only on the internet. In terms of precedents you can not simply rely on the official journal, because important rulings are sometimes "only" posted on the internet.

- Fifthly, as I have already said, the judicial organisation and the limits on the possibilities to appeal restrict the binding effects of precedents: If there is no claimant, or the claimant can not appeal due to procedural reasons, a decision that is in contradiction to a precedent will stand.

Departure from Precedents

The constitutional right to equal treatment under the law (Art. 8 (1) of the Constitution) requires that the Supreme Court observes its own precedents (BGE 1C-356/2009, 12.2.2010, E. 3.1.). However, it is admissable to depart from precedents, if there are serious and objective reasons and if *"the new solution better reflects the ratio legis, changed circumstances or altered legal views"* (BGE 5A-333/2009, 4.12.2009, E. 3; BGE 127 II 289, E. 3a; Kramer, op. cit., p. 251 ff.). The longer the current case law has been applied, the more weight these reasons have to carry (BGE 136 III 6, 6; BGE 135 II 78, 85; BGE 133 III 335, 338). The departure from a precedent must not just be the expression of a momentary fluctuation or a singular deviation. Rather it has to be a fundamental adjustment for all similar cases (BGE 2A-573/2002, 21.5.2003, E. 3.2; Reich/Uttinger, Praxisänderungen im Lichte der Rechtssicherheit und der Rechtsrichtigkeit, ZSR 129 (2010) I, p. 163, at p. 164 ff.). It has been said that there is a rebuttable presumption in favor of precedents (Kramer, op. cit., p. 254).

On the level of the Supreme Court I also like to point out Art. 23 FASC entitled *"departure from case law and precedent"*. It states the conditions that need to be fulfilled for one chamber to depart from a precedent set by another chamber. Art. 23 FASC is necessary because the Supreme Court has, as I mentioned before, seven chambers. It is clear that a certain amount of coordination is needed to guarantee a consistent case law. Art. 23 FASC assumes that the legal question at hand relates to the ratio decidendi and not only to an obiter dictum (BGG-Komm/Seiler, Art. 23 N 3).

According to Art. 23 (1) FASC a chamber of the Supreme Court is only allowed to depart from a precedent established by one or more of the other chambers, if two thirds of the Meeting of Justices of these other chambers agree. Their decision is binding. It is interesting to note that disregard of Art. 23 FASC does not establish a ground on which an appeal on issues of law can be based.

The new practice is to be applied immediately and in all pending proceedings (BGE 4A-161/2009, 8.6.2009, E. 2.2; BGE 135 II 78, 85; BGE 132 II 153, 159). There are exceptions, though they are more relevant to procedural questions than to matters of substantial civil and commercial law. If the departure from or clarification of the precedent e.g. relates to the calculation of time limits for filing an appeal and a party would suffer a detriment, it is allowed to rely on the old precedent (BGE 135 II 78, 85). It is disputed if a departure from precedents should have a retroactive effect; in tax matters the Supreme Court has a tendency to give the new case law such effect (see Reich/Uttinger, Praxisänderungen im Lichte der Rechtssicherheit und der Rechtsrichtigkeit, ZSR 129 (2010) I, p. 163, at p. 175 ff.). The effect "ex nunc et pro futuro" has been criticized as unjust. Instead it has been proposed that the Supreme Court should announce a departure from a precedent in an obiter dictum and thus "warn" the legal community (Kramer, op. cit., p. 256 f.).

I researched the Supreme Court decisions of the last 50 years that were published in the official journal and that concerned matters of civil and commercial law. I found 62 departures from precedents that were labelled as such of the published decisions. Of course, I might have missed one or the other, esp. because the Supreme Court had in some cases not published such decisions (e.g. Entscheid Anklagekammer v. 5.8.83, *Staatsanwaltschaft Kt. AG gg. Staatsanwaltschaft Kt. BS*, only cited 9 years later in BGE 118 IV 301) or the departure is disguised. A study conducted about 20 years ago shows that between 1875 and 1990 there were 731 departures from precedents, roughly 2.5 % of *all* the published decisions. Comparing these figures we can draw the conclusion that the Supreme Court is more willing to depart from precedents in the last decades than it used to be. This seems to be an interesting trend.

Conclusion

To sum up: It is safe to say that the courts in Switzerland respect and follow the ratio decidendi of precedents to a wide extent due to the rule in Art. 1 (3) CC. With the typical Swiss pragmatism they try to strike a balance between the advantages of the doctrine of precedents (certainty, consistency, predictability and uniformity of the law) and the necessity to decide every case on the merits and find a just and adequate solution with respect to the individual circumstances of the case at hand.

This concludes my remarks and I thank you for your attention.

Precedent in Common and Civil Law

RICHARD PLENDER[1]

In a speech delivered in London on 10 May 2009, Lord Neuberger, formerly a judge of the Supreme Court and now Master of the Rolls, gave voice to a concern perceived by several of the superior judges of England and Wales about the impact upon the common law of European law (both in the Convention on Human Rights and in the European Union). Lord Neuberger proposed that the European Court should adopt *"a more acute appreciation of the validity of the differential approaches taken by Convention states to the implementation of rights."*

We owe to Oliver Wendell Holmes the observation that the inspiration of the civil law is logic; that of the common law experience. In his words the common law *"embodies the story of a nation's development through many centuries, and it cannot be dealt with as if it contained only the axioms and corollaries of a book of mathematics."*

The source of the common law is not the command of the legislature but the customs of the people; identified by judges. To this day, for example, no English statute makes murder an offence. It is an offence against common law, since the custom of the realm has made it so from time immemorial.

Because the source of common law is custom, the common law attaches the greatest importance to precedent. It is, of course, a fact that customs change: so no modern judge would accept the account given by Blackstone in 1768 of the husband's right to inflict chastisement upon his wife. But save in exceptional cases, changes in custom are gradual; and a change in the common law does not come about by reason only of the fact that one judge differs with the opinion of another judge of equal jurisdiction. The former is expected to apply the judgement of the latter even if he disagrees with it. It is not a case, as in civilian jurisdictions, of merely taking account of precedent established by another judge. The common law concept of precedent imposes an obligation upon one judge to follow another judge's reasoning, even if the former judge disagrees with it.

---

1 Professor of European and Business Law, Royal University of Groningen, formerly Justice of the High Court of England and Wales.

It is also important that on a question of law there should be only one judicial interpretation of the customs of the realm; and this interpretation should be authoritative. From this it follows that each court is bound to follow decisions of superior courts. In an unusually trenchant judgement, Lord Hailsham, Lord Chancellor, said in *Cassell v. Broome:*

> "[I]t is not open to the Court of Appeal to give gratuitous advice to judges of first instance to ignore decisions of the House of Lords in this way and, if it were open to the Court of Appeal to do so, it would be highly undesirable ... The fact is, and I hope it will never be necessary to say so again, that, in the hierarchical system of courts which exists in this country, it is necessary for each lower tier, including the Court of Appeal, to accept loyally the decisions of the higher tiers."[2]

Precedent attaches, of course, to the reasoning of the judgement, the *ratio decidendi* including the identification and articulation of the law. It does not extend to comments made by the way, that is *obiter dicta*, which do not form part of the reasoning.

In recent years there has been some tendency in common law courts to adopt civilian notions that used to be foreign; and there has been a modest relaxation of the rules of precedent in the House of Lords. Lord Gardiner issued a practice statement in October 1966 stating that the House of Lords will in exceptional cases depart from its own previous decisions[3] (although it has not yet done so). The statement was an acknowledgement of the rapidity with which social change was coming about. All courts will, of course, fail to apply otherwise binding precedent when persuaded that the precedent was established by error. So in *Dixon v. British Broadcasting Corporation*[4] the Court of Appeal refused to follow its own decision on the ground that other relevant provisions which threw light on the words in question had not been brought to the attention of the court. Moreover, a judgement of a superior court will not be followed by an inferior one when the superior court's judgement is inconsistent with one of the European Court of Justice. See *ReMedicaments and Related Classes of Goods (No. 2) [2001]* CA.[5] Subject to these exceptions the principle remains that a precedent, once established, must be followed.

As I have observed, judges in common law jurisdictions are seldom well informed about the civil law, so it comes as a surprise to the common lawyers to read of European Courts departing without explanation from their own precedents. The European Court of Justice in *Dassonville*[6] gave a broad interpretation of Art. 28 (ex Article 30) of the Treaty of Rome to include all trade measures or trading rules enacted by the Member States which are capable of hindering,

---

2   *Cassell v. Broome*, [1972] 1 AC 1028.
3   *Practice Statement*, [1966] 1 WLR 1234.
4   [1979] ICR 281, CA (5 October 1978 – Lord Denning M.R., Shaw and Brandon L.JJ.)
5   [2001] ICR 564, [2002] 1 WLR 700, [2001] UKHL 67, [2002] 2 WLR 37, [2002] 2 AC 357, [2002] 1 All ER 465. This principle does not apply to decisions of superior courts which are contrary to decisions of the European Court of Human Rights: *K & Ors v. Lambeth Borough Council*, [2006] 2 AC 465 at paras 43–44 per Lord Bingham; applied in *GC & C v. Commissioner of Police of the Metropolis*, [2010] EWHC 2225 granting leave for a leapfrog appeal to the House of Lords.
6   Case 8/74 *Procureur du Roi v. Benoît and Gustave Dassonville* [1974] ECR 837.

directly or indirectly, actually or potentially, into community trade but in *Keck and Mithouard*[7], the same Court did not apply that formula to a non-discriminatory restriction. Since the judgement in *Köbler*,[8] an English court might even have considered that it would render the United Kingdom liable in damages if it failed to follow faithfully the *Dassonville* formula.

In May 2010 the Grand Chamber of the European Court of Human Rights granted Latvia's appeal against the chamber's ruling of 24 July 2008 that the conviction of the Soviet World War II veteran Kononov for the May 1944 killing of Latvian citizens suspected of collaboration with Nazis breached the Convention.[9] The chamber's judgement had been based on Article 7 of the European Convention of Human Rights, which prohibits retroactive punishment for crimes. The Grand Chamber's decision is, of course, far from a reversal of the earlier decision but it contemplates the possibility that there may be a reversal of precedent in a most important (and apparently clear) case. In the view of the Russian Parliament the upholding by the Strasbourg Court of Latvia's prosecution of Mr Kononov could lead to a "*change in the legal approaches to the evaluation of World War II events.*"

The perception that the European Courts do not apply the doctrine of precedent as rigorously as do the highest courts of the Member States is much to the disadvantage of the former courts. The European Court of Justice has not yet formally disclaimed its own judgement in Case C-338/91, *Emmott*, but in *Poole and Others v. HM Treasury*[10] a High Court judge sitting in London acted on the premise that *Emmott* is no longer good law. If the European Court of Justice shares that view, it may consider that the time has come to administer the *coup de grace* to *Emmott*.

Hitherto, I have identified some of the difficulties which, in my view, arise when civil or common lawyers, insufficiently familiar with each other's legal system, are confronted with issues of precedent. You are entitled to ask whether this really matters. I believe that at a time of European integration, entailing the superimposition of supreme courts in Luxembourg and in Strasbourg, such imperfections of understanding matter a great deal. Let me explain why I take that view, illustrating my reasons by decisions of the Court of Human Rights and the Court of Justice.

I take first the judgement of the European Court of Human Rights in *Application no. 7511/76, 7743/76 Campbell and Cosans v. United Kingdom*.[11] The case concerned the use of corporal punishment in schools, a subject which is controversial in several Member States of the Council of Europe.

Under Scottish law, the use of corporal punishment is controlled by the common law. Under that law an assault may give rise to a civil claim for damages or to prosecution for a criminal of-

---

7   Case C-267/91 and C-268/91 *Keck* [1993] ECR I-6097.
8   Case C-224/01 *Köbler* [2001] ECR I-10239.
9   Case 36376/04.
10 [2006] 2 CLC 865.
11 25 February 1982, Series A no 48.

fence. However, teachers in both state and other schools are, by virtue of their status as teachers, invested by the common law with power to administer such punishment in moderation as a disciplinary measure. The teacher's power of chastisement, like that of a parent, derives from his relationship with the children under his care and is not a power delegated by the state.

The applicants, Mrs Campbell and Mrs Cosans live in Scotland. Each of them had one child of compulsory school age at the time when they applied to the Commission. Mrs Campbell's son Gordon was attending a Roman Catholic Primary School in which corporal punishment is used for disciplinary purposes. For misconduct in class corporal punishment could be administered by a teacher who strikes the palm of the pupil's hand with a leather strap or tawse. Gordon was, in fact, never so punished whilst at that school but the Strathclyde Regional Council had refused Mrs Campbell's request for a guarantee that he would never be so punished.

Mrs Cosans' son Jeffrey used to attend a High School in Fife. He was told to report to the Assistant Headmaster to receive corporal punishment for having tried to take a prohibited short cut through a cemetery on his way home from school. On his father's advice, Jeffrey duly reported, but refused to accept the punishment. He was suspended from school. After three months he was readmitted to the school on the condition that he must accept the rules, regulations and disciplinary requirements of the school. His parents refused to accept those rules, maintaining that he should not be subject to corporal punishment. He never returned to school.

Mrs Campbell and Mrs Cosans maintained that the maintenance of corporal punishment in these circumstances constituted torture or inhuman and degrading treatment contrary to Article 3 of the Convention or a violation of Article 2 of the First Protocol to the Convention which provides that *"the State shall respect the right of parents to ensure ... education and teaching in conformity with their own religious and philosophical convictions."*

The Court found that no violation of Article 3 was established. This is not surprising since neither boy had in fact been subjected to any corporal punishment at any time.

The Court found, however, that there had been a violation of Article 2 of the First Protocol. It concluded that the two boys had been denied education in conformity with their parents' philosophical convictions. The difficulty with this reasoning is that there may be very strongly held beliefs on the processes by which schools seek to achieve their educational objectives, including the segregation of sexes, the streaming of pupils according to ability or the existence of independent schools. To characterise these issues as "philosophical" is to demand a result that is incapable of achievement, namely the right of each parent to demand that his own child shall be schooled in accordance with the parent's strongly-held belief, in the face of objections from other parents that their children shall be schooled in accordance with their contrary beliefs.

Had it looked for guidance in the common law, which applied in the first instance to the rights of the applicant parents against the schools, the Court would have found that the right to the instruction of a child in conformity with the parents' philosophy demands that the schools shall respect the parents' philosophical convictions *in the relation to the content of the information con-*

veyed and knowledge imparted. (I remind American colleagues present of the judgement of the Supreme Court in *Newdow v. United States Congress, Elk Grove Unified School District, et al.*)[12]

That interpretation would also have been consistent with the judgement of the European Court of Human Rights in *Kjeldsen, Busk Madsen and Pedersen*[13] where the Court itself said that:

> "The second sentence of Article 2 (P1-2) implies ... that the State, in fulfilling the functions assumed by it in regard to education and teaching, must take care that information or knowledge included in the curriculum is conveyed in an objective, critical and pluralistic manner. The State is forbidden to pursue an aim of indoctrination that might be considered as not respecting parents' religious and philosophical convictions. That is the limit that must not be exceeded."

Had the Court been better informed of the common law it might have reached a different decision, and one consistent with its own judgement in *Kjeldsen, Busk Madsen and Pedersen*. It might even have been invited to have regard to the precedent established by the Supreme Court of the United States when construing the European Convention.

In its judgement of 21 January 2010 in Case C-456/08 *Commission v. Ireland*[14] the European Court of Justice concluded that Ireland had failed to implement Council Directive 89/665/EEC on the award of public supply and public works contracts. Ireland pleaded that it had implemented the Directive by Order 84A (4) of the Rules of the Superior Courts – which applies in Ireland the elementary rule of administrative procedure applicable also in England and Wales, that any application for judicial review must be made as soon as possible and in any event within three months. The European Court responded that this rule was inadequate as it gave rise to uncertainty as to which decision must be challenged and as to how periods for bringing an action are to be determined. It is difficult for a common lawyer to understand that objection. The decision to be challenged under Order 84A (4) is any decision that the claimant wishes to challenge. In the context of the case, which concerned a tender for the building of a by-pass west of the city of Dundalk, the decision that the applicant wished to challenge was the decision to award the contract to a competitor. The period for bringing the action is determined by enquiring how much time elapsed between the date of the contested decision and the initiation of the challenge. If a common lawyer found any uncertainty in Order 84A (4) of the Rules of the Superior Courts, he would resolve the ambiguity by precedent. The European Court made, however, no reference to any precedent. The Advocate General in her opinion both in this case and in the *Uniplex* case did consider Ireland's submission that the provision needed to be interpreted in accordance with case law but regarded such a situation as "*complex*

---

12   542 U.S. 1 (2004).
13   Cases 5095/71, 5920/72 and 5926/72 *Kjeldsen, Busk Madsen and Pedersen v. Denmark* 17 December 1976.
14   Not yet reported in ECR. See also Case C-406/08 *Uniplex*.

and non-transparent".[15] I am not, of course, concerned to attribute responsibility for a misunderstanding; but rather to point to its existence. Those in a position to draw to the European Court's attention any precedent which may correct the impression that there is a lack of precision in a statutory provision must do so.

A similar failure of communication can be detected in the controversy over *Turner v. Grovit*.[16] In that case an English solicitor, initially employed in London, was transferred at his own request to Madrid where he resigned his appointment alleging that he had been the victim of efforts to implicate him in illegal conduct. He instituted legal proceedings in London for unfair dismissal. The employment tribunal dismissed the defendant's challenge to jurisdiction and awarded damages to Mr Turner. The defendant then applied to the Spanish courts which made an award of damages of 85 million pesetas against Mr Turner. The English Court of Appeal considered that in order to protect Mr Turner's interest in the English proceedings it was necessary to grant him an injunction against the defendants restraining them from persevering with the Spanish proceedings. On a reference from the House of Lords, the European Court ruled that:

> *"The Brussels Convention is to be interpreted as precluding the grant of an injunction whereby a court of a Contracting State prohibits a party to proceedings pending before it from commencing or continuing legal proceedings before a court of another Contracting State, even where that party is acting in bad faith with a view to frustrating the existing proceedings."*

The Court of Justice reasoned that the injunction undermined the Spanish court's jurisdiction to determine the dispute and must be seen as constituting interference with the jurisdiction of the Spanish court. This, it said, was incompatible with the system of the Convention and ran counter to the principle of mutual trust.

It is unfortunate that the European Court gained the impression that it was confronted with a case involving a breach of the principle of mutual trust, since the injunction issued by the Court of Appeal was no different to one that might have been issued if the defendant had gone to another English court to claim the relief that it sought in Madrid. The relief had nothing to do with distrust of the Spanish court and everything to do with the defendant's conduct.[17] Indeed, if the defendant had gone to another English court, instead of a Spanish one, its claim would in all probability have been struck out as "frivolous and vexatious". That is so because the judgement against it given by the Employment Tribunal established an adverse precedent.

Mr President, ladies and gentlemen, common lawyers, who are often ill-informed on questions of civil law, have no right to expect that judges from civilian systems will fully understand the

---

15   Paragraph 61 of Advocate General Kokott's Opinion in Uniplex: *"the referring court is required above all to deal with the limitation period under Regulation 47 (7) (b) of the PCR 2006, in harmony with the directive, in such a way that in the case of proceedings for declarations and compensation it does not already start to run from the time of the breach of procurement law, but only from the time at which the applicant knew or ought to have known of that breach of procurement law."*
16   Case C-159/02, 27 April 2004.
17   As described for example in the discussion of Dillon LJ in *Derby v. Weldon* (No. 6) [1990] 1 WLR 1139 at p. 1149 in relation to injunctions and orders for receivers with apparently extra-territorial effect.

common law; but they are entitled to expect appreciation of the fact that both civil and common law may implement the standards to which the Contracting States have subscribed. The common law, which is applied to approximately one third of the world population, is in Europe a small minority. It is in force only in less than two of the 47 States belonging to the Council of Europe or of the 27 Members of the Council of Europe that is, in Ireland and the United Kingdom (with the qualified exception of Scotland); and the repercussions of its system of precedent are often imperfectly comprehended.

I doubt that the solution to this difficulty lies in the promulgation of common laws in identical terms in all the Member States (or legislation by way of Regulation rather than Directive, which amounts to the same thing). Even the use of common terms in a common language is not enough to eliminate differences in perception, which derive from our separate histories and cultures.

In his play *The Caretaker*, the Nobel prize-winner Arnold Pinter is reputed to have established the proposition that there is no true communication between humans. I say that he is *reputed* to have established that proposition; because if he really established it, nobody could be quite certain that he did so.

Cross-border Commitment to Precedents in European Civil Courts

ILKA KLÖCKNER

Thank you Mr Chairman. Let me first thank you, dear Professor Baudenbacher, and the members of the organisation committee of the University of St.Gallen for giving me the opportunity to be here and speak to you all.

Ladies and gentlemen, Mr Chairman, I would like to lay out a concept of a cross-border commitment to precedents between courts of the EU Member States in the application of harmonised law.[1]

In this context, a number of theoretical and practical issues are at stake. I would briefly like to recall the European court system, its preliminary reference procedure and proposals for its reform. In a next step, I would like to address potential legal foundations of a transnational system of precedents. I will then outline the scope of such a concept. Finally, I will briefly indicate some of the limits and practical preconditions of this concept.

I. European Court System

In Europe, the now so called Court of Justice of the European Union (CJEU) was created almost 60 years ago to ensure the effective and uniform application of EU legislation and to prevent divergent interpretations. The courts of the Member States, however, are part of the European judicial architecture. They are the ordinary courts in matters of European Union law. They are engaged in both a vertical dialogue with the CJEU and a horizontal dialog with courts of other Member States.

The preliminary reference procedure according to Article 267 of the TFEU (former Article 234 TEC) does establish this vertical dialog between national courts and the Court of Justice of the European Union. In its third paragraph, as Professor Baudenbacher already mentioned, the provision lays down the conditions under which a national court of last instance is obliged to refer a question for a preliminary ruling.

---

[1] For a more detailed presentation of the concept and further references see Klöckner, Grenzüberschreitende Bindung an zivilgerichtliche Präjudizien (Mohr Siebeck, 2006), p. 170 ff. et passim.

In 1982, however, and this has been mentioned by Professor Baudenbacher as well, the Court rendered its famous CILFIT decision.[2] It held that Article 267 (3) TFEU does not impose an obligation on the courts to refer the case if the correct application of community law is *"so obvious as to leave no scope for any reasonable doubt as to the manner in which the question raised is to be resolved"*[3].

This is generally referred to as the so called *acte clair* doctrine. As part of the applicable test, *"the national court or tribunal must be convinced that the matter is equally obvious to the courts of the other Member States and the CJEU"*[4]. There seems to be a difference, however, between, on the one hand, the rather strict interpretation of the *acte clair* doctrine by the CJEU itself and, on the other hand, the more relaxed interpretation actually applied by national courts of last instance.[5]

Over the years, the European court system as such, its preliminary reference procedure and more specifically, the CILFIT-criteria, have been subject to comprehensive discussions and have attracted a lot of criticism.[6] Several proposals to decrease the Court's workload have been made, amongst others by three Advocates General in their opinions to the Court.[7] They pleaded in favour of a greater independence of national courts and for an adaptation of the CILFIT-criteria to the demand of the times.

To date, however, the Court itself has rejected all attempts to review or relax its *acte clair* doctrine and to increase the national courts' discretion to refer a case.

In the course of the last few years and despite the Community's enlargement, the duration of preliminary proceedings indeed has decreased from 20.4 months in 2005 to 17.1 months in 2009.[8] This still entails a considerable prolongation of the main action.

Moreover, the amount of European law is still growing. Therefore, proposals to reform the European judicial system still seem worth discussing.

If one supports the idea of giving national courts of last instance a wider discretion to refer, this would have to be accompanied by an appropriate mechanism to ascertain a uniform and correct application of harmonised law. Cross-border commitment to precedents on EU and harmonized national law could be a solution to prevent divergent interpretations.

---

2   Judgement of the Court of 6 October 1982, Case 283/81 *Srl C.I.L.F.I.T. and Lanificio di Gavardo SpA v. Ministry of Health* [1982] ECR-03415; hereinafter simply referred to as CILFIT.
3   Ibid., para. 16.
4   Ibid.
5   See, for example, Broberg, *Acte clair* revisited: Adapting the *Acte Clair* Criteria to the Demands of the Times, CMLRev 45 (2008), p. 1383.
6   Ibid.; see Klöckner (footnote 1), p. 60 ff. with further references.
7   AG Jacobs in Case C-338/95 *Wiener* [1997] ECR I-6495; AG Tizzano in Case C-99/00 *Lyckeskog* [2002] ECR I-4839; AG Colomer in Case C-461/03 *Gaston Schul* [2005] ECR-I 10513.
8   Court of Justice of the European Union, Annual Report 2009, p. 94; available at http://curia.europa.eu/jcms/jcms/Jo2_7000/.

This applies particularly in the field of civil law. I may remind you in this context of the still existing idea of a European Civil Code which the European Commission described as a possible option in its Green Paper on policy options for progress towards a European Contract Law from 1 July 2010.[9]

Certainly, the CJEU alone cannot sufficiently ensure uniform interpretation of such an European Civil Code. Stronger trans-border cooperation between the Member States' courts could turn out to be a suitable instrument to guarantee the uniform application of such unified civil law.

II. Legal Foundations of a Transnational European System of Precedent

Courts of the Member States are already bound to consider case material of other Member States. Presently, such an obligation can be founded in both EU law and national law.

To begin with the EU law, one can argue that the CJEU has already developed this obligation of the courts of last instance to consider precedents of other Member States in its just mentioned CILFIT judgement: *"The national court or tribunal must be convinced that the matter is equally obvious to the courts of the other Member States and the CJEU"*.[10]

Thus, in order to determine whether the matter is equally obvious to the courts of the other Member States, a court is obliged to consider existing precedents of other Member States' courts.

Moreover, Article 4 (3) TEU (the former Article 10 of the EC Treaty) – *de lege lata* – already serves as a legal foundation for the Member States' courts obligation to give uniform interpretation of European harmonised law.[11]

This obligation to ascertain uniform interpretation of harmonised law results in an obligation to consider precedents of other Member States. Article 4 (3) TEU embodies the general principle of a European *Comitas* and provides for the *"principle of sincere cooperation"*.

This concerns not only the relationship between the Union and the Member States but also the relationship between the Member States themselves. They *"shall, in full mutual respect, assist each other in carrying out tasks which flow from the Treaties"*.

---

9   Com (2010) 348 final.
10 See CILFIT (footnote 2), para. 16.
11 See Klöckner (footnote 1), p. 173 with further references.

The Member States, hence also their courts, shall take any appropriate measure, to ensure fulfilment of the obligations arising out of the Treaties or resulting from the acts of the institutions of the Union. The said provision thereby obliges national judges to be Community law judges.[12]

National law based on European provisions needs to be construed by means of a harmonising interpretation and in conformity with EU law's purposes. Such harmonising interpretation also implies an obligation to consider and discuss other Member States' relevant case law.

Finally, a further argument to establish the obligation to consider other Member States' relevant case law can be derived from the European principle of equality. This principle constitutes a general principle of European law and is also laid down in Article 20 of the Charter of Fundamental Rights, which reads *"Everyone is equal before the law"*.

The principle demands that *"like cases must be treated alike"*. Based on this principle, national courts are at least obliged to consider and discuss foreign relevant case law and give arguments if they want to depart from relevant previous decisions.

As regards national law, a normative foundation of the national courts' obligation to consider and discuss other Member States' decisions can be seen in the respective national legislator's expressed or presumptive will to implement EU law in a correct and uniform manner.

According to Article 20 (3) of the German Constitution (*Grundgesetz*), for example, the national judge is bound by law and justice. He, therefore, has to respect the expressed or presumptive will of the legislator to prevent divergences from other Member States' implementation laws. In doing so, he is obliged to make use of a harmonising interpretation and – as a part of this – to consider foreign precedents.

III. Scope and Limits of a Cross-border Doctrine of Precedent

A. De Lege Lata

As regards the current scope of a cross-border doctrine of precedent, there can be no European *stare decisis*, since there is no genuine community court system with a real hierarchy and several instances.

This still holds true although some indications may point towards a more hierarchical structure.[13] In this respect, one can notably refer to the Court of Justice's *Köbler* decision[14], which has already been mentioned by Professor Plender, and which establishes state liability for loss

---

12   As regards the role of the national judge in the European judicial system, see also the European Parliament's resolution of 9 July 2008 (2007/2027 (INI)).
13   See Klöckner (footnote 1), p. 51 ff.
14   Judgement of the Court of 30 September 2003, Case C-224/01 *Gerhard Köbler v. Republik Österreich* [2003] ECR I-10239.

or damage caused by a decision of a national court adjudicating at last instance which infringes a rule of Community law.

Although courts are, therefore, presently not bound by existing case law stemming from other Member States, one can argue an obligation to consider and discuss relevant case material. This might be described as a "presumption of correctness" of existing precedents from other Member States. However, so far, courts are free to depart from foreign precedents as long as they give reasons for their departure.

B. De Lege Ferenda

De lege ferenda, a system of "relative authority" could be envisaged, which would provide for a somewhat tempered binding effect: Courts would generally be bound to follow other Member States' precedents, but they would be allowed to depart from them under certain circumstances, yet to be specified.

This could particularly be of use in the case of a reform of the preliminary reference procedure establishing a wider margin of discretion for the national courts. A transnational European system of precedents could then constitute a suitable instrument to ensure uniform interpretation of EU law.

However, as long as the various national systems of precedent are not harmonised, only decisions of foreign courts of last instance would have to be considered. Otherwise, the paradoxical situation might arise where a court of higher instance of country A could disregard a precedent of a lower court of the same country according to its national system of precedents whereas the highest court of country B would have to follow such a precedent.

So far, in Europe, no consistent and uniform method regarding the use of foreign precedent can be observed.[15] This contradicts, if you will, the much discussed convergence thesis. In practice, courts in both common law and civil law jurisdictions do sometimes take foreign case law into account as persuasive authority.[16]

The traditional perception of precedent in German law and many other civil law countries has been laid out by Professor Baudenbacher already. It is that courts may and do in practice follow judgements of a superior court, yet they are not bound to follow them. A German court of first instance may even depart from a decision of the Federal Court of Justice.

---

15 See, for example, Hondius, Precedent and the Law, Electronic Journal of Comparative Law, Vol. 11.3, December 2007, available at http://www.ejcl.org; Tjong Tjin Tai/Teuben, European precedent law, Tilburg Institute of Comparative and Transnational Law Working Paper No. 2008/4, electronic copy available at http://ssrn.com/abstract=1148115.
16 See examples in Klöckner (footnote 1), p. 125 ff.

So, *de lege ferenda*, to establish criteria as part of a system of "relative transnational authority" in European uniform law, one might, therefore, rather borrow from elements of the common law technique in interpreting precedents, i. e.:

- only the *ratio decidendi* of a court's decision should be binding. Propositions of law which are not part of the *ratio decidendi* are called *obiter dicta* and have no more than persuasive authority;

- Member States' courts should be allowed to distinguish on the material facts of a case;

- the CJEU should be allowed to overrule precedents; and

- national courts should be allowed to depart from a precedent if it was decided *per incuriam*, i.e. if the judge was misinformed of the law or another precedent and did not apply a relevant statutory provision or has ignored a binding precedent.

In case of conflicting precedents, the respective Member State's court should deal with the diverging opinions and propose a solution to the CJEU.

As a limit of a cross-border doctrine of precedent it can be submitted that courts cannot be bound when they do not have the possibility and resources to obtain a translated version with reasonable effort.

Otherwise, this might lead to delayed proceedings and the principle of effective legal protection might be affected. Thus, *de facto* only courts of last instance would be obliged to consider the decisions of other Member States.

IV. Practical Difficulties to Gain Access to Relevant Case Material

So far, there are few examples of the use of European precedents in Member State courts' decisions. Currently, manyfold barriers to the study of national case law on harmonised private law do still exist.[17]

Relevant national decisions would have to be systematically collected, analysed, commented in European commentaries and translated, maybe into the English and the French language as *the linguae francae*.

---

17 See Klöckner (footnote 1), p. 211 ff.; Martens, Rechtsvergleichung und grenzüberwindende Jurisprudenz im Gemeinschaftsrecht, in: Jahrbuch Junger Zivilrechtswissenschaftler 2009, p. 27, p. 43 ff.; Tjong Tjin Tai/Teuben (footnote 15), p. 11 f.

In this respect, it could prove to be useful to develop a European Law Institute, as proposed by the European Commission in its Action Plan of 2010[18] implementing the Stockholm Programme.

Moreover, national courts' practices would have to be modified in order to have them explicitly make reference to foreign precedents and indicate the European dimension of their decisions.

A European training scheme for judges is on the agenda of the European Institutions. Again, in its Communication on the Action Plan, the Commission has announced that it will launch pilot projects on "Erasmus-style" exchange programmes for judicial authorities and legal professionals.[19]

It remains to be seen whether these first steps will lead the way towards a greater importance of foreign precedents from other Member States in interpreting uniform European law.

Thank you all very much for your attention.

---

18 Communication from the Commission to the European Parliament, the Council, the European Economic and Social Committee and the Committee of the Regions – Delivering an area of freedom, security and justice for Europe's citizens – Action Plan Implementing the Stockholm Programme (COM/2010/0171 final).
19 Ibid.

Discussion

FRANZ WERRO
We have heard three very interesting presentations, each of them had its own centre of gravity around the notion of precedent. I see already hands waving at me. Please, Professor Rau.

ALAN RAU
I am not sure if this is a question, but I will try and tack on a question mark at the end of it. The whole notion of a regime of precedent – of precedential constraint – depends on the practice of reasoned opinions by which I mean that the very fact of giving reasons necessarily involves a commitment to some principle or rule that operates at a higher level of generality than the case before us but which will be applicable in future cases.

Now, if that is what this is about, I do not begin, no common law lawyer can begin, to understand, for example, Article 5 of the French Civil Code, which says that judges are forbidden from ruling on the basis of general dispositions. To a common law lawyer that is an oxymoron, unless as Mr Werro suggested it is just a historical relic that dates back to the revolution. But the differences with respect to our practices of giving reasons or how we treat reasons explains a lot. It explains the form of a reasoned opinion. The Anglo-American reasoned opinion reads like an argument. The French reasoned opinion reads like a syllogism and this must be considerably less satisfactory to the common law lawyer, n'est-ce pas?

JOHN TEMPLE LANG
One thing struck me listening to Professor Klöckner's very interesting and practical comments; it seems to me that it would be desirable for European courts, the Court of Human Rights, the EFTA Court and the Court of Justice, to include in their advice to counsel a recommendation or a request that the lawyers should, as far as possible, refer to judgements of other European courts and other national courts.

You cannot expect lawyers to know everything. I hope as a practicing lawyer that this is accepted. However, I think it would be useful if the courts would encourage lawyers to refer to the case law of other courts because, at present, you really do not know whether you ought to be doing that or not and it would be desirable to be encouraged.

CARL BAUDENBACHER

Thank you very much for a very stimulating panel. I have a very simple question to my colleague Professor Müller-Chen here from St.Gallen. You mentioned Art. 23 FASC which says that if one chamber in the Swiss Supreme Court wants to depart from the case law of another chamber, there is a procedure that they have to sit down and vote. Only if they reach two thirds of the votes, they can go ahead and change the precedent. That can easily be disregarded, obviously. How is that in practice? How often do they sit down and formally decide on whether to overrule or not?

MARKUS MÜLLER-CHEN

It is not applied too many times. There is no sanction if one chamber does not follow the provision. There would be potentially enough opportunities to apply this provision, since civil and commercial law issues are often disputed and dealt with by different chambers. I know of at least some cases where one chamber clearly deviated from precedents of another chamber and there was no procedure according to Art. 23 FASC.

CARL BAUDENBACHER

You also mentioned that if a case involves a value which is below the threshold to be challenged in the Supreme Court, the lower judge can deviate. You made reference to a case in which a lower court judge did deviate and then the party which was affected tried to bring the case before the Supreme Court based on the ground that it involved a fundamental question. However, the Supreme Court said that its case law is clear. That is just unbelievable.

MARKUS MÜLLER-CHEN

Yes it is. I totally agree with you.

FRANZ WERRO

If I may react, it seems to me that we have been repeatedly saying that courts with a civil law tradition do not have an obligation to follow precedents, but they do so in practice. There is something we have not mentioned so far. It seems to me, and that is the techniques of common law courts, to go around precedents and to do as if one would be adhering to one, even when one is in fact moving away from it.

Keynote

The Doctrinal Paradox without Doctrine

LAWRENCE SAGER[1]

My topic centers on something called the doctrinal paradox, which was discovered by Lewis Kornhauser and me some years ago.[2] Somewhat surprisingly, this paradox can occur in arbitration as well as in multi-judge adjudication and is rather easily overlooked – and mishandled – in each of these settings.

My objective in this talk is to introduce you to the doctrinal paradox, to make some general observations about it and then to turn to some musings about the treatment of the paradox in arbitration. I hope to show you how the paradox can occur in arbitration and to make some suggestions about how to respond to it in that setting.

I am a genuine neophyte in the domain of arbitration, so my last remarks are tentative and should be read as an invitation to a conversation, not as definitive pronouncements.

I. The Doctrinal Paradox

Imagine a three judge court ruling on the liability of a defendant for the breach of a contract. There are two issues: Was there a valid contract and was there a material breach? If, and only if, we answer both of these questions in the affirmative there will be liability. So, there are two issues ("Liability" is in italics, because it is synonymous with the outcome of the case).

Imagine that the judges' views of the case are as follows:

	Contract?	Breach?	*Liability?*
Judge A	Y	N	N
Judge B	N	Y	N
Judge C	Y	Y	Y

---

[1] Dean and Alice Jane Drysdale Sheffield Professor of Law at the University of Texas at Austin. I want to thank Prof. Carl Baudenbacher, our host, and the participants in the St.Gallen International Dispute Resolution Conference in October of 2010 for the opportunity to develop these ideas and for the many helpful suggestions I have received.

[2] Our joint work in this area includes: The Many As One: Integrity and Group Choice in Paradoxical Cases, 32 Phil. & Pub. Affairs 249 (2004); The One and the Many: Adjudication in Collegial Courts, 81 Calif. L. Rev. 1 (1993); and Unpacking the Court, 96 Yale L. Rev. 82 (1986).

What is remarkable is that rather a long way into the history of the Anglo-American legal system, we do not have a settled view who should prevail in this case or why. One way of aggregating the votes in this case is the following:

	Contract?	Breach?	Liability?
Judge A	Y	N	N
Judge B	N	Y	N
Judge C	Y	Y	Y
			N

Each judge casts her vote for the case outcome, in effect, and the court simply totals those votes and rules with the majority.

But there is a very different – and altogether plausible – alternative. The court could total the votes on each of the salient issues and then reach the outcome through what we might call "doctrinal arithmetic". In this case that process would look like this:

	Contract?	Breach?	Liability?
Judge A	Y	N	N
Judge B	N	Y	N
Judge C	Y	Y	Y
	Y +	Y =	Y

For convenience we can call our first way of aggregating the judges' votes by majority vote on the final outcome, "case-by-case" voting. The alternative, in which we have totaled the votes on each outcome, is called "issue-by-issue" voting. It is altogether possible, as in the simple contract action we have been looking at, that the outcomes of these two voting protocols can be diametrically apart:

	Contract?	Breach?	Liability?
Judge A	Y	N	N
Judge B	N	Y	N
Judge C	Y	Y	Y
	Y	Y	(Y/N) ?

This lurking problem in multi-judge adjudication is the doctrinal paradox. Remarkably, it went largely unnoticed in Anglo-American common law adjudication for centuries and was, therefore, bereft of analysis.

II. An Example: The *Tidewater* Case

This is not to say that the paradox did not make trouble from time to time. One especially vivid instance of troublemaking was the decision of the Supreme Court in *National Mutual Insurance v. Tidewater Transfer Co.*[3] That case involved the Congress's extension of diversity jurisdiction to include citizens of the District of Columbia – an innocent idea, but one with constitutional difficulty. The problem is that Article 3, widely regarded as the exclusive reservoir from which Congress can draw in conferring jurisdiction on Article 3 courts, provides for jurisdiction between the citizens of different *states*. There appears to be only two possible ways to justify diversity jurisdiction that includes citizens of the District of Columbia (or at least the Justices in *Tidewater* could only identify these two theories). The first could be called the "Squint" theory: For these purposes, at least, we could read the word "state" in Article 3 to include the District of Columbia. The problem is that John Marshall and his early Supreme Court rejected that reading and subsequent courts have never deviated from his interpretation. Alternative-ly, there is what could be called the "Lagniappe" theory: An otherwise well-formed Article 3 court can accept some additional jurisdiction of a kind otherwise within Congress's legislative, or Article 1, authority. This view, unfortunately, represents a fairly brazen heresy in conventional federal courts understandings.

In *Tidewater*, the judges were divided as follows ("Y" indicates acceptance of the relevant theory; "N" represents the emphatic rejection of that theory):

	DC = "state"	A Little Extra is OK	Valid?
2 judges	Y	N	Y (2)
3 judges	N	Y	Y (3)
4 judges	N	N	N (4)

By now, you are probably anticipating the problem. This is how the Court in *Tidewater* actually proceeded – without asking itself whether it was obliged to do so or even justified in doing so:

	DC = "state"	A Little Extra is OK	Valid?
2 judges	Y	N!	Y (2)
3 judges	N!	Y	Y (3)
4 judges	N!	N!	N! (4)
			Y (5–4)

---

3   337 U.S. 582 (1949).

The rub, of course, is that the extension of diversity jurisdiction was upheld on the basis of two rationales, each of which was emphatically rejected by a substantial majority of the justices:

	DC = "state"	A Little Extra is OK	Valid?
2 judges	Y	N!	Y (2)
3 judges	N!	Y	Y (3)
4 judges	N!	N!	N! (4)
	N! (6–3) +	N! (7–2) =	N!

If this does not move you, consider another sort of case with the same abstract structure as *Tidewater*. Suppose that a three judge court is hearing an appeal to a criminal conviction, with two distinct grounds of error put forward. Judge A agrees that ground I error constitutes reversible error, but rejects ground II; Judge B rejects ground I but agrees that ground II constitutes reversible error; and Judge C rejects both asserted grounds of error. If the court engages in case-by-case voting, the conviction is reversed and a new trial is ordered. But note the quandary of the trial judge: A majority of the judges on the appellate court supported both of his rulings/actions. How should a trial judge proceed in a different case, where only one of the two grounds of error raised in the first case is implicated?

III. Responses to the Doctrinal Paradox

When Lewis Kornhauser and I worried about the paradox, we came to several conclusions:

— First: When it crops up, the paradox ought to be noted and resolved, not swept under the rug.

— Second: One size emphatically does *not* fit all neither case-by-case voting nor issue-by-issue voting will always be the right course. I will not take the occasion here to substantiate that proposition, but let me say that we arrived at this view through a kind of adversarial induction. When we began, Mr Kornhauser was a firm partisan of case-by-case voting and I championed the issue-by-issue protocol. Each of us would find a hypothesized circumstance where our protocol of choice was clearly the better and confront the other with the power of the example. After a while, we realized that the voting method needed to vary with features of the case at hand.[4]

---

[4] We make our case for this in Kornhauser/ Sager, The One and the Many: Adjudication in Collegial Courts, 81 Calif. L. Rev. 1 (1993).

- Third: The choice between voting protocols should be made by the court as a whole. That might seem the only possible way, but there is another: Any individual judge who is outvoted on an issue critical to her view of the case as a whole could choose to change her vote because a majority of her colleagues disagrees. This has actually happened in the Supreme Court. In *Pennsylvania v. Union Gas*[5] Justice White did not believe that Congress had evinced the requisite intent to abrogate the immunity of the state, but he took the majority view of his colleagues to the contrary to govern, and so cast his vote on the final disposition of the case in favor of the vulnerability of the state to suit. His vote was decisive in the 5-4 outcome. No other member of the court in that case embraced this personal version of the issue-by-issue voting protocol. Two years later, in *Arizona v. Fulminante*[6], Justice Kennedy, who was unmoved by the call of personal issue-by-issue voting in *Union Gas* suddenly felt obliged to change his vote to conform with the majority of his colleagues on a salient issue. Neither Justice White nor Justice Kennedy, nor any other member of the court in either case, took up the question of the propriety of such deference, let alone the broader question of the choice of voting protocols that was right under the Court's nose.

In the end, Mr Kornhauser and I argue that a court faced with a paradoxical distribution of judgements should take a *metavote*, on the proper voting protocol. The judges should discuss why, in the circumstances of the case, one method or the other should be followed. This might have to do with the firmness of the convictions of the judges as between outcome and rationale; or it might concern the need for guidance to the court below, the state of precedent, or the kind of case (criminal cases, for example, might qualify for distinct treatment).

IV. The Doctrinal Paradox and Arbitration

Let me now move to my ultimate target, arbitration.[7] Suppose we have a contractual dispute before a panel of three arbitrators. Broadly, the questions are whether there is liability (contract plus breach), and if so, what are the damages. And suppose that the distribution of views among the arbitrators is this:

	Liability?	Damages?	Award?
Arbitrator A	Y	250 million	250 million
Arbitrator B	Y	None	0
Arbitrator C	N	250 million	0

---

5   491 U.S. 1 (1989).
6   499 U.S. 279 (1991).
7   I composed these remarks before I encountered an essay by Manuel Conthe, Introducing the question of the doctrinal paradox in arbitration, Majority Decision in Complex Arbitration Cases: The Role of Issue-By-Issue Voting, Revista del Club Espanol del Arbitraje (8/2010).

Now it might seem obvious that arbitral tribunals, which are often heavily outcome oriented, silent as to rationale and relatively oblivious to precedent (and, therefore, we might assume, to doctrine), would clearly vote case-by-case:

	Liability?	Damages?	Award?
Arbitrator A	Y	250 million	250 million
Arbitrator B	Y	None	0
Arbitrator C	N	250 million	0
			0

But suppose (and this can happen, to be sure) the arbitrators meet twice. They meet first in Paris and decide the question of liability. And then some months later, they meet in New York to decide the question of damages. From this decision to segment the proceedings, which could well have been made on grounds of convenience, the availability of the members of the arbitral tribunal, or possibly the availability of witnesses, profound substantive results might follow. Consider the following, in which the segmentation of judgements follows mechanically and as matter of course from the segmentation of the proceedings:

	April in Paris	*September in New York*	
	Liability?	Damages?	Award?
Arbitrator A	Y	250 million	
Arbitrator B	Y	None	
Arbitrator C	N	250 million	
	Y +	250 million =	250 million

Unnoticed, we assume, is the paradoxical nature of the outcome: Had the tribunal voted case-by-case, Arbitrator B and Arbitrator C would both have favored an award of 0, and that outcome would have prevailed.

This story is borrowed more or less directly from the real world and there are several lessons it carries. The first is that it does not take much doctrinal detail or nuance to provide the segmental structure that can produce paradoxical distributions of judgements, and further, that paradoxical cases can and do occur in arbitration. A conceptual division as crude as liability and damages is sufficient for the paradox. The second lesson is that modern, complex, international arbitration may carry with it a special danger associated with the doctrinal paradox, namely, the risk that a decision to segment the proceedings based on various considerations of convenience that ought to have nothing to do with the choice of voting protocol may inadvertently commit an arbitral tribunal to issue-by-issue voting. Permitting the outcome to turn on the length of proceedings, the location of witnesses or the availability and preference of the arbitrators, is surely a misfortune.

How should we respond to the doctrinal paradox in the domain of arbitration? My suggestions parallel the conclusions that Mr Kornhauser and I reached with regard to the paradox in conventional adjudication and go along with some observations meant to calibrate those conclusions in this new setting. My first suggestion is that the paradox has to be noticed and addressed, not simply bungled into, as it seems to be the case in *our April in Paris example*. Because arbitration is modeled in some reflective detail in the prior agreement of parties to submit their disputes to arbitration, or in the standard form agreements of various arbitral associations or tribunals, it is possible, in principle, for parties to consider the possibilities of paradox *a priori* and to choose how to deal with the problems if it raises. Anglo-American common law may be condemned by centuries of heedless practice to bungle on, but arbitration offers the possibility of a fresh and self-conscious look at the doctrinal paradox. The growing trend of segmented international proceedings ought to be a goad to make some appropriate provision for the possibility of paradox.

My second suggestion is that, here too, a blanket embrace of either case-by-case or issue-by-issue voting would be a mistake. In arbitration, there are, as we have observed, some intrinsic reasons for favoring case-by-case voting. But they are far from absolute, and there are reasons why, in some contexts issue-by-issue voting should prevail:

- even in arbitration, there are some contexts or some particular cases where the parties and the world in which their controversy is embedded will benefit from articulate legal rulings and, possibly, precedent;

- in some cases, one or more of the issues may be fraught with controversy or important policy questions, or overriding questions of domestic or international law; and

- as with adjudication there may be some arbitral decisions where the distribution and firmness of views or general presumptions of one sort or another may push towards one voting protocol or the other.

My third suggestion is that, as in orthodox adjudication, the voting protocol in paradoxical cases should be decided by a metavote, that is, by deliberation and decision among the members of the arbitration panel. The structure of arbitral panels does offer an alternative possibility: The neutral chair of an arbitration panel could be charged with choosing the appropriate voting protocol in paradoxical cases. In regard to this issue I am on somewhat thin ice, given my lack of sophistication on the domain of arbitration, but I am strongly inclined to favor deliberation and voting among all three members of the panel. My argument is blunt: All the reasons we have for structuring arbitration panels as we do, with a neutral chair and an additional member chosen by each of the protagonists, ought to apply in full to the choice of voting protocols in paradoxical cases.

Discussion

ALAN RAU
I want to pick up on the last remark you said. It reminds me of a very common problem in arbitration where the dynamics of a three party arbitral tribunal make it impossible, or may make it impossible, to get a majority decision at all. The majority may not be different, but you cannot get a majority at all. The paradigm case is in labour law, where an employee has been fired and the union want him reinstated with full back pay. The employer, however, just wants him out. Imagine that each party, the union and the employer, names their own arbitrator. The independence of the party appointed arbitrators may not be completely guaranteed. So, the employer's arbitrator wants the employee out. The union's arbitrator wants him reinstated with full back pay. But the chairman, the presiding arbitrator would like, for reasons of his own future acceptability, some sort of compromise – maybe a reinstatement but no back pay. The two party appointed arbitrators, however, will not agree. They each want to take an extreme position. The chairman, the neutral arbitrator, could engage in some sort of mediation or arbitration between them in an inept kind of negotiation. What he actually might do in the alternative is, however, to control the agenda. He could suggest to take a vote first on reinstatement and he will vote in favour of reinstatement. The union representative votes in favour of reinstatement, too. So, the group has decided on reinstatement. Afterwards, they take a vote on giving him back pay. The neutral arbitrator does not think that they should. The employer does not think that they should, either. As a result, no back pay. So, the neutral arbitrator has attained a kind of compromise where in the absence of this agenda setting any decision might have been impossible as any majority decision might have been impossible in the first place. So, the power of the chairman to set the agenda can be a very powerful tool to get an award when an award might be impossible.

LAWRENCE SAGER
That sounds very sensible to me. I told you I was on thin ice. The question would be two-fold: Are you comfortable with that agenda setting control? And does that cover the potential paradoxical cases broadly enough that you would conceive this power as a whole? I am not. I am happy to stop here because I warned you that there are aspects of the internal dynamics of arbitration that puts me on thin ice.

DANIEL HOCHSTRASSER
I would like to make a short comment on your example. There is one phenomenon which favours the appearance of that problem, and that is bifurcation. You see it more and more in arbitration that you actually bifurcate the case, first looking at liability and then having an interim award on liability, which is a formal decision which stands. Afterwards, you move on to the quantum. One downside of bifurcation is that you are more likely to encounter that phenome-

non. The second downside is that it increases the costs terribly, because if you have a case that starts as a $ 250 million case and you only look at the liability, both parties treat it as a $ 250 million case. Afterwards, when you come to the quantum, you actually see that it is only a $ 25 million case which might cause parties to deal with it with less effort. That is something that you should keep in mind when you bifurcate.

LAWRENCE SAGER

I think that this is a very helpful comment. One instruction of this presentation should be that bifurcation ought to be evaluated against the possibility of this kind of paradoxical distribution so that if, for example, you think the paradoxical distribution is problematic that you favour case-by-case adjudication.

CARL BAUDENBACHER

Thank you very much, Dean Sager, for this fascinating speech. I have been thinking about my own behaviour as a European judge and the behaviour of fellow judges. Mr Hochstrasser's point is an important issue. In an arbitration proceeding the arbitrators can decide on the method and they can even make the first vote binding by issuing an interim award. But in a court proceeding in a European court, even if you take a vote issue-by-issue, that does not hinder the judge from saying at the very end that he wants to come back to what he would have voted on the issues because he wants a different outcome.

LAWRENCE SAGER

That is right and I would argue for the court revising its chronic revisitation.

RACHEL BREWSTER

I have a question about strategic voting. It seems like that even if you have a situation where you have a meta decision on how we are going to vote, someone can look ahead and realise that simply if I think that there is liability then I just change my liability vote, because I know what the other people think about the damages. So, even if we bifurcate, I can act strategically. I wonder how often you see this happening. To some extent it might be that judges never called the doctrinal paradox before you identified it, but how often did it actually happen. Can the strict strategic element really even undermine making a meta rule?

LAWRENCE SAGER

If you think of judges as strategically aiming at their outcome instead of the right outcome, then the meta vote is irrelevant. You are essentially at case-by-case voting one way or the other. You have to believe in the good faith of judges to make the meta vote interesting. On the question, how often do you see it? What you see are strange artefacts that suggest that the court is just stumbling around in the dark rather than voting. For example, if you go back to *Tidewater*, Justice Frankfurter is by himself. He asks his colleagues if they are serious: Do you realise what we have done here? We have upheld a statute on the grounds of two totally flawed and repudiated theories, but he does not ask why they are voting case-by-case. Do we need to? Is there a reason? Is there a rule in our voting? He does not even whisper that, which is pretty remarkable. If you go to the criminal case, I have described, where Justice White defers to his colleagues and

Judge Scalia pulls ahead, no one on the court observes what the two of them did. No one talks about the propriety of changing your vote by your colleagues. The notion is that if you were to infer with a rule of the Supreme Court, it is every judge for herself or himself. But that seems implausible. So, self-consciousness is an improvement. There just seems to be a kind of blindness to the question, which is pretty surprising.

RACHEL BREWSTER
So, is your presentation today and your writing about this actually bringing it more to the front and do leading people now become more strategic about it? What do you think?

LAWRENCE SAGER
I am a child of the Warren Court, a lover of judges and I actually believe, for various institutional reasons and some cultural reasons, that lots of judges behave in good faith lots of times. There are several judges on both sides that are behaving right at the margin of ethics in not saying what is really on their minds, in covering up. I do not think that judges are perfect but I think that you do better in asking judges to articulate what they are doing and why, even if cryptically, rather than just letting, for example, Judge Scalia decide not to change his vote when Judge White changed his vote. Or letting *Tidewater* come out the way it is. Maybe it should have come out that way. It seems extremely benign but sort of permitting a law to be upheld on the bases of two repudiated doctrines is a little uncomfortable. So, I would put more in the mix.

SUSAN FRANCK
I just want to add an example that actually helps you in another understanding. The first example is about arbitration. It is not bifurcated, it is trifurcated if you are also thinking about jurisdiction. How does that affect your model? The reason I started thinking about that were two known inconsistent cases, which are almost identical in terms of facts and laws but six arbitrators voting in four to five different ways. The reason I would suggest that this is actually helpful to your analysis as it shows now two tribunals were doing different things.

In the second case, there was a change of arbitrator involved, namely there was one arbitrator in the liability phase but a different arbitrator in the damages phase. So, how does that affect the concept that Mrs Brewster was leading you towards, namely strategic voting, not issue-by-issue voting?

LAWRENCE SAGER
Both of the two variations, in this simple theme that involve more arbitrators and more issues, increase the likelihood of paradoxical distributions.

JOHN TEMPLE LANG
Have you thought about the application of your theory to cases where the court in question is not allowed to have concurring and dissenting judgements? The reason why I ask is that I can think straightaway of several judgements of the Court of Justice, which without having any confidential information of any kind, I am pretty certain were the result of something like that.

LAWRENCE SAGER

I have not until you mentioned it. My former colleague and still good friend Lewis Kornhauser and I have thought about millions of things and argued about most of them. But I cannot really remember systematically thinking and certainly never writing about the unanimous court phenomenon. In the United States intermediate state appellate courts have a tradition of unanimity, for example. I believe, at least at one time, intermediate appellate courts in California always issued unanimous opinions. In arbitration arbitrators on the whole just come out with an answer. There is a version of unanimity built into some arbitral awards. Assuming that the judges or the arbitrators are behaving systematically makes the problem even more invisible.

MLADEN STOJILJKOVIC

I have a remark on your meta vote theory. I was wondering if the meta vote decides the case? Does it not, actually, resemble the case-by-case decision? Should not more often than not the meta vote be identical to the case-by-case vote?

LAWRENCE SAGER

I take that to be a variation of Mrs Brewster's question. If you take the judges to be driven by the outcome of the case, then the meta vote will indeed simply replicate the case-by-case vote. But it is reasonable to expect some, if not substantial, monotonism of conscientious judicial behaviour.

2nd Panel
Precedent in Arbitration

Introduction

DANIEL HOCHSTRASSER

Thank you for having me here, particularly to Professor Baudenbacher. It is an extreme privilege for me to be among this group of speakers, who are all very reputable academics. Some, of course, also have considerable practical experience, but, nevertheless, they have earned academic praise which I have not; I am a simple-minded practitioner. So, for me, it is really a great honour to be among the speakers and in some areas I might be able to add some practical experience. It is also, of course, an honour to be in this room and in this building. I have never been an elected delegate to any parliament in my country and we have many parliaments on several levels. Almost everybody I know, at some point in time, is a member of some parliament. I have never and I never will but now, at least from what I can say, speak in a parliament. It is a great privilege. When I sat in the audience and looked forward to holding this speech, I actually wondered about these various podiums that you see behind us. They seem to be above, so whoever is sitting here has at least three levels of additional, higher authority above him or her and then, of course, God at the very top. So, what a frightening prospect. We have nobody up there, so we can say we are only under your control.

We have already heard from the preceding panellists Professor Werro, Professor Müller-Chen, Professor Klöckner and Professor Sir Richard Plender about precedent in common and civil law and the somewhat different concepts. In his keynote, Professor Sager has enlightened us further in that he has explained the enigmatic ways that precedents might come about. So, the question is whether in fact it is such a good idea to rely on precedent. But, since he has also provided some solutions, we should still continue to look at them.

We are now getting a bit more specific and we will look at the special role of precedent in arbitration, or maybe I should say the lack of role of precedent. I have two distinguished panellists that will help us to come to conclusions. They are Professor Susan Franck and Professor Alan Rau.

Let me make some introductory remarks. I can be rather brief as we have already heard a lot about the role of precedent. It used to be almost common knowledge that there is no doctrine of precedent in international commercial arbitration; certainly not in the way it exists in the common law system. Nevertheless, arbitral tribunals and arbitrators issue reasoned awards. Certainly in my area, international commercial arbitration, reasoned awards are the rule. You have, therefore, awards that run over dozens, sometimes hundreds of pages, and they make frequent reference to precedents. Usually, arbitrators quote a variety of sources when they refer to precedents. Most obviously they refer to court decisions from the judicial system of the law that the parties chose to be applicable to their dispute or that is considered to be applicable by the tribunal after application of the relevant conflict of law rules. Thus, they refer to substantive law decisions from the legal system which they apply to the dispute. And then, they also refer to precedents that are more concerned with jurisdictional issues and they are usually decisions of other tribunals. These can be decisions from arbitral institutions, for example, about the validity of an arbitral clause. Finally, what I consider to be quite an important source for precedents in international arbitration, are decisions of courts that were faced with challenges against arbitral awards. In that regard, I can make reference to Switzerland, where the case law on arbitration almost exclusively comes from the Swiss Federal Supreme Court, and these decisions are rendered in the framework of challenges against arbitral awards.

One important set of decisions, are the decisions that the Swiss Federal Supreme Court has rendered about 15 to 20 years ago about the duty of arbitral tribunals to apply competition law rules from the European Union to disputes that are taking place in Switzerland. Swiss law is applicable where the tribunal finds that the relationship between the parties had sufficient contact with the European Union market. Later, there were other decisions. About five years ago, the Swiss Supreme Court held that European competition law is not a part of Swiss Public Policy, something which was heavily criticised. This is the type of decision where the Supreme Court of Switzerland renders decisions in cases that then serve as precedent in arbitral tribunals.

If you move away from national legal systems and ask yourself if there are precedents in international law, you will find decisions of the International Court of Justice and the World Trade Organisation Appellate Body, for example, where undoubtedly precedents are recognised and are important for practice. You will hear more about such decisions, I think, not only in the presentation we have later but also in the ones we will hear tomorrow.

International commercial arbitration in a narrow sense and investment treaty arbitration, for example, are the actual topics that we are trying to cover here. There are a numbers of interesting articles that have investigated this topic in recent years. If one wants to look at Swiss sources, I should mention the 2006 Freshfields lecture of Professor Gabrielle Kaufmann-Kohler, who you all know as a member of the magic circle of international arbitrators. She is not only active in commercial arbitration but also in sports arbitration. She has been a member of the arbitral tribunals at the Olympic Games several times and she is also involved in investment treaty arbitration. She concludes in her article, based on an analysis of several hundred awards by one of her research assistants, that arbitrators do what they want with past cases and that there is no clear practice in this field. This is the starting point for our discussion and since this is based on an empirical analysis of the reality, we should accept it as it is and look forward whether that is a good situation or whether something must be changed. I am pretty sure that the two panellists have differing views or perspectives in that regard.

Why do arbitrators, as a general rule, not seem to be overly inclined to rely on precedents? Is it because they are not formally bound? They are definitely not part of a system that would declare them to be bound by precedents. Or is it because they do not feel that they owe respect to early decisions which were rendered by people who were not themselves? I am pretty sure that there are people in international arbitration who feel that this is the true reason. They believe that world class and well-known arbitrators simply feel that they do not need to look at decisions rendered by other people, because they can do that themselves. Or is the real answer rather that they are not controlled in a way which would force them to keep their decisions in line with precedents? As a matter of fact, there is no court of appeals above an arbitral tribunal, normally. In most countries, and certainly in those countries where most of the international arbitrations take place, there is a very limited review system over arbitral awards. In countries such as Switzerland, the USA and England it takes a lot until an arbitral award is rendered void by a court of appeals or a supreme court. In Switzerland, for example, there are a lot of procedural reasons that you might invoke to invalidate an award, like the right to be heard and the right of a due process. However, if you look at the substance of the award, the award has to result in a violation of public policy to justify annulment. That is a very, very high threshold. If you look at the area where precedents play a role, one talks about the specific application of a specific provision of law or of a specific decision on a point of law. Quite often, where it needs a precedent to decide or to give guidance whether to go one way or the other, it does not lead to questions, that if the tribunal decides to go the other way, the violation is so severe that it would amount to a violation of public policy. So, all of these decisions in that area fly below the radar of the Swiss Federal Supreme Court.

Of course, there is also another explanation why precedents might not be that important or might not play an important role in many arbitral awards. That is the number of arbitral awards and the number of arbitration cases, which is rather small compared to, if you look at a country like the USA, the hundred thousands of court cases. It is quite likely that if you have a specific question of law that it has been the subject of earlier decisions. Whereas, in international arbitrations, many times you find that cases are quite unique and you would be hard pressed to actually find a case where the fact pattern and the questions of law were so similar that you would actually find a precedent with very similar circumstances. At least in my practice, when I look back on my 20 years in international arbitration, I do not think that I ever had two cases which were really so similar that I could use this earlier case from five or ten years ago as a precedent for what I am doing here.

Professor Kaufmann-Kohler focused in her article on ICC cases. ICC cases are interesting because the percentage of actually published cases is higher than for any other institution. There are specific collections that focus on ICC awards so you have at least a database that you can look at. The research found that only approximately 15% of the awards quoted other arbitral decisions, which is quite a few. However, most of these citations concerned matters of jurisdiction and procedure, such as questions of timeliness of an objection to jurisdiction or such as objections to the power of the tribunal, the composition of the tribunal, determination of the governing law, and not the type of legal question where you would usually look at precedent.

When thinking about this topic, I asked myself whether, and to what extent, I would use or quote precedents when I am an arbitrator. I actually found that my inclination to do so would be quite similar as to what it was when I worked in the Swiss court system. If I have a legal question, I would certainly do some research and see whether I find a Supreme Court decision that talks about this issue and if "yes" I could go along with it. I would certainly quote it. But, I do not think I would find it an absolute necessity to do so. In arbitration, I would probably stop at the level of Supreme Court decisions. It is very unlikely that I would go down to the level of the Cantonal Courts of Appeal. Maybe, if there was a decision of the Commercial Court of Zurich, which is a court with a high reputation, I would quote it. But, other than that, in a national arbitration setting, I would probably not be inclined to quote such cases. This is also a question of the expectation of the parties in international arbitration. Do parties in international arbitration really want their tribunal to go to the nitty gritty details of the applicable national law? Professor Müller-Chen has mentioned the very interesting example of Article 404 of the Swiss Code of Obligations, which is the most important example of the Swiss Contract Law where you have case law that is very important in many cases. This mandatory character of the revocability of a mandate is something that parties are not used to, that is often changed or that parties often try to deviate from in their contracts and then they are called back by the courts. This is certainly something where one would quote Supreme Court case law. But, other than that, I think, the expectation of the parties is not necessarily that you would do that in their decision.

The question is, and hopefully we will get closer to an answer to the question, whether in fact this freedom that arbitrators and arbitral tribunals have is something that should be protected in that they should use their discretion which is granted to them. The discretion stems from the fact that the parties have opted out of a national court system and gone to a level of internationalism. Should they maintain that discretion, or should they be called back into the same constraints that state court judges have? I think there are good reasons for both views and I hope that we can use the discussion after the presentations to hear more about your views in that regard.

Let me perhaps make one final remark. There are areas of arbitration where the cases are in fact so similar that there is case law and that there are precedents which are important. One classic area is sports arbitration. As you know, Switzerland is the seat of the Tribunal Arbitral du Sport in Lausanne, which is basically the world sports court. All important sport disputes are decided there, regardless whether they arise from Olympic Games, whether they arise from Soccer World Cups, whether they arise from transfer of football players or whether they are in the area of doping. You find rich case law there, particularly in the area of doping. The main reason is probably that there is no fixed legal regime, so the entire legal framework is actually formed in that jurisdiction. Another area are investment treaty cases, but you will hear more about those later. Other than that, we are in an environment where precedents play a role but they do not play the same role as in state courts.

Precedent in International Arbitration

ALAN RAU

A few weeks ago I was talking to one of my colleagues at the University of Texas Law School about this conference, and mentioned what the topic of my talk was going to be: "Precedent in international arbitration." His reaction was, "Oh, is it going to be a very short talk then?" I think he was reacting to the common view that the notion of precedent as a tool for arbitral decision making is thought to be somewhat incompatible with the nature of the arbitral process. Whatever arbitration is, it is not "law" – not, at least, in the sense of a findable, studiable and "restateable" body of law.

Some of the peculiar virtues of arbitration like confidentiality and secrecy may in fact be in conflict with the production of law. Above all, there is the fact that in commercial arbitration, in particular, there is no standing bench and that there is no institutional continuity. There is a continually changing series of decision makers chosen on an "ad hoc" basis. So, to begin with an obvious point, consider the paradigm case of arbitrators who are asked to settle a dispute between two private parties over the sale of goods by applying the Convention on the International Sale of Goods. Here, arbitration is a substitute for national court adjudication. It may be chosen for reasons of efficiency, speed, finality or neutrality, but there is already going to be a very rich, thick body of national law that addresses these questions. Where arbitrators are expected or likely to look to such national law, there is really little space for the notion of "precedent" that is peculiarly "arbitral": The parties' attorneys, and the arbitrators themselves, will go back and look directly to the source of the law, which alone is going to have precedential value. And only the most doctrinaire of writers (I am thinking here of the French literature in this respect) could think that arbitrators can pretend in any sense to have a co-equal status with the law or to be the equals of state courts in generating an independent system of law.

In such cases it is fair to say that arbitrators usually do try to model their awards on what courts will do. That is what the empirical evidence suggests.[1] What courts have previously done is a natural starting point. It appears to be the path of least resistance for arbitrators. It is also congruent with the ex-ante expectations of contracting parties, who when they agree to arbitrate

---

1 See Soia Mentschikoff, Commercial Arbitration, 61 Colum. L. Rev., p. 846, at p. 861 (1961). This often-cited study of commercial arbitrators found that 80% of the respondents *"thought that they ought to reach their decisions within the context of the principles of substantive rules of law, but almost 90% believed that they were free to ignore these rules whenever they thought that more just decisions would be reached by so doing."* Note that the survey was conducted a time long before it became commonplace to entrust arbitrators with questions of mandatory, regulatory law – although Mentschikoff still found the results *"curiously parallel to the attitudes that seem to be implicit in our appellate courts."*

do not really expect to be entirely at the whim of arbitrators in isolation from the positive law.[2] In addition, to follow the official public law is very useful for the members of an arbitral tribunal themselves. It not only seems to help insulate their awards against the possibility of legal challenge, but, in addition, the typical member of an arbitral tribunal – the elite law professor or the elite lawyer – wants the chance to show off and advertise his skills, the usual skills by which he has come to define himself. So, for all those reasons the arbitrators are likely to look directly to the publicly-enunciated positive "law". There is really little need for any special concept of arbitral precedent.

As Mr Hochstrasser suggested, the matter may be different when arbitrators are faced with issues as to which there is no well developed body of national law. Issues of arbitration law and practice, like the jurisdiction of the tribunal, the group of companies doctrine or the question whether a non-signatory can be bound to an arbitral clause are matters for which it may be difficult to look to national courts. In addition, there may be gaps in the national law, or more properly, the transaction may have a transnational character where it is uncertain what the applicable national law should be – it may even be uncertain to what extent the usual rules of national law happen to be adequate for the needs of international commerce. The usual and pejorative term is that the rules of contract of the national law may be "parochial". In his case, there may be an opening for the very vague notion of a "lex-mercatoria", which is different from what the national courts will do. But, those are the limited circumstances where arbitrators may develop their own precedent in private commercial matters.

Here is the main point I want to make. When we reach this question of the liberation of arbitration from positive national law, we are getting into something very important. The first point is that any regime of precedent or any regime of precedential constraint, depend in the first instance on the presence of reasoned opinions and on the publication of those opinions. That is all taken for granted within most systems of national law with respect to the functioning of courts. If the giving of reasons involves a commitment to some rule – a rule operating at a higher level of generality and applicable as well to future cases – then imposing a requirement to give reasons may be an attempt to impose on the decision maker a practice of such commitment. A reasoned opinion can thus serve a function of guidance for private parties – supplying predictability with respect to the outcomes of future disputes, facilitating reliance and informed planning in both their dispute settlement and their primary conduct.

But that is very far from being the case in arbitration. To start with the American domestic practice, arbitrators do not write opinions. They are in fact discouraged from doing so by the

---

2   See William W. Park, National Law and Commercial Justice: Safeguarding Procedural Integrity in International Arbitration, 63 Tul. L. Rev., p. 647, at pp. 659–660 (1989) (a lender will "*want to know that the loan agreement, as well as any security agreement or third party guarantee, will be enforced under the applicable law*" and "*[n]either the banker nor the customer is likely to authorize that disputes be resolved under a shade tree, according to an adjudicatory's intuitive sense of fairness or momentary impulse*"). It is one thing, though, to say that in some sense contracting parties are likely to be counting on the arbitrator's application of "the law" – it is something very different to recognize that it was after all his "take" on it – his reading and his own working out of legal principles – that they were bargaining for. This includes their necessary appreciation of the fact that there will be somewhat more play in the joints here than before a state tribunal.

principal administering institution, the American Arbitration Association. To some extent that gives them enormous freedom from any sort of judicial review at all. It is a familiar enough proposition that an arbitrator's freedom from the need to explain or justify his award is closely linked to his lack of accountability in terms of judicial review: The naked award that is the norm in domestic commercial arbitrations can be explained as much by a desire to insulate decisions from judicial scrutiny as by any desire to avoid the delay or added expense that written opinions would entail. And this tactic of insuring the finality of arbitration by harnessing Delphic decisions to a hard-to-rebut presumption of validity has been extremely effective: For example, when one American court found it had no alternative but to confirm an award, even though, there was no expressed reasoning, no findings of fact, no conclusions of law, the court said, *"for all we know the arbitrators concluded that the sun rises in the West, and the earth is flat"*, but we have no alternative but to confirm the award.

While this American practice is only a "default rule," my general impression is that it is rarely reversed in practice.[3] Such an acquiescence in naked awards might serve to reassure us that our usual rule is in fact an efficient one – that it is, as I suspect, appropriately tailored to the expectations and wishes of contracting parties. But of course, that one rarely sees a requirement of reasoned awards can just as plausibly be attributed to the "stickiness" of legal presumptions. Transaction costs incurred in negotiating over unlikely eventualities may deter contracting around the default rule. An even more powerful explanation is that the presumption itself will inevitably affect the preferences of bargainers, as well as their perceptions as to what the customary norm, the "standard, widely accepted solution to a contracting situation" may be. Some support for this latter explanation might be found by looking at actual practice in other legal systems where an opposite presumption – one that favors reasoned awards – prevails, and where the parties must expressly provide for a naked award if they wish one. Apparently in such jurisdictions contracting parties almost always acquiesce in this presumption as well.

The absence of reasoned opinions is not, of course, what we see in international commercial disputes, where reasoned awards are the norm.[4] Many states take it for granted that a reasoned award is necessary for any true adjudicatory function. For example, the UNCITRAL Model Law lays down specifically that the award must be reasoned unless the parties agree otherwise.[5] In some legal systems, the notion that the award must be reasoned is a matter of pub-

---

3   However, where parties arbitrate under the CPR's Non-Administered Arbitration Rules, they do reverse the usual presumption by opting for a reasoned award. The CPR's Non-Administered Arbitration Rules provide that awards *"shall state the reasoning on which the award rests unless the parties agree otherwise."* CPR, Non-Administered Arbitration Rules Rule 13.2. See also *Western Employers Ins. Co. v. Jefferies & Co.*, Inc., 958 F.2d 258, 262 (9th Cir. 1992) (parties altered a standard agreement to arbitrate under NASD rules by requiring the arbitrators to accompany any award with a statement of their findings of fact and conclusions of law; the claimant later demanded such a statement – apparently for collateral estoppel purposes in connection with a related class action pending against the respondent – but the arbitrators refused; held, award vacated, that the claimant should not *"be held to the terms of a contract for which it did not bargain"*).

4   Ph. Fouchard et al., Traité de l'Arbitrage Commercial International 775 (1996) (in international arbitrations *"virtually all [la quasi-totalite] awards are accompanied by reasons"*).

5   See UNCITRAL Model Law, Art. 31 (2): The award *"shall state the reasons upon which it is based, unless the parties have agreed that no reasons are to be given or the award is an award on agreed terms under Article 30"*.

lic policy that the parties cannot agree to vary.[6] Strangely enough, the UNCITRAL Model Law has been enacted not only in a number of important nations, but has also been enacted in six or seven of the largest American states. This in fact is a whole other subject that I unfortunately do not have the time for as it would be interesting to consider and to talk about the extent to which American arbitration law has been deformed by this insistence on mimicking more sophisticated European continental models. The adoption of the UNCITRAL Model Law in many American states is theoretically accompanied by the legal requirement – rarely if ever enforced to my knowledge – that there be a reasoned award.

Even when the award is reasoned, however, publication is rare. Publication takes place largely in arbitrations that are administered by institutions. Mr Hochstrasser said that the ICC does publish some awards but probably not more than 10-15% of their awards. And publication usually requires the express consent of the parties, either their prior consent, or their consent after the fact. The Swiss Rules on international arbitration say something about that, but I could certainly use some help in understanding just what it is that they provide: Article 43 (1) of the Swiss Rules says that unless the parties *"expressly agree in writing to the contrary"* the award shall be confidential, and that undertaking also applies to the arbitrators. That is pretty clear. Sub-section 3 then says, *"an award may be published unless no party objects to such publication."* So Art. 43 (3) seems to say that publication is the norm unless there is an objection by a party;[7] by contrast, Art. 43 (1) seems to say that there should be no publication unless the party has expressly agreed ahead of time.[8] I assume that somebody knows which of those two is the proper result, but I do not. But in any event, the critical point is that publication requires consent at some stage, and is unthinkable if there is a serious objection by the parties – and as a result publication is rare.

In the United States awards are not reasoned and, of course, there is no publication. What is the effect on the arbitral process when there is no requirement of a reasoned opinion? You might think that when there is no requirement of a reasoned opinion, it makes decision making pretty easy. It leads to lazy, uninformed judgement. The parties do not know why the arbitrators reached the decision they did. There is no safeguard against arbitrary decision. People say that, but I confess that I am rather sceptical about this proposition. I suspect that a requirement of a reasoned award is less likely to affect the outcomes and is more likely to be a challenge to the craftsmanship of the arbitrator. That is to say, an arbitrator who is obligated to write an award, a reasoned award, is going to deploy his rhetorical ability, his imagination, his

---

6   In France, arbitral awards must as a matter of public policy (*ordre public*) be reasoned, although this is no longer true for international awards made subject to a foreign law under which reasons are not required. See Jean-Louis Delvolve, Essai sur la Motivation des Sentences Arbitrales, 1989 Rev. de l'Arb. p. 148, at pp. 148–149. For a similar position in Italy, see Bobbie Brooks, *Inc. v. Lanificio Walter Banci*, Corte app. di Firenze, Oct. 8, 1977, 4 Yrbk. Comm. Arb. p. 289, at p. 292 (1979) (American award; *"the fact that the reasoning constitutes a principle of the Italian Constitution is not important because what is fundamental in Italian law of procedure may not be considered as such by foreign legislative and judicial authorities"*).

7   See Tobias Zuberbuhler et al., Swiss Rules of International Arbitration: Commentry (2005) at pp. 368–369 (Art. 43 (3) *"does not require the Chambers to obtain the parties' expressed consent to be able to publish arbitral awards"*).

8   Cf. Alexis Mourre, Precedent and Confidentiality in International Commercial Arbitration: The Case for the Publication of Arbitral Awards, in Emmanuel Gaillard (ed.), Precedent in International Arbitration at pp. 39 and 60 (2008) (Art. 43 (1) of the Swiss rules *"require the parties' written consent prior to publication of an award"*).

creativity and his ingenuity in articulating the narrowest possible, plausible and most conventional rationale for his decision.

A few years ago I had a very interesting conversation with a distinguished European academic and arbitrator, who expressed some surprise that it was only in the United States, which is after all supposedly a common law based judicial system, arbitrators do not have to write opinions and we dispense with written reasoned opinions. This arbitrator found that very strange and very paradoxical. But my reaction was that there is nothing paradoxical about it at all – because it is precisely our common law background that enables us to dispense with written opinions. Our entire legal education specialises in deconstructing legal opinions and debunking their power of explanation. We no longer believe that the presence of a reasoned opinion has very much to do with a just decision. And we do not believe that the process of crafting awards is congruent with the decision making process. That the process of crafting reasoned decisions is not congruent with the decision making process, is a common place of a realist insight. Oliver Wendell Holmes once said in one of his letters: "*I always say in conference [that is, in judicial conference among the judges]*", that no case can be decided by general propositions and that "*I will admit any general proposition you like and still decide the case either way.*"[9] Imposing an obligation of reasoned opinions is not a guarantee of a just decision. It is a challenge to the craftsmanship of the arbitrators.

But there is a second point, which is that reasoned opinions, even though they do not dictate decisions, constrain choice more than we would like. If an arbitrator is free from writing a reasoned opinion, he is free from overbroad rules and he is able to pay maximum attention to the context. For example, let me describe two actual arbitrations, one of which I was involved in:

– The first involved a sale of goods over a period of time, an instalment agreement. The buyer refused to perform, refused to take delivery. The arbitrators awarded damages to the seller for breach, but at the same time they relieved the buyer of any further future obligations to buy. Now, I teach contract law and I would despair of trying to rationalise that result in the terms of the contract doctrine. Yet, the decision may make some rough sense in terms of the business situation of the parties.

– Another example involved a claim that had been made for rescission of a joint venture agreement on the ground of fraudulent inducement. The arbitrators were sympathetic to the plaintiff: They felt that fraud had been shown, but felt that the plaintiff was at least in part responsible for his own dilemma and partly responsible for his own reliance. So they decided that since the plaintiff was responsible for 30% of the fault, they would award 70% of the damages. That, too, is not possible in terms of the ordinary contract doctrine. If the

---

9   Letter from O.W. Holmes, Jr. to Harold Laski, 19 February 1920, in 1 Holmes-Laski Letters 243 (Mark DeWolfe Howe ed., 1953); see also Jerome Frank, Law and the Modern Mind 137-38 (1935) ("*those judges who are most ... swayed by the 'perverting influences of their emotional natures', or most dishonest, are often the very judges who use most meticulously the language of compelling mechanical logic, who elaborately wrap about themselves the pretense of merely discovering and carrying out existing rules, who sedulously avoid any indications that they individualize cases*").

arbitrators are required to justify their result in terms of a reasoned opinion, they are likely to do so in terms of the existing doctrine which may forbid such a result.

If the two cases I described are not compatible with existing positive law, yet they are not arbitrary, not law-less and not lazy, they may respond to some sense of commercial understanding, good business practice and some sense of honourable business behaviour. It is only the freedom not to write an opinion that allows the arbitrators to do this.

The third point is that there is no reason to believe that arbitrators cannot share in the shaping and development of their own law. There is no reason to believe that courts have a natural monopoly over the elaboration of the law. Arbitrators may, as in the case I gave, be more responsive to the business needs of the parties than courts would be. And we have all seen many examples of business law which evolves over time and which might be 30 years out of date. Arbitrators who are intimately involved with the business community may be more sensitive to that and may be able to push the law in a particular direction. One of the founders of Legal Realism, who I have to admit was a colleague of mine when he was in his 90s, Leon Green, once wrote that after all *"the decision of a court is no more 'the law' than the light from yesterday's lamp is electricity."* That is deep indeed, but requires some thought.

What I have been talking about are the commonplaces of Legal Realism, but one further point is this. Left to themselves, arbitrators, as private judges, would have very little incentive to produce precedents. What is the incentive for a private arbitrator to produce a precedent? To write an opinion, which is going to confer some benefit on third parties or on future competing arbitrators – where is the incentive on their part to confer this benefit on people who are not hiring them? Arbitrators may well have reasons to do something. They want to appear to be honest. They want to appear to be competent. They want to appear to be impartial. They want to show that they can do standard legal analysis. So, in many cases an opinion that an arbitrator writes is going to be a piece of advertising or self-promotion to indicate that he, the arbitrator, is able to do this kind of impartial and competent legal writing. But even if he does that, the system is very strongly biased against the creation of precise rules, because any rule that an arbitrator lays down that may indicate just how he is likely to decide a case, will assure that no case involving this issue will be submitted to him in the future because we know exactly how he feels about it. There are powerful pressures even on arbitrators who write opinions to be obscure or to be open-ended so as not to give their hand away. How else to explain the many cases that I have seen where the question arises which law governs that dispute? And the typical arbitral decision will be very careful to scrupulously canvas every conceivable possibility and every conceivable national law and to conclude that they would have reached the same result regardless of what law they were applying. They do not need to make any definitive decision with respect to what law to apply, because they would reach the same result anyway. All of the biases are against the production of anything other than the most vague and obscure doctrines, because the most important consideration for an arbitrator is future acceptability in future cases.

One more point and then I am going to stop. This will lead to what Mrs Franck is going to talk about. I have been talking about private commercial arbitration as if it was a fairly consistent monolithic block, but obviously, it takes different forms. For example, in the United States collective bargaining agreements between unions and employers – although a very small piece of the economic pie these days – will always contain arbitration clauses. Arbitrators decide thousands of these cases in labour disputes every year. These awards are always reasoned awards and quite a few are published. Many are distilled into treatises about the law of the workplace. The labour awards are also increasingly relied on by other arbitrators in similar cases.[10] This is a very different paradigm from the commercial case I first started to talk about. Why? What makes it different? We were talking about this at lunch and Mr Hochstrasser said, in a slightly different context, that this is blindingly obvious. That took a little bit of the wind out of my sails, because what was going to be a subtle and elaborate discussion is now, in light of what he said, going to be very short. In the labour cases I was describing you have an agreement which is the constitution for the plant. It is governing the future relationship between the parties. There are going to be recurring disputes between these same parties and the parties who are subject to these recurring disputes need some guidance as to how an arbitrator is likely to consider the case in the future so they can adjust their behaviour. And in addition, these are not disputes which will ever find their way into court, given the separate institutional structure of collective bargaining. There is no need for arbitrators to look to the supposedly superior court system, because these are disputes which are only settled in arbitration. In cases like that, arbitrated disputes would naturally lead themselves to reasoned opinions and publication.

The same structural features, that might explain the use of precedent in labour cases, may also explain a very robust system of precedent in investment arbitration and in sports arbitration, where we also have a running series of recurring disputes. Also, there is in such cases a strong interest in maintaining a level playing field so that one party is not disadvantaged and that one's competitors do not have an advantage by a separate kind of treatment. In investment arbitration, in particular, the stakes are enormous. The economic repercussions affecting bodies of citizens are vast and so there has developed a self-contained system of regulatory law where again such disputes are never and cannot ever be committed to state judges. And so, of necessity to maintain a certain level playing field, arbitrators have to develop precedent. The development of a system of precedent in investment and sports cases can be expected to be very different for those structural reasons from the ordinary commercial case.

---

10 See Frank Elkouri/ Edna A. Elkouri, How Arbitration Works, pp. 414–419 (4th ed. 1985) (an "*extensive survey of labour arbitration disclosed that 77% of the ... responding arbitrators believed that precedents, even under other contracts, should be given 'some weight'*").

Costs in Investment Arbitration

SUSAN FRANCK

Thank you to the conference organisers for having me here. In light of the absence of Jim Loftis, I should provide a bit of a background on investment treaty arbitration as it is a relatively new innovation. Creating a common doctrinal framework will enhance our discussions. I would first like to give you a background on what an international investment agreement is and how it results in an international arbitration. This will permit us to focus on the primary aspect of my talk, namely how costs are treated in investment arbitration and the role that precedent plays within that particular aspect of arbitration.

What is an international investment agreement? It is an international treaty that some have called a "grand bargain" where a sovereign state (in an effort to attract foreign investment and its concomitant benefits) decides that it is worth the risk and related costs to create substantive investor rights and to provide a set of procedural rights that offer a forum for the resolution of the substantive disputes. At present, there is a "spaghetti bowl" of more than 2600 bilateral and multilateral treaties in this area that offer investors a series of substantive economic rights. For example, investment treaties offer compensation for expropriation, freedom from discrimination, guarantees of fair and equitable treatment and can transform domestic law contract claims to international law violations. Although, some actions have traditional international law antecedents, some substantive rights have been unique innovations.

As Professor Rau suggested, there are certain bodies of law that are thick and some that are thin. Investment treaty arbitration is an area in which I would suggest that the precedent and other doctrine is on the rather "thin" side. But the real innovation of these treaties was not actually the specification of substantive rights, rather it was the procedural rights granted by states to private investors. So, rather than the government-to-government dispute resolution that Rachel Brewster and others will discuss tomorrow, investment treaty arbitration is about private citizens (whether private individuals or corporate entities) initiating arbitration immediately against states. Generally, national courts are not provided as an option for resolving disputes (although some treaties may permit this option): Instead, treaties provide an opportunity – where an investor believes that one of its international law rights in the treaty has been violated – to more or less immediately bring the host state to the bargaining table of international arbitration.

Let me give you an example to make that scenario sticky. A rather straight-forward case might involve an investor from the United States who owns a bank in Estonia and whose banking license is revoked by a state regulatory body. The US investor in the Estonian bank may be in a position to claim a violation of the US-Estonia investment treaty and hypothetically make a claim for a denial of "fair and equitable treatment" by the Republic of Estonia for alleged damage to the bank in the order of $ 50 million. Or, one might also look to cases related to the Argentinean currency crisis, where a government decision to change the link between the US Dollar and the Peso arguably decreased the value of foreign investments and arguably damaged investors. These claims against Argentina are no small matter and have resulted in hundreds of millions of dollars claimed against the government of Argentina. Nevertheless, these types of cases are a relatively new historical phenomenon. One of the first cases in my own dataset came about in the early 1990s. UNCTAD now has information about over 250 disputes arising under international investment treaties.

One critical normative question is: Are the costs of the treaties worth it? In other words, are the purported benefits of foreign investment and agreeing to limit a state's regulatory space to become part of a larger international economic playing field worth the costs? While there are a variety of political and social costs, today I would like to focus on the actual fiscal costs of investment arbitration.

To offer a sense of why this matters, investment treaties and investment treaty arbitration are now somewhat contentious aspects of the international political economy. The United States and Norway are either revising or have thought about revising their international investment agreements; and the European Union is contemplating the implications of its approach to international investment. Although some countries have been joining the ICSID Convention, others have been withdrawing from it as well as from other investment treaties. As this area has landed on the pages of the Financial Times, it makes a considered and careful analysis of this area all the more prudent.

My thesis is that costs in investment treaty arbitration are in need of further rationalisation. While the data I analyzed suggested that there was a degree of incoherence, there were also pockets of rationality and consistency. Yet there was little reliance on precedent in tribunals' treatment of costs. I would suggest that, when it comes to the fiscal costs of investment treaty arbitration, it would be appropriate to create incentives to encourage better behaviour and more transparent decision making. This creates an opportunity to enhance the integrity and perceived legitimacy of the dispute resolution system as well as permitting investors and states to make more informed assessments about both their dispute resolution risks and the net value of investment agreements and arbitration. So, let me break down how I am going to address that.

First, I would like to provide you some data about the investment arbitration process to give you a sense of what I collected and why, so that you can make an assessment about its utility. Second, I will offer some basic data about cost outcomes and show you some divergence with a bit of balance. Third, I would like to provide information about both authority and rationale that investment tribunals used to make their decisions about cost. Then I will mention a few areas of reliability and sum up what I think it all means.

There are various processes that might be used to create reliable data sets. Using publicly available awards before 2007, we identified 102 awards in 82 different cases. We coded data about who were the parties, who were the winners, who were the losers, what amounts were claimed and various issues related to costs. For investment treaty arbitration, there are two costs that I focused upon. One is the parties' legal costs, namely their lawyers and experts. That is one variable (namely, PLC). A second variable, which is doctrinally distinct, was the tribunals' costs and expenses (TCE), namely how much do the arbitrators get and how much the institutions. These are doctrinally separate but potentially quite similar. This matters particularly as different national court systems have – within their national court systems – different doctrinal approaches to cost allocation in national court litigation. The US approach has what is often referred to as the "American Rule" or what I call the "pay-your-own-way" that requires parties to pay for the totality of their own costs and expenses. A more traditional UK or continental approach is called the "Loser Pays" approach, namely you pay if you lose. But there is a third approach championed by the Swedish academic Lars Wellamson, which is interested in various factors and has advocated for parties paying for their relative success amongst other aspects. Different approaches to how costs can be addressed in investment treaty arbitration may derive in part from a purported baseline that potentially emanates from traditions in national court litigation; or it may be a function of the treaty terms or the parties' agreement.

Now, I would like to honour my promise to give you some basic data about investment treaty arbitrations. The awards occurred during different phases, jurisdiction, merits, damages etc. Theoretically, tribunals could address costs at each and every one of those junctures. But the data says that tribunals did not and instead decided costs primarily in final awards. In non-final awards, there were only about five that make cost decisions and 26 reserved their decisions. This was arguably a lost opportunity to permit parties to think systematically about what cost rules may be applied to their case, adjust their arbitration behaviour accordingly and perhaps even facilitate an early settlement. But there is more. It is not just that tribunals could make cost decisions or offer cost guidance at various temporal junctures; there are also issues related to the net result of cost decisions. Remember we have two variables, what the lawyers cost (PLC) and what the tribunals cost (TCE). There were potentially seven different permutations about how costs could be decided at the end of the day. What the data shows is that there was variation in how tribunals decided and apportioned costs. The most prevalent approach was the "pay-your-own-way" approach, where the parties paid their own attorney's fees and half of the tribunal's fees. But what does it mean in terms of actual fiscal costs? What it means is the average cost shift of the parties' fees (not the total party cost but the shift of PLC) was approximately $ 500,000–700,000. But the tribunals make about $ 600,000 on average. So, you start to think, what are the potential costs of arbitration? And this is a very conservative measure given that it does not fully reflect the totality of both parties' total cost for lawyers. But it is worth considering the value of pursuing arbitration given the scope of potential costs, the uncertainty of who will pay those costs and the fact that the average amount awarded in the order of $10 million.

As one example, which is an arguable outlier because there was a clear legal error involved, I will mention the *Eureko v. Poland* award. In a case that had been discussed in the Financial Times and that had a claim against the Republic of Poland for $ 1.34 billion, a rather prominent tribunal rendered an 86 page award on the merits of the claim, which decided against

Poland. In a quick reference to cost, the tribunal explained the: *"Claimant has prevailed. Consequently, its costs and those of the Tribunal shall be borne by the Respondent."* There was nothing further. Unfortunately, there was no citation to legal authority; but if there had been a reference to the underlying treaty, the tribunal would have learned that its shift of cost was expressly prohibited. While a press release issued by the Republic of Poland suggests this was redressed in a subsequent decision (i.e. why this case is an arguable outlier), it was typical of other cases in two respects. First, it failed to cite any sort of legal authority for its justification. Second, it cited only one reason for its ultimate adjudication on costs.

I also promised to tell you about how tribunals decide and to offer a sense of what tribunals do both in terms of authority they cite and the rationale that they provide. Here using the metric of tribunals' costs and expenses (TCE) as the data is more complete. As a general matter, tribunals exhibited minimal reliance on legal authority for their cost decisions. The average number of authorities cited was less than one, and the average number of rationales cited was less than two. This was striking given how generous we tried to be with the coding. We would have even coded authority as a rule that permitted tribunals to act according to their own discretion or a tribunal indicating that they were acting in accordance with their discretion. But many of the awards did not even cite that. To be fair, there is a thoughtful article by W. Mark C. Weidemaier from the University of North Carolina in which he suggested that sometimes these decisions are made in accordance with precedent the tribunals implicitly recognise. While I appreciate that, I would nevertheless encourage tribunals to be more transparent in this sensitive political area. Let me give you a little bit more details. What were they citing? What were these tribunals relying on? Again, I tried to code for just about everything. The ICSID Convention, UNCITRAL Rules, Stockholm Chamber of Commerce Rules, investment treaties themselves, arbitration awards, other tribunals, national courts, and other sources, such as even law review articles. But what we see generally is that there were only three awards where tribunals actually referred to other tribunals (such as other investment treaty tribunals or the Iran – US Claims Tribunal). The other noteworthy aspect was that in the 24 cases involving ICSID, only nine cases cited the ICSID Convention, the ICSID Arbitration Rules or the ICSID Additional Facility Rule. In other words, more than half of the ICSID tribunals did not cite their own authority, whereas the subset of Stockholm and UNCITRAL tribunals cited their own internal rules more than 90 % of the time. This suggests that there may be a disjunction between ICSID and other tribunals as regards their willingness to cite authority for costs.

Costs are more than legal authority. It is also about what rationale the tribunals provide. Some literature in investment treaty arbitration recommends following a "cost-follow-the-event" rule. In some of my own early scholarship, I suggested (perhaps wrongly) that there should not be a concern about unmeritorious behaviour by parties because tribunals would address impropriety by shifting costs and making parties pay for their bad behaviour. However, that does not appear to be what tribunals did. This idea of punishing bad behaviour or rewarding good behaviour was cited some of the time but not always. Rather the tribunals were much more interested in parties' relative success and general conceptions of equity and justice. There was also a category we defined as "substantive," which was a little bit of what we thought of as a "I know it when I see it", i.e. there is a bit of a problem here and we will use these underlying substantive issues about the substantive claim itself as a basis for shifting costs. But what was not cited were concerns related to stare decisis, making informed decisions or some other sorts of concern related to precedent. In other words, both as regards citation to legal authority and underlying rationale for costs, investment treaty arbitration tribunals did not seem terribly interested in precedent and legal doctrine.

Now, I would like to contrast this with other research, which I have not done personally but I have been fortunate to learn from. Both Jeffrey Commission and Ole Kristian Fauchald have done a reasonably equivalent look at ICSID cases in a similar time frame to see what happens on the merits, jurisdiction and substantive claims and how tribunals cite authority. Their evidence about the scope of tribunal's reliance on precedent is markedly different. Jeffrey Commission's study suggests that at the beginning of investment treaty arbitration jurisprudence, tribunals only cited one case on average for arbitral precedent. That makes a great deal of sense because there was very little precedent to cite at that point in time. However, as the caseload has evolved, Mr Commission found an increasing number of citations to other awards. So, for example from 2000 to 2001, he found 2.5 citations per case. But by 2006 that rose to 10 citations in every case. This suggests that citation to precedent in investment arbitration is reflexive; and to the extent that there are increases in the number of available decisions, there may be more authority to draw on, so we begin to create, as Professor Rau suggested, a more "thick" body to evaluate. Mr Fauchald found something similar except he did not simply look at cases that were citing precedent. He considered what type of precedent tribunals relied upon. Mr Fauchald found that the most "precedent" referred to consisted of other ICSID awards, general legal doctrine and state practice; he also observed that what tribunals did not refer to were things related to party agreement or general principles of law. His overall thesis was that tribunals were more likely to rely on specific rules and specific decisions rather than generalised conceptions of international law or legal standards.

I may have painted a rather bleak picture of investment treaty arbitration, at least as it regards costs and the lack of coherence within the system. But there are pockets of consistency. Namely, there are issues related to a link between the two different types of legal costs (namely PLC and TCE) that were statistically significant. I interpret this as meaning "in for a penny, in for a pound." If the tribunals shifted the parties' legal costs, they were also likely to do something relatively similar with the tribunal's costs and expenses. But there was a lack of a statistically significant relationship with a cost shift and which party lost the dispute. I was unable to find evidence that the "loser-pays" rule was reliably linked to a cost shift either for the legal costs of the parties' lawyers or the tribunal itself. There was no relationship between winning and losing and a party's legal cost shift. There was likewise no relationship between winning and losing and shifting the tribunal's cost. This suggests that the "American Rule," namely the "pay-as-you-go" approach, predominated at least this dataset of investment treaty arbitration awards.

But there are also a few other points that are worthwhile to note. There is an intriguing empirical literature in the United States that considers domestic national litigation that variables related to litigation costs. Recent studies from the US Federal Judicial Center by Lee & Willging consider how increased costs can be associated with large law firms being involved in cases, more electronic discovery and larger time spent on cases. Those are very interesting variables that we should keep our eyes on. But Lee & Willging were looking at the party's legal costs in US national court litigation, rather than those costs in international arbitration or the cost of international tribunals. I was interested in exploring whether or not there was any kind of a reliable relationship between the tribunal's costs (TCE), largely because the public data is more complete on this variable, and links between what amounts investors claimed in damages and the ultimate outcome. What I found was an intriguing pocket of consistency where – even when controlling for energy disputes – the lower the amount claimed, the lower the cost of the tribunal. Likewise, the higher the amount claimed, the higher the cost of the tribunal. This finding is quite important, particularly as the investor is the only party that can initiate a claim and establish the amount in controversy in investment treaty arbitration. In other words, foreign investors kick off the cost of the entire dispute and the potential costs of the proceedings by the amount that they claim in damages. So, to the extent that we want to encourage useful behaviour in international dispute resolution, I might suggest that there are normative changes that we may wish to consider. Some of it may relate to requiring claimants to have a good faith pleading obligation or to particularise their claimed damages at an early time. While this data does suggest that the higher the net cost of the tribunal the more the parties claimed, this is not a causal relationship. We cannot say definitively that higher claims will necessarily lead to higher total costs of proceedings. It is, however, a critical first step in moving the discussion forward.

As an interesting counterpoint, there was no reliable relationship between the total tribunal costs and the actual amount awarded. The inference from the data is quite simple. Based upon the data and our measures, we were unable to demonstrate that the arbitrators' payday depended upon the amount they actually awarded. The variable appeared to function independently, which suggests that arbitrators do not necessarily have a stake in an individual outcome at the macro level. That is a very intriguing piece of evidence as regards the legitimacy of the investment arbitration system.

I know that we are going to have a rather interesting discussion, so, I would like to wrap up briefly. However, I would like to mention what I think this means normatively for investment treaty arbitration.

For me, this means that we need to address cost-related issues (both PLC and TCE) at an early stage so that parties will have a sense of what rules and standards tribunals will be using. This should help parties adjust their arbitration conduct and strategies as well as giving them a sense of variables that affect the potential value of settlement. I also think it means that we need to encourage tribunals to be transparent about cost decisions in the same way that they have become increasingly transparent about the reasons for their adjudication on the merits of claims. This may involve various approaches. We might consider mandating criteria for tribunals to consider. One can hardly be surprised at the variation in tribunals' reasoning when there is little guidance about what reasoning is determinative and when arbitration rules and treaties themselves are silent. If stakeholders decide it is normatively desirable, it might be appropriate to either mandate particular categories of rationales or indeed incentivise the use of particular rationales through a soft law or normative practice. There may also be value in implementing a procedural mechanism for controlling variance related to claimed damages. But these options and normative implications will, of course, develop over time.

So, what means this overall? It means that the data suggested that there was a partial rationalisation of costs in investment arbitration, but that precedent and stare decisis had a small role to play in that rationalisation. It means that there were pockets of certainty but we need to continue the process of rationalising investment arbitration, at least in my view, because there is far too much at stake from a normative matter with the creation of international law and the continuing validity of international economic agreements in a time of globalisation and economic transformation. Future research is needed and may shed light on the use of precedent and arbitration costs, particularly as the population continues to evolve and statistical insights will no doubt also shift. For now, my suggestion is that we create a system that offers greater reasoning and authority to enhance the legitimacy of investment treaty arbitration and international investment agreements to a broader constituency of stakeholders.

Discussion

DANIEL HOCHSTRASSER
Thank you, Susan. This brings us to the discussion part and maybe I can kick this off with two comments that I would like to make regarding your presentation. The first is that I was a bit surprised about your finding that fees are not somehow related to the amount of the award. It would be a pretty bad sign if it was otherwise, because it would basically mean that the fee of the tribunal is some sort of tax on the award or, to put it differently, I would not want to be a defendant in a system where the tribunal has an incentive to make a higher award to get higher fees. The other question is: would in your view a system like ICC arbitration, where the fees are set by an institution, help to lead to a uniform cost regime?

SUSAN FRANCK
I was surprised because I was not exactly sure what I was going to find. There have been certain critiques of the international investment treaty arbitration and I think it is critical to stick to the data and focus on the facts. It is a *Freakonomics* approach to international investment law. I was not sure what I was going to get in part because of the critiques about the legitimacy of the system. I agree that it could appear to be the equivalent of a tax on the award. To the extent that all of the respondents are states who are the parties who were drafting the treaties, it is a key piece of information for the respondent states.

As it regards the fees set by the institution, I am not necessarily troubled by a case that takes longer to trial and is, therefore, more expensive because the facts and law warrant that. What I am more concerned about is when the tribunals do articulate their reasoning or their authority for making their decisions, tribunals should do so in a coherent and transparent matter that permits parties to potentially predict what rules the tribunals might use and how they will exercise their discretion. Because, if you know that they are going to be following a "loser-pays"-model you may behave differently in deciding whether to make certain types of claims in your pleading and in terms of making particular defences or in terms of requesting particular types of evidence. To the extent that it is affecting the litigation strategy and parties' pay off matrixes, it is helpful to be able to assess whether parties will have to internalise these costs or indeed whether it might be that they will pay for their lawyer's fees, the other side's lawyers' fees and the tribunal's fees. Giving guidance at an early stage is very useful in that respect for investment arbitration.

ALAN RAU
I have one point: I have never had an investment case and if I continue to say the things that I am going to say, I probably never will. If I were to have one, I would probably start with the presumption that the loser should pay, because that would be my best guess as to what the ex-

pectation of the parties would be. But, I would certainly feel compelled to embellish that result with equity considerations. I wonder about the utility of taking arbitral rationales at face value. I would fear that if I was simply to rely on a simple metric like a "loser-pays", I might lose face with the relevant peer group. A related point is in regard to who is doing this arbitration. Unlike commercial arbitration we are talking about a very limited group of very elite arbitrators who see themselves as the equals of state judges with whom they exist on a parallel basis and whose decisions are regularly commented on and analysed as if they were judges of a supreme court. The arbitrators, who are writing opinions, are writing for this peer group who are fellow arbitrators. They want to show-case their legal understanding of proper principles so a simple crude "loser-pays" or the American rule – you bear your own costs – would have to be tarted up with a certain amount of other considerations that you talked about. In other words, the stated rationale of the tribunal does give you the transparency that you are claiming for.

DANIEL HOCHSTRASSER
Let us open the discussion for the audience. We have a number of interventions.

MICHAEL WAIBEL
Thank you very much for two highly interesting presentations. I was particularly fascinated by Mrs Franck's collection of data on the costs and I summarised, for myself and I may be wrong, what you said on precedent. We cannot really say that, at a macro level, precedent plays an important role in investment arbitration. You really need to look deeper. It seems to play a fairly important role when it comes to the merits of jurisdiction. It plays almost no role as in regard to costs and that is because there is very little reasoning in the cost decisions. I wonder whether you have some hypothesis for why that is. Is it because of the ICSID Convention's license to arbitrators to use their discretion as it regards cost decisions? Is it because they think that cost decisions are not important? Is it that there are no other awards with reasoned cost decisions? Is it that arbitrators are tired by the time they get to the cost decisions after they have concluded a hundred pages reasoning through the merits and the jurisdiction?

SUSAN FRANCK
Mr Weibel, you summed it up with your usual alacrity. Yes, it does seem that precedent matters more on the merits but much less on the costs. If it was indeed just simply a question of the ICSID Convention, for example, which grants discretion without guidelines for exercising that discretion, I would at least have expected a little bit more reliance on the legal authority of the ICSID Convention. There is a forthcoming article in the Cornell Law Review that talks about repeat appointments for arbitrators. One of the interesting findings of this particular study is that repeat arbitrators are less likely to reach compromise awards. The conclusion of that article is essentially that there are no compromise awards in investment treaty arbitration on the merits. That is the working hypothesis of the article that is supported by that particular data set. So, there may be more analysis on the merits, particularly when there is a 200 page award. It makes me wonder whether or not costs, which are typically decided quickly at the end of an award, are an effort to split the proverbial baby. For example, one of the things I

found, when looking at the specific sub-set of those investment arbitrations that have specific fiscal information about costs, those cases were more likely than the general population to have a separate opinion. So, it suggests to me that perhaps, although tribunals may want uniformity on the merits of the claim, costs are more of an afterthought. That may have something to do with what Dean Sager was talking about today in terms of splitting things in a particular way if you do not agree on the case matter. Perhaps that means that the tribunal will separate this tiny costs issue and decide issues differently. However, I would not go much further than that, but the idea did occur to me. If you arenot wiling to split on the merits, maybe you are willing to split on costs.

DANIEL HOCHSTRASSER
Would you not, as an arbitrator in an ICSID case, rather write more about why you allocate costs a certain way if you have discretion as opposed to when you have no discretion? If you are operating in the "loser-pays" regime, you do not have to say anything; if you have total discretion, that is when I want to explain why and under what principles I allocate costs.

RICHARD PLENDER
May I add to your contribution an account of a very recent ICSID decision, which appears to me to be unprincipled, counter to precedent but wise and exactly what one should expect from a well constituted tribunal? The dispute was between the world's largest dimensional stone quarry – it quarries marble, granite and other stone sold by the square meter or yard – and the South African government. The South African government was defending the centre piece of the ANCs legislation, the Mineral and Petroleum Resources Development Act, which requires mines in South Africa to ensure progressively that a proportion of their share holding and of their management is in the hands of black South Africans over a period of 25 years. The objection of the quarries to this was that this quarry was established in Italy and, therefore, a closed Italian company. The owners are all multi-billionaires and since the days of Marco Cicero, the same family has owned the company. Indeed, they were rather proud in telling me that they had sold the marble to Michael Angelo to build his famous statue. The complaint was that by requiring disposal of shares to South Africans, irrespective of colour, the legislation expropriated a portion of the company. That complaint seems to me pretty unarguable. The quarries made it plain at the outset that their real objection was that they were not in the same industry as the mines and the petroleum companies and that they were swept up by careless drafting in the same legislation. After fairly prolonged ICSID proceedings, the South African government announced that it was prepared to make an exception and to amend the legislation in favour of the quarries. The tribunal thereafter awarded costs against the quarries. The quarries were delighted with the result. They got what they wanted. The costs, although astronomical by your and my bank manager's standards were trifling in relation to the value of the successful company. The last thing they wanted was to penalise the South African government in costs. As they explained, they are in a long term business. They were investing now for profits in 30 years time. They wanted good relations with the South African government. The award of the tribunal, although in favour of the quarries, was against them in costs. Even though it was probably wrong in principle to do so, it was wise having regard to the commercial relations be

tween the company and the government. One should not look for too much logic in awards of tribunals in relation to costs. Sometimes wisdom prevails over logic.

DANIEL HOCHSTRASSER
That almost sounds like a final word, but we are not there yet.

LUCIUS CAFLISCH
Thank you very much. I have seen a recent ICSID arbitration and have been struck by the following elements regarding costs. The plaintiff, who had invested in a foreign country and was represented by a very large firm specialised in that kind of business, lodged a claim against a country. The firm was drowning the poor three fellows who sat on the board of arbitration in all kinds of documentation, and its bill was simply colossal. On the opposite side you had the state working more cheaply, with its own employees, that is, with no outsiders except a few experts, and making its own people work. That meant that the plaintiff had enormous expenses and the state very little. If you apply the own-cost rule, that is all right. But if you do not, if expenses are shared, this will cost the state a packet. And this rule also would have the effect of tempting the plaintiff to spend a lot more money than warranted by an economical way of proceeding. What do you think of this problem and do you see a way of solving it?

SUSAN FRANCK
I think that you have hit the nail on the head and that you understand why it matters. This is precisely why I was interested in costs. There may be a mismatch or there may be equals. We do not know about it, particularly when rules related to cost allocation are assessed not knowing what kind of dispute is going to arise, because the agreement is part of an ex ante arbitration agreement. But once you have a live dispute, what do you do about it? That is the question. Professor John Gotanda has recently written a bit about costs and investment arbitration and as a normative matter he would very much recommend the "pay-as-you-go" approach to redress precisely those types of issues that you have suggested; namely you want to prevent an imbalance which incentivises poor behaviour on the part of the investors. That is Professor Gotanda's approach and I actually think that that is potentially a very useful approach. I, however, prefer a more normative approach that focuses on certain behaviours to incentivize party conduct. For example, tribunals will decide the case on the basis of the factors before it. So that to the extent the tribunals do have discretion, they can take that into account as regards the particular dispute before them but they have to be clear about when and why they will be using those rules, because there is a flip side to the scenario. What happens if there is a very small Costa Rica banana investor, whose plant is worth no more than $ 1 million. Imagine that the costs of hisown arbitration are $ 1 million and with cost shifting it could be $ 5 million. In this circumstance, you have the costs of investment arbitration that outweigh the cost of the investment itself, which is potentially a significant inhibition from bringing arguably wrongful government conduct before an international tribunal. That issue concerns me as well as I am trying to look for procedural integrity in the system itself. This is one of the reasons why I prefer clarity about expectations – whether in a treaty, arbitral rules or an upfront assessment by the tribunal – on how they intend to handle arbitration costs, so that investors and states can

know at the outset, what the likely consequences are and parties can use that information to weigh up the costs and benefits of pursuing investment arbitration.

DANIEL HOCHSTRASSER
This strikes me as a problem which is not specific to investment treaty arbitration. It is a very general problem which you also encounter in litigation, but there it might be less of an issue. You certainly see it in commercial arbitration, where you sometimes see one party (it might be the bigger party, but it might be just the more desperate party) coming to hearings with a football team of lawyers and the other one sits there with one lawyer, who sometimes does a better job and a more focused job in any case. If you then reach the stage where you have to award the costs, at least general arbitration rules such as the ICC rules and the Swiss rules say that what you do compensate under the "loser-pays" rule are costs that were reasonably incurred. I have been in cases where the tribunal have actually said, that, they do not see why a party needed two law firms and why they had to bring six or seven lawyers to a hearing in a case with an amount in dispute of $ 4 million. That was simply unreasonable. There were cases where we simply did not award the cost that the party was claiming.

The question is really whether this problem speaks in favour of the "loser-pays" rule or for the pay-as-you-go-rule. Definitely, the risk for the small guy under the "loser-pays" rule is that he has to compensate the other side if he loses. On the other hand, if the small guy wins, your banana grower from Costa Rica, at least if the "loser-pays" rule applies, gets his $ 1 million back that he invested in this case. I think it works either way.

LAWRENCE SAGER
I was just trying to sort out two very different reasons for precedent that our two speakers gave. On the one hand, Mr Rau stressed a sort of legal process school reason, which is the guidance of parties in the world, broadly speaking. And Mrs Franck stressed integrity of tribunal decisions. I was thinking about both of those reasons and was trying to understand where costs fit in that picture as opposed to the substance of contractual relations. Here, I have a kind of naivety that undercuts my instinct. But my instinct is that in order to guide parties in the complex set of arrangements that they face in the world of commerce, you may need a fairly rich and subtle body of precedent, if you can get it, confidentiality notwithstanding. But you would think some fairly blunt propositions about costs could suffice. They might be varied over time but any of these rules for the moment would seem as though you could place a fairly blunt set of cost rules. If it were well published and stable, it would do the guidance job and the integrity job. It would seem as though the substantive decisions require a much more complex set of principles to produce guidance. Both of them seem to give over to integrity.

SUSAN FRANCK
Theoretically, what I want us to be able to do is to create litigation or arbitration insurance as regards issues related to costs. As you have said, if we can price it out, then parties are more likely to know their dispute resolution risk. But again, it is as if we are in the early days of investment arbitrations costs clarity. So, to the extent that we can get more predictability, certainty and a few guidelines or even if parties wanted to include provisions in their treaties them-

selves or there was a particular protocol in institutions like ICSID to provide a little bit more guidance about even just the base line, that would be useful. I cannot fault the arbitrators for coming up with divergent decisions if they have no guidance whatsoever. The parties then get exactly what they want, namely, divergence and uncertainty. So, to the extent that they want that, that is fine, but to the extent that we can provide procedural integrity and price out the cost aspects, that I think has long term merit.

DANIEL HOCHSTRASSER
Maybe the certainty you get when you agree on arbitration is not the certainty about the outcome, but the certainty that you have three competent, neutral, objective, experienced arbitrators who will decide and who will do the right thing. And maybe that is one of the reasons why the users of arbitration, at least as far as the merits are concerned, are not so much interested in having a lot of precedents quoted. They want to make sure that they have an arbitral tribunal who hears them and who does the right thing and who takes a wise decision. That decision might not be influenced at all by what some local court has decided on similar issues. And you could even go one step further and say, why should parties have to pay? And that goes, I think, in Mr Rau's direction: Why should parties have to pay for arbitrators to kind of develop their own reputation by writing elaborate awards, when all they want is the right and the wise decision. If they trust the three arbitrators, they might not really want to know the legal details that caused them to decide that way. For me, the main purpose of having a reasoned award is to improve acceptance by the parties, so they do not only get the result, but they also get some explanation why the tribunal reached that result. But do they really want to hear elaborate legal discussions of precedents and why the tribunal thinks this is the right precedent, and the other one is not to be followed? I am somewhat doubtful.

ALAN RAU
That is interesting and I would like to hear sort of general people's views about this. I suspect if you ask people who make the decision whether to include an arbitration clause in a commercial agreement and if you ask the commercial council who are doing it what they expect out of the process, you will not get the answer that they want justice or that they want a wise decision because that is dangerous. They are likely to say that they want a decision where the arbitrators follow the law. The last thing in the world they want to do is to put themselves in the hands or their head in the jaw of someone whose idea of justice is very different from theirs. And that is why I think that arbitrators do tend to follow the law more often than not because it is consistent with the ex-anti expectations of the parties. They know that they are accepting the arbitrator's take on the law, but that the arbitrator is some wise person sitting under a tree who is just going to do justice, and is just going to dispense justice as he sees it is alien to the expectations of corporate council.

DANIEL HOCHSTRASSER
I tend to disagree, not totally but to a certain extent. I tend to believe that there is some more to the decision to agree on arbitration, particularly in an international setting, where you have two parties from two sometimes quite different countries; different in terms of culture and different in terms of the quality of the judicial system. The starting point of the discussion is quite

often that both parties say, whatever happens, we do not want to end up in the courts of our opponent's home country. So, that leaves, for example the High Court in London, and it leaves arbitration. Not surprisingly many then opt for arbitration. Is that the wise man sitting under a palm tree? No, but there are three, or at least two trustworthy people who take a wise decision – or not so wise but least a neutral decision –, which are not biased and they are not in the other parties' pocket.

THOMAS STEPHEN BURKE
As in-house counsel, when it comes to choosing for arbitration, one of the things that we are acutely aware of is cost. What does it cost you to go to arbitration? This is usually the singular defining point when it comes to whether we will or we will not go to arbitration, because it is definitely not just quick and cheap. And that is no reflection whatsoever on the skill or the ability of the arbitrators but it usually relates to the complexity of the types of disputes that arise. I work in the oil and gas business. Everything we do is insanely expensive and if there is a dispute, it can go on for a very, very long time. One example: In 2008 we were to lay 86 km of pipeline in the North Atlantic and we had a vessel that was to come in and do that. The cost of the vessel was somewhere in the region of $ 1.2 million a day and for that then to take between 40 to 60 days, depending on the weather. When the operators of the vessel were testing it, they damaged the pipe-lay vessel on the seabed. They broke off the piece of what is called the stinger that sits on the back of the pipe-lay vessel. There was no other pipe-lay vessel in the world that can do the job we needed done and the vessel had to be repaired. Because of the time window to do that, it put our operations out by over 12 months. It caused a project delay and an increase in costs – and those costs are enormous. Will we go to arbitration on something like that? Most likely not. We will sit down and try to hammer it out because it is far more effective and far more useful for us to do that. I am very interested in the ICSID case where the company was quite happy to absorb the costs because they ultimately got what they wanted in South Africa, because sometimes the exercise of your legal rights is not really what you want. It is certainly not what a business wants. A business wants clarity on what it can do. If clarity comes at a price, the legal departments are often very reluctant to have to pick up the tab out of their budget for clarity, but the business overall is often very happy to say that we can do that.

To just come back very quickly to the analysis of the costs, it was very heartening to know that the arbitrators are not invested in the outcome, but quite disheartening to note that if as an investor in a state where your only option can sometimes be to go to investor state arbitration under the ICSID rules, you are going to be so heavily penalised because the decision on the equitable element of cost is removed. That is a very bitter pill for a business to have to swallow. And it is not a particularly pleasant pill for the lawyers in the company to have to administer.

SUSAN FRANCK
This is why I started the empirical research. It was also because of a promise that I made to my friends, namely I said, „I hope I never create useless legal research but rather create something that is of value". Having spent time in practice both in the US and in the UK, I was vitally sensitive to the impact that cost can have on clients. Part of what I hope this research leads to, not just this but other people building on it as well, is helping us to think more systematically about

the value of arbitration, because in investment disputes, arbitration is the baseline. But as your comment earlier today suggested, we need to be able to bargain in the shadow of the law, which means we need to be able to do some sort of a rational cost-benefit analysis of the arbitral baseline to think about the value of other forms of dispute resolution. Sitting down and hammering it out on the basis of interests as opposed to legal rights is one way to do it. But we do not get there in terms of making an informed assessment until we first have the information about the default process. That is a very critical point.

LAWRENCE SAGER

Sitting here thinking about what parties would want, I had two thoughts. One is what parties want does not just arise at the moment of conflict. What parties want has a great deal to do with the risks they will take. So, in an area like oil and gas exploration the risks that a relatively small company will take in investing a great deal of money has something to do with the stability of the legal environment and that they have relatively precise expectations. That conduct prior to the disagreement is going to be impacted on what the legal system will produce. What the legal system will produce will include in this case arbitration. Therefore, what they need or want from arbitration in an area where almost everything is arbitrated, starts at the contracting moment.

The second thing that occurred to me was, there might be very different kinds of consumers of arbitral awards even in the same area like oil and gas. On the one hand, you might be talking about a very large private company like Exxon Mobile, dealing with even larger nation states. What it wants first of all is not to be in the courts of Russia or other courts that it cannot trust. It is a repeat player. It wants to be in the hands of reasonable people in these repeated transactions. It does not want high variance. It does not want insanity and it does not want unfairness. On the other hand, if you are a relatively small company making a staggeringly large investment because you are gambling on an one-off investment in resources, the outcome of this transaction is huge and you want more than just fairness and want to be in the hands of a wise person. Then you really do want to be able to predict with some accuracy how likely things go as you hope they will and how likely it is that the legal outcome is the one that you predict and hope for.

You may want something more than wise persons at that point. You may want to know what the rules of the road are and whether you are able to depend on them. Depending on if you are Exxon Mobile or you are a small intrepid adventurer, your requirements may be quite different from each other.

DANIEL HOCHSTRASSER

One of the concerns I do hear from clients we represent in arbitrations, if they are not the Exxon Mobiles of this world, is whether we believe that the arbitrators will look for repeat assignments. If you are a small company opposing against a multi-national big player who has a lot of arbitrations, it is one of the concerns, whether we believe or we see a danger that the arbitrators look for repeat assignment, which, of course, they are more likely to get from the big global player as opposed to this small company who only has one arbitration in a decade.

THOMAS STEPHEN BURKE
The international arbitration circle is so small that I know myself personally so many of them that you actually have to trust them. And you have to trust that the other party to the arbitration also trusts the people into whose hands you put the making of a decision. It is such a small circle and there are not so many of them; some are very, very well known not alone to each other but also to the people who appoint them. The people who use arbitration relative to the number of people who go to court on a daily basis, is very, very small.

DANIEL HOCHSTRASSER
That is true, but to give you a different example: when I started my legal career I was a staff attorney at a small district court outside of Zurich and we only had two divorce lawyers in that district. In any divorce, almost inevitably you had the two lawyers opposing each other. I can tell you that we liked one and we hated the other. This is not singular to arbitration, and ultimately, there is no guarantee that you get justice in any forum. To assume that arbitration is kind of the best of all worlds is probably naive, and if you have an alternative like a negotiated settlement before you even start an arbitration or litigation, that is always better. But in many cases and in many instances, arbitration is simply the best alternative. You know, when you buy commodities from Central Africa that there is no other choice than arbitration. There simply is not. And, in such cases, it is probably always ICC arbitration.

THOMAS STEPHEN BURKE
I absolutely agree, but the point really was rather more that the consummate professionalism of the people who work within that very small circle is so high that they can actually be trusted to a very, very high level. There is the occasional stray and vagrant who blows himselves completely out of the water for one reason or another. But once they wash out of the system, they never really come back. So, it keeps the calibre and standard of practitioner very, very high.

DANIEL HOCHSTRASSER
That is probably not what you are afraid of. You are not afraid of the arbitrator who does something completely crazy. You are afraid of the arbitrator who is more subtle than that, who decides, with very good reasoning, being seemingly very objective but simply decided for the other side for reasons which you are not really sure about. And that is not what I as a counsel am worried about, but that is what parties are particularly worried about. To give you an example: I was once a chairman in an ICC tribunal appointed by the ICC where one party was German and the other was Chinese. The Chinese party challenged me and the reasoning was that Switzerland and Germany were eventually the same thing! Everybody who is Swiss in this room knows it is not really the case. And to assume that somebody who is from Switzerland is per se deciding in favour of a German party in an arbitration is also not an entirely correct assumption. I give credit to that party, the Chinese party, that they actually thought that this was the case. They were just afraid that, maybe because I speak the same language, that I will decide in favour of the Germans; which when the challenge was rejected and the case was heard, neither did I nor did the tribunal. These are the concerns that you have.

SUSAN FRANCK

This is why the point about systemic integrity matters so much. The legitimacy of the dispute resolution system hangs by the thread of those who are adjudicating the disputes. At least in the pool of data that I have, out of the 82 different cases we had 145 different investment treaty arbitrators, which was very surprising to me because I had actually thought it was a small, tiny club. And in fact when I looked for repeat appointments, there were a small number of arbitrators in that pool that had more than five appointments, which was also very surprising to me. However, the Cornell article that I mentioned before, suggests that things are moving on and that in fact we do potentially have more elite arbitrators coming up the pipeline. But, we have to begin to think: What is the purpose of the arbitrators? Whose interests are they serving? Is it an elite group that is essentially decreasing variance because we know who the subset of the population is? The point is, what do we want arbitrators to be doing? Do we want them to be neutral adjudicators that are providing rule of law institutions or not? And that is a normative question. And we have to ask ourselves as users and consumers of law.

Keynote

Precedent in International Trade Negotiations

CHRISTIAN ETTER[1]

Introduction

Precedent is a concept normally used in relation to jurisprudence, i.e. the interpretation and application of enacted or otherwise effective law by courts or other judicial bodies. Regarding international law, precedent may be a relevant concept when it comes to the resolution of disputes, e.g. by arbitration panels, relating to the interpretation and application of international treaties. However, what may be the meaning of "precedent" in international negotiations?

The negotiation of international treaties is a law making process (or part of the law making process)[2], not a process of application of law. Therefore, the concept of precedent does not seem to be of straightforward relevance for international negotiations. Nevertheless, due to the specific process that the creation of international public law is following, and due to the peculiar nature of such law, it may be worthwhile to examine whether there may be relevance for "precedent" in international negotiations.[3]

The Specific Context of International Trade Negotiations

The *process* of international trade negotiations, which is the subject of this contribution, takes place in an ad hoc context, quite different from the formally established rules and procedures national law making normally follows. In contrast to this, the negotiators – law makers are not elected representatives or members of a constitutional body such as a parliament, but are envoys appointed by the governments they represent, cooperating in intergovernmental teams. This means that there are no common predefined rules, let alone binding statutes, negotiators would have to follow or could rely upon, e.g. on how to proceed, whom to consult or what to

---

1   The author is a member of the executive board of the State Secretariat for Economic Affairs SECO, Berne, Switzerland, and head of the Special Foreign Economic Service Division of SECO. He was the Swiss chief negotiator for GATS/services in the Uruguay Round negotiations leading to the WTO. He is the chief negotiator and head of Swiss delegations in the negotiations of free trade agreements. The views expressed in this contribution are the personal responsibility of the author and do not engage the SECO or the Swiss Confederation.
2   In some national legal systems international public law is not self executing, i.e. before it becomes applicable law the relevant provisions have to be transposed into national law according to the national constitutional order.
3   International (trade) negotiations throughout this contribution refer to negotiations leading to traditional intergovernmental agreements such as free trade agreements or investment protection agreements, or the Agreements forming part of the system of the World Trade Organisation, WTO (as opposed to agreements with supranational elements such as the treaties establishing the European Union, EU).

do in certain instances. There may be some diplomatic customs or habits available, but these cannot be taken for granted.

Due to the peculiar circumstances under which the provisions of intergovernmental agreements come about and are applied, such provisions have a different *nature* compared to national laws and regulations. First, there is no superior constitution, whether codified or customary, from which the provisions could be derived, or against which the provisions could be tested once in force. Second, unlike in national or supranational legal systems, there is no court system, hierarchical or otherwise, to supervise the coherence of the legislation and to ensure application of the laws in conformity with constitutional principles.[4] While intended to secure compliance, the dispute settlement mechanisms normally found in trade and investment agreements, typically taking the form of consultation and arbitration procedure or mechanisms for taking rebalancing measures, do not come with an enforcement mechanisms based on powers comparable to those of government and public authority available to domestic legal system.

The procedural specifics of intergovernmental negotiations, together with the special nature of treaty provisions, imply that systemic considerations in international trade negotiations cannot, and indeed do not, play the same role as in a national law making context. This is even more the case when international trade negotiations take place in an intercultural context, where the cooperating national delegations, as it is often the case, come from different historical, political and legal backgrounds.

When systemic implements are available to a limited extent only, "precedent" in the sense of looking into examples from previous negotiations or into jurisprudence relating to treaties already in force, may receive particular importance. "Precedent", in this sense, cannot mean binding precedent, as e.g. when precedent is set by a higher court to be observed by lower courts in a hierarchical court system. Rather, similar to advisory precedent, trade negotiators may look into previous agreements serving as reference or indication of best practice, in order to further develop ideas or options when looking for solutions in the course of an ongoing negotiation.

Precedent in Negotiations on Agreements on Trade in Services

Looking into the example of the national treatment provisions of the services and investment chapters of the North American Free Trade Agreement (NAFTA) concluded in 1992 and of the

---

[4] There are some hierarchical aspects in international law relevant for trade treaties: Preferential agreements concluded by Members of the WTO have to observe the relevant provisions of the WTO Agreements, particularly Article XXIV of the GATT and Article V of the GATS; the conclusion, entry into force and application of international treaties, including trade treaties, are subject to the Vienna Convention on the Law of Treaties of 1969. However, the Vienna Convention and the WTO Agreements only provide for limited aspects covered in trade agreements and, more important, they are themselves intergovernmental agreements to which the limitations, in particular those relating to enforcement, as described in this contribution, apply.

General Agreement on Trade in Services (GATS) of the WTO concluded in 1994, I attempt to show that precedent in the sense described above was indeed at work.

The NAFTA[5] concluded between the USA, Canada and Mexico in 1992 is an early example of a comprehensive international trade agreement including obligations regarding market access for trade in services. With the GATS[6], negotiated during the Uruguay Round of multilateral trade negotiations that were concluded in 1994, trade in services became a subject of the multilateral trading system. Analysing the negotiation history and looking into the resulting provisions suggests that the national treatment provisions of the NAFTA, among other sources, served as "precedent" for the negotiators of the GATS. Similarly, from free trade agreements concluded between various countries around the world in the last 10 to 15 years[7] it can be inferred that precedent plays a role in such negotiations, too.

NAFTA

The basic national treatment obligation of NAFTA is set out in Paragraph 1 of Article 1202 of Chapter 12 (Cross Border Trade in Services[8]) as follows:

> *Article 1202: National Treatment*
> *1. Each Party shall accord to service providers of another Party treatment no less favorable than that it accords, in like circumstances, to its own service providers.*

This clause, as straightforward as it may seem, leaves at least two important questions open:
(1)   What does "in like circumstances" mean?
(2)   What does "treatment no less favorable" mean?

While "in like circumstances" was certainly meant to avoid that apples and oranges are compared when treatment of foreign suppliers is measured against treatment of domestic suppliers, it could also be read to include an element of reciprocity, e.g. that foreign services and service suppliers could be excluded from the benefits of national treatment if the host country deems the regulations applied to the specific service in the home country of the foreign supplier not to be equivalent to the corresponding regulations of the host country, thereby denying that like circumstances prevail. In an even more extensive interpretation, the provision could be read as providing for the possibility to exclude services and service suppliers from a contracting party not providing reciprocal market access conditions. This situation leads to further refinements of the national treatment discipline in the context of the GATS negotiations (see below).

---

5   http://www.nafta-sec-alena.org/en/view.aspx?conID=590.
6   http://www.wto.org/english/docs_e/legal_e/26-gats.pdf.
7   http://rtais.wto.org/UI/PublicAllRTAList.aspx.
8   Chapter 11 "Investment" of NAFTA provides the same national treatment standard, applicable to the supply of services through commercial presence. Chapters 11 and 12 of NAFTA do not apply to financial services, which are subject to the provisions of Chapter 14 of NAFTA (see below).

Regarding "treatment no less favorable", the NAFTA negotiators recognized an inherent ambiguity, leading them to include Article 1205 into the agreement:

Article 1205: Local Presence
No Party may require a service provider of another Party to establish or maintain a representative office or any form of enterprise, or to be resident, in its territory as a condition for the cross-border provision of a service.

At first sight, this article may seem redundant. However, without this specification, it could be argued that a local presence requirement is in conformity with Article 1202. Such reading would mean that the requirement to establish a commercial presence by a foreign supplier in order to be allowed to supply services in the territory of the host country would not constitute less favourable treatment, given that the suppliers of the host country, by definition, would also have a local presence.

If we look into this question from an economic point of view, it is obvious that a local presence requirement indeed may de facto constitute less favourable treatment. A local presence requirement means that the foreign service supplier, in addition to the establishment he has in his home country, has to open and run a second business establishment located in the host country, even if this is commercially not necessary in order to supply cross-border services (e.g. database services, or consulting services). In such cases the local presence requirement imposes additional costs on the foreign services supplier diminishing his competitiveness compared to the suppliers of the host country. By including Article 1205, the negotiators made it clear that the "no less favourable treatment" standard, at least when it comes to measures relating to local presence, has to be interpreted not to mean merely formally identical treatment, but requiring treatment no less favourable in economic terms.

In relation to the supply of financial services, the NAFTA agreement goes a step further. Negotiators recognized that there are other measures than local establishment requirements putting foreign suppliers de facto at a disadvantage compared to domestic suppliers, even if such measures accord formally identical treatment. One could, e.g. in the context of the supply of a service through commercial presence in the host country, think of the requirement to hire nationals of the host country to run a subsidiary by a foreign supplier. In order to avoid such de facto discrimination through measures according de jure no less favourable treatment, paragraphs 5, 6 and 7 were added to article 1405 (paragraphs 1, 2 and 3 state the same basic obligation in relation to the various forms and aspects of the supply of financial services as Article 1202 does for non-financial services):

Article 1405: National Treatment
5. A Party's treatment of financial institutions and cross-border financial service providers of another Party, whether different or identical to that accorded to its own institutions or providers in like circumstances, is consistent with paragraphs 1 through 3 if the treatment affords equal competitive opportunities.

> 6. A Party's treatment affords equal competitive opportunities if it does not disadvantage financial institutions and cross-border financial services providers of another Party in their ability to provide financial services as compared with the ability of the Party's own financial institutions and financial services providers to provide such services, in like circumstances.
> 7. Differences in market share, profitability or size do not in themselves establish a denial of equal competitive opportunities, but such differences may be used as evidence regarding whether a Party's treatment affords equal competitive opportunities.

By paragraph 5, the negotiators made clear that the "no less favourable treatment" standard had to be read, regarding all conceivable measures, to mean requiring treatment affording "equal competitive opportunities". This standard clearly rules out that granting de jure non-discriminatory treatment will be sufficient in any case to comply with the national treatment obligation. The concept of "equal competitive opportunities" itself is specified by paragraphs 6 and 7. In paragraph 6, the concept is defined by "... not disadvantage ... [foreign suppliers] ... in their ability to provide financial services ...". Recognizing that this could lead to an extensive interpretation, paragraph 7 hastens to clarify that "competitive opportunity" and "ability to provide services" is not meant to require that foreign services providers have to be helped to attain the same market share, profitability or size as national suppliers.

GATS

The national treatment standard of the GATS is set out in Article XVII, paragraphs 1, 2 and 3:

> **Article XVII: National Treatment**
> 1. In the sectors inscribed in its Schedule, and subject to any conditions and qualifications set out therein, each Member shall accord to services and service suppliers of any other Member, in respect of all measures affecting the supply of services, treatment no less favourable than that it accords to its own like services and service suppliers.
> 2. A Member may meet the requirement of paragraph 1 by according to services and service suppliers of any other Member, either formally identical treatment or formally different treatment to that it accords to its own like services and service suppliers.
> 3. Formally identical or formally different treatment shall be considered to be less favourable if it modifies the conditions of competition in favour of services or service suppliers of the Member compared to like services or service suppliers of any other Member.

Looking at paragraph 1, the concept of "treatment no less favourable" is there, however qualified by "like services and service suppliers" instead of by "in like circumstances" as in NAFTA. This substitution is an improvement over the NAFTA-"precedent", as the qualification of "like services and service suppliers" makes equally sure that there is no comparison between apples and oranges, but at the same time inhibits interpretations that would allow for reciprocity requirements.

Paragraphs 2 and 3 take the "precedent" of NAFTA Article 1405 as a starting point, making sure that "treatment no less favourable" not only means de jure, but de facto non-discrimination, whether accorded through formally identical or formally different treatment (paragraph 2). The standard of de facto non-discrimination chosen by the GATS negotiators is "modification of the conditions of competition" (paragraph 3). By transforming the "precedent" of NAFTA Article 1405 ("equal competitive opportunities") into "(no) less favourable ... competitive conditions", the GATS-standard avoids the possible misreading that foreign suppliers could be entitled to anything more (such as equal market share) than fair framework conditions to enter the competition. By this modification, the GATS negotiators did not need to include a clarification similar to NAFTA paragraph 7 of Article 1405.

Other concepts of the NAFTA services and investment chapters did not make it as precedent into the GATS. For example, in NAFTA, market access commitments are recorded by the so called negative list approach, where all services sectors are subject to the national treatment obligation, except when a party inscribes a specific non-conforming measure in its list of reservations. The GATS-negotiators have not followed this approach but have settled on the so called positive list approach, where the application of the national treatment obligation is limited to those sectors and subsectors that are specifcally listed in the national list of specific commitments of a party. While the same level of market access can be committed by either approach, experience shows that it is easier for a party to limit the scope of commitment under a positive list approach. As the 150 Member States of the WTO (which are at very different levels of development) are parties to the GATS, the more flexible positive list approach had to be chosen.

Free Trade Agreements

Free trade agreements concluded by various countries in the world in the last 10 to 15 years, in addition to trade in goods, increasingly also cover trade in services. The USA[9] follow in their free trade agreements, with very few exceptions, the NAFTA-precedent, both regarding the concept of national treatment and the negative list approach to reservations. Those free trade agreements of the EU[10] which include market access obligations on trade in services follow the GATS approach, both regarding the national treatment and the scheduling of commitments according to the positive listing approach. Switzerland's free trade agreements[11] also mostly follow the GATS precedent on both accounts. However, in the free trade agreement concluded between Japan and Switzerland in 2009, a GATS-type national treatment clause was combined with a negative list approach to reservations. This decision is another example where "precedent" was used in trade negotiations as a creative tool.

---

9   http://www.ustr.gov/trade-agreements/free-trade-agreements.
10   http://trade.ec.europa.eu/doclib/docs/2006/december/tradoc_111588.pdf , http://trade.ec.europa.eu/doclib/docs/2006/december/tradoc_118238.pdf.
11   http://www.seco.admin.ch/themen/00513/00515/01330/index.html?lang=en.

Conclusion

The example of the national treatment provision relating to the supply of services found in the NAFTA, the GATS and a number of free trade agreements shows that "precedent" is at work in trade negotiations. "Precedent" in this context means that trade negotiators draw on existing agreements, negotiation history and jurisprudence when recombining and refining ideas in order to develop options with a view to find solutions for new agreements.

Discussion

RICHARD PLENDER
May I, as a frequent member of WTO dispute resolution panels, identify a problem, which I have often found and believe to be common in such panels, as well as a proposed solution and ask whether you agree with the identification of the problem and the solution?

The problem that I have encountered is that the panels, which are commonly composed of an ambassador plus two international lawyers, soon come to a stage of disagreement. The international lawyers which are presented a particular text can agree upon its meaning. Sometimes they agree extremely forcefully upon its meaning and say that it can only have one particular meaning. The ambassador, who has participated in the negotiation of that very article, says it did not have that meaning at all. The negotiators were thinking of something entirely different. When pressed by his colleagues to explain how the language can be reconciled with a different meaning, the ambassador has to respond that he remembers the negotiations very well. He might say something like: "We had an earlier text and then the Brazilian delegate raised a question about servicing of aero engine parts, so we amended it." The international lawyers will then ask why the negotiators did not note that there was a particular problem relating to aero engine parts, to which the ambassador will reply that it was perfectly obvious. My proposed solution to this problem is that panels, both the dispute resolution panels and the Appellate Body, when called upon to interpret WTO provisions, should be free to refer to the negotiating text. I am well aware that as a general matter of international law, Article 32 of the Vienna Convention from the Law of Treaties limits substantially the freedom of parties to do so. However, it is the technicality of WTO texts, including GATS, that if we are really to interpret them consistently, with the actual intentions of the drafters, those who have to interpret them would be much assisted if they could have reference to the negotiating history. Does that idea appeal to you as an ambassador?

CHRISTIAN ETTER
As far as I am aware of it there is at least access to a part of the negatiation history. Having been myself a part of these negotiations in the Uruguay Round, there was a technique called green banding of documents. Green banded documents are accessible today. Such documents would be more than just first drafts or texts by particular persons or delegations. So, there is some access to the negotiation history and the Secretariat was very busy during the Uruguay Round negotiations to establish analytical documents which sort of summarised what was discussed when it comes to the intentions behind certain provisions. I can mention the so-called scheduling guidelines, for instance, which would explain particular wordings.

I do not take sides in the debate whether the historical or the theological interpretation should prevail. There are various techniques how you read a text which, of course, once the negotiation is concluded becomes a self-standing text. I fully agree that recourse to the negotiation history may be important. To the extent that the material is relevant, I have the impression that some access is possible. If you had access to each and every scrap of paper that was produced in the negotiations, this would rather enhance the confusion than reduce it.

RICHARD PLENDER
There is, however, still a question of accessibility for Member States and for the Secretariat, particularly at the negotiating phase and before a tribunal when it has to determine upon a dispute which cannot be solved just by negotiation. In the latter case, it has been my experience, we were denied access to these documents.

CHRISTIAN ETTER
You were not able to get the green banded documents?

RICHARD PLENDER
No. They were admissible during the negotiation of a proposed dispute, but not once it came to the formal resolution by a tribunal. What you say about the green banded documents only strengthens the case for the tribunals to have access to these materials which in public international law are generally denied to international tribunals.

CHRISTIAN ETTER
I am well aware that if you read through the GATS Agreement, which I know from its inception, the text is sometimes difficult to understand. Indeed, some provisions are as such not really coherent or consistent, so panels would have to interprete them. I do not see any other solution because just relying on what the Brazilian or the Hong Kong delegate said back in 1991 should in my view not be decisive for what a panel finds.

CARL BAUDENBACHER
I have discussed with Mr Planzer whether we should use the notion of precedent in the context of your speech but you have shown that it is not wrong to do so, because negotiators would rely on past decisions or past agreements to insert some sort of continuity into new trade agreements pretty much in a comparable way as courts do. You have focused mainly on substantive law approaches, but there is also the enforcement and the dispute resolution side. We can see a development if we start looking at the old free trade agreement concluded by the EFTA States and the European Community in 1972. The only one which is of relevance is the one between Switzerland and the European Union. It only mentions a Joint Committee which would take care of potential conflicts, whereas in the meantime we can see free trade agreements of a newer generation with an arbitration clause or an arbitration tribunal (for instance: the agreement concluded between the European Union and Korea). Is that also some sort of precedent which would be used in similar agreements again? We both know that there are people in Switzerland

who seem to dream of the possibility to subject the bilateral agreements concluded between Switzerland and the European Union to an arbitration clause.

CHRISTIAN ETTER
Very interesting question, and, indeed, I think you could also identify strands of precedent when it comes to the dispute resolution mechanisms in various agreements. The examples of agreements concluded between the EFTA States and the EU in the early 70s – the only still relevant is the one with Switzerland – has served as a strong precedent for the first generation of free trade agreements which the EFTA States have concluded with the Eastern European states after the fall of the iron curtain as well as with South-Eastern and Mediterranean states. The EFTA has more or less copy-pasted the approach of not having arbitration but of just providing a joint committee. If you look into the agreements concluded by the EU in the 1990s and early 2000s and the ones of the EFTA with Mexico and Chile in the same period, you can see a difference. The EU did not negotiate many agreements until recently when they negotiated one with Korea. EFTA went on with Singapore, Korea, Canada and many more way before the EU did so with other states. The EU has also an agreement with South Africa. If you look at all these agreements, there is an evolution in the sense that arbitration was included in addition to at least when it came to the differences in interpretation of provisions. So, there was a gradual development towards including arbitration first for the interpretation issues and then – starting with the agreement with Mexico – for a fully fledged arbitration mechanism for all disputes under the agreement. The EFTA concluded in the year 2000, with a few months delay after the EU, a similar free-trade agreement with Mexico. There was also a fully fledged arbitration mechanism. In both cases, this was at the request of Mexico because they said that it is unfair just to apply rebalancing mechanism without having the possibility to have arbitration before going to that step. Early EU agreements were, of course, agreements between the big and very small partners, the newly independent states of Eastern and South-Eastern Europe. They were very happy to be included in the Western European system of trade and they did not ask many questions. But then, once the EU and the EFTA states started to negotiate with partners beyond Europe and the Mediterranean area, this approach was not acceptable anymore.

So, there is also some sort of precedent here and you will not see agreements in the future which do not provide for proper arbitration. This was really a very particular approach chosen by the EU in the early 70s and then through the early 90s.

CARL BAUDENBACHER
Would this also be feasible for the relationship between the European Union and Switzerland?

CHRISTIAN ETTER

Feasibility is a multi-dimensional concept, of course. It is technically and legally feasible and I would think it would be nice. However, whether the EU would agree is, if you look at feasibility from that perspective, at least very doubtful, because the EU is not inclined to accept arbitration decisions by the European Court of Justice. Given that the Swiss approach to the bilateral agreements with the EU is very much to be associated to the arbitration convention, I doubt that under these circumstances, arbitration in the sense of international public law would closely be feasible.

SIMON PLANZER

Ambassador Etter, you mentioned in your presentation that the free trade agreement between Japan and Switzerland may stand for a new precedent, potentially. Could you possibly elaborate on the reasons why you chose to go for this mixed approach?

CHRISTIAN ETTER

The negative list approach to scheduling has a bias towards more rapid and more profound liberalism. It is the position of Switzerland that with every partner which is prepared to go for the negative list approach, Switzerland would also choose to go for the negative list approach because Switzerland being a small open economy, which is very much depending on foreign trade and international exchange, seeks to do away as much as possible with obstacles to international trade also regarding services. So, why the combination? We tried to combine the best of two worlds. That is basically the idea behind it and the Japanese shared this approach, because the NAFTA is a very complex agreement and there are many other aspects, like the so-called stand still and ratchet effects. The NAFTA is also a very US tailored agreement as they tailored it to their federal system of constitution. It was an agreement with Canada and Mexico, two important countries, but they were still junior partners to the USA. For instance, when the EFTA negotiated with Peru, Chile and Colombia which were influenced by the US approach as they had concluded free trade agreements with the US before, they wanted to stick to that approach as much as possible.

If free trade agreements have a disadvantage it is the disadvantage of the spaghetti bowl, as it is called. For example, a Swiss company has to check a dozen or more agreements depending on where it wants to export to. As a result, you want to have as much similarity as possible, but once you start to negotiate with various parts of the world, it stops somewhere. Therefore, these merged or combined approaches are a natural development. We fought very hard with Colombia, Peru, Chile and the others to avoid the NAFTA approach when it comes to the national treatment provision and to the stand still and ratchet issues. They have a concept of reservations for future measures which, if extensively used, can void an agreement very much of its contents. Switzerland, except in relation to Peru, succeeded at the price that we had to accept the positive list approach. Japan was a bit more flexible and they thought it was manageable.

AKIO SHIMIZU

I would like to ask you more about the new Japan – Swiss approach that you talked about. Did you think it worked because it was the pair of Japan and Switzerland? Do you think it will work with other countries if you try to negotiate new FTAs?

CHRISTIAN ETTER

We currently try it with Hong Kong. They have agreed to the basic approach, namely, to take the GATS type of provisions and to combine it with a negative list. But we are still in a relatively early stage of the negotiations. As I mentioned, taking market access commitments according to the negative list approach is quite a demanding proposition. As a result, we have to see how far Hong Kong can get when working on that approach. Keep in mind, that we are talking about free trade agreements between rather highly developed countries and emerging countries. If we were negotiating with Canada, we would try to convince Canada of this mixed approach. The Canada negotiations, which started before the year 2000, was in the first generation phase of agreements. But then it was interrupted and only concluded 2007. However, it is still a first generation agreement. It does not include services, for instance. One particular reason for this is, that Canada seems to have big difficulties to depart from the strict NAFTA approach, apart from their particular federal system which makes negotiations for the Canadian Federal Government difficult with any partner.

THOMAS STEPHEN BURKE

To what extent do you think that the Swiss approach will influence the speeding up and potentially the conclusion of the Doha Round? Will this round have this bilateral approach? And to what degree will that Swiss approach, as it may be called, possibly leverage and perhaps even encourage the conclusion of the Doha Round of the talks?

CHRISTIAN ETTER

I would like to caution to talk about the Swiss approach. There are now hundreds of free trade agreements in force or being negotiated and it is a bit like looking into the universe. Maybe there are others trying similar things.

I think the link to the Doha Round negotiations is a very loose one. You could, of course, debate whether the general tendency of countries in the world to go for preferential agreements, mostly bilateral agreements or small groups of plurilateral agreements, helps or rather detracts from the conclusion of the Doha Round. You can make both arguments. You may say that the more of these agreements are negotiated and come into force, the higher the pressure to make order again and to combine everything into the multilateral context because the manageability, obviously, gets more difficult. On the other hand, you could say that it is a resource issue. The trade negotiators are working on other issues, so they have less resources for the WTO. Secondly, you could say that the government also lose incentive to conclude a multilateral agreement in the WTO because when they have concluded free trade agreements with their major trading partners, their economies are basically served. You have to look at the general evolution in this preferential trade area and the Doha Round. Doha Round is really not moving as very important partners have internal difficulties.

RACHEL BREWSTER
I will ask a quick question. Since you are one of the negotiators of the Uruguay Round and since we are having a panel on it tomorrow, I was curious what you think about the designers of the WTO system. What did they think about a system of precedent in dispute resolution? When you look at the dispute settlement understanding, it certainly does not mention precedent. It says that, you know, the system should create stability. At the same time it says that it should not create new rights and obligations or take away from them. As a result, there has been some push within the WTO to have a more formal system or even some system of precedent at all. I was wondering what you thought as a negotiator. Is this in coherence with the initial ideas of what dispute resolution would do or not?

CHRISTIAN ETTER
It is unavoidable in a way that precedent plays a certain role because sitting in a panel, as it has been mentioned before, can be a very difficult job and whenever you can find models or good practices you are not forced to use them, but they might help. It is very good if you have such precedents, however, they need to be carefully assessed. Whether it would make sense to formalise this, I cannot judge. I would personally find it very difficult because someone would have to decide what a relevant precedent is. This is the challenge in international public law. There is no world superior court, there is no world police, there is no world prison and there is no real enforcement in the end. We all are happy to believe that the arbitration mechanism we design in our agreements are enforcement mechanisms, but in the end they are not really. An international agreement is followed as long as it is in the interest of the parties, otherwise they just break it or cancel it. There are many international agreements from the late 19th century which have very demanding obligations but nobody thinks they are still to be followed.

SIMON PLANZER
We still have a few more minutes for questions. I may have a question, maybe to round up the discussion and to give an outlook. You mentioned that you were just about to start negotiations with China, not an unimportant trade partner. You certainly have your favourite approach with regard to the Swiss position, but maybe you can dare an outlook what might be the favourite approach of the Chinese side with regard to the different models that you have described.

CHRISTIAN ETTER
Switzerland is a relatively small country and even if we negotiate with the EFTA as a group, we are still a small group; but not an unimportant group. However, we do not have political clout like the US, Japan, the EU, China or Russia. So, we have to follow a rather unassuming approach. China has only been a WTO member since 2002 and they took great efforts, particularly also in trade and services, to come up with a reasonable schedule of commitments. As often, a late-comer to the club pays a higher price than those who were originally there. The Chinese schedule is better than many schedules of long time WTO members, particularly in comparison to developing country or emerging market WTO members. When it comes to services it is probably smart to agree on a GATS approach, as well in regard to the provisions as far the scheduling. And just to make a footnote, when I talk about the GATS approach for provisions,

I mean that the national treatment provision is pretty much perfect. Again, I am not a lawyer and you may have a different view on that. Also, I am, of course, biased because I was part of the team that worked on that. There are other provisions in the GATS that I am less proud of. For example, a certain delegation wanted a small change, but it made the affected article less coherent or less understandable. Therefore, we try in our free trade negotiations, when we negotiate the provisions of the service chapter, to improve on some GATS provisions. It is necessary for the national treatment, but also for other provisions. How far we will get with China is an open question because negotiations are just about to start.

SIMON PLANZER

If there are no more questions, I would like to simply state that we will not take your final remarks as binding precedent and thank you for the honest answer. I would like to thank you for the insights that you have offered us; you offered us a different perspective on precedent. As Professor Baudenbacher said himself, it was certainly justified to have you here, to have your very valuable input and your view on this topic. With this I would like to thank everybody and conclude the first day.

3rd Panel
Precedent in European High Courts

Introduction

PAUL MAHONEY[1]

I. A Common Analytical Framework?

"Discretion inheres in the judicial function", it has been said.[2] The exercise of interpretative choice, giving one meaning or content to the law rather than another, necessarily confers on the judges a lawmaking power.[3] But this judicial interpretative discretion, and the resultant lawmaking power, evidently cannot be unlimited. On the contrary, as counterpoints to judicial discretion, objectivity and neutrality – assuring the highest degree of certainty and predictability of the law are considered to be essential qualities attaching to the judicial function. In legal systems where some institutionalised doctrine or stabilised practice of precedent is present, it is usually seen as a constraining concomitant of judicial discretion.[4] Indeed, although precedent is customarily presented as a particular attribute of the Anglo-Saxon common law, there are good reasons why any legal system needs a doctrine of precedent, if only because like cases should be decided in like fashion.[5]

If this admittedly obvious, if not even platitudinous, introductory point is evoked, it is as a preliminary to attempting to offer a common analytical framework for getting the most from the richness and diversity of this session's contributions.

At the core of that framework, there is evidently the technical aspect of precedent: In this or that legal system, what, if any, are the particular rules, principles or practices governing when a court should follow its own case law or that of a higher court; how constraining on the courts is any doctrine of precedent that may exist within that system; and what are the conditions de-

---

1   Any opinions expressed are personal.
2   The opening words of Alec Stone Sweet and Margaret McCown, "Discretion and Precedent in European Law", in: Ola Wiklund (ed.), Judicial Discretion in European Perspective, pp. 84–115, at p. 84 (Norstedts Juridik/ Kluwer Law International, 2003).
3   See, e.g., Paul Mahoney, Judicial Activism and Judicial Self-Restraint in the European Court of Human Rights: Two Sides of the Same Coin, 11 Human Rights Law Journal, pp. 57–88, at p. 60 (1990).
4   See the remarks in Stone Sweet and McCown, footnote 2 above, p. 84, discussing when *"precedent [can be analysed] as an evolving constraint on discretion"*; p. 90, citing the argument of another author that *"the development of doctrine and precedent reduces the possibility that the [ECJ] will abuse its discretionary powers, enhances the coherence of the Court's case law and constrains the Court in other ways"*; and p. 96, referring to *"judges, and [two scholars], along with legal positivists more generally, who portray precedent as an inherently legal constraint on discretion and lawmaking"*.
5   As to what "precedent" should be taken to mean, see Jan Komarek, Precedent and Judicial Lawmaking, in: Cambridge Yearbook of European Legal Studies, Vol. 11, 2008–2009, pp. 399–433, at p. 403. For Komarek, the phenomen of "precedent" is best understood as not being limited to previous judicial decisions that are "legally binding" – which he defines as *"having a strict formal binding force that would require the courts to choose between recognising a relevant previous judicial decision as binding and following it, or overruling it"*; rather, he finds it preferable to think in terms of a broader definition: *"a previous judicial decision that has normative implications going beyond the context of a particular case in which it has been delivered"*.

termining when precedents may be overturned or departed from? How well have the courts in question done their technical job of following the relevant doctrine of precedent?

There is also the more general issue of the role of any doctrine of precedent as it exists within a given legal system. How does precedent contribute to the development of the law in that system?

As far as the three "European High Courts" (namely the European Court of Human Rights in Strasbourg – "the Strasbourg Court"; the Court of Justice of the European Union, commonly known in English as the European Court of Justice – "the ECJ"; and the EFTA Court) are concerned, any discussion of precedent, therefore, depends, I would say, on a number of preliminary questions, such as:

- What is the judicial discretion conferred on the European judges by the respective treaties?

- How does the exercise of the judicial function by the European judges relate not only to the European legislature but also to the national authorities in the Member States, and in particular the domestic courts?

- For what (policy or other) purposes can the European Courts be seen to have used their lawmaking power?

In the light of their actual practice, we can then ask:

- Can the manner in which the European Courts have gone about their technical task of precedent-building be linked to the pursuit of these perceived lawmaking purposes?

- Do the nuts and bolts of their practice in relation to the recourse to precedent tell us anything about the role of the two main European Courts, and in particular their lawmaking and policy-making power, in their respective systems?

II. European Court of Human Rights

The European Convention on Human Rights ("ECHR") is an interpretative paradise for judges. Like many national constitutions or human rights charters, it uses wholly indeterminate language that necessarily calls for interpretation. To transpose what the American judge and scholar Learned Hand said of the American Constitution, the words of the ECHR's open-textured clauses can be characterised as *"empty vessels into which [a judge] can pour nearly everything he [or she] will"*.[6] The filling of the empty ECHR vessels over the last 50 years of judicial activity has produced impressive results – namely a veritable ECHR law made up not only of the text of the treaty but also, more substantially, of the interpretative jurisprudence.

Unlike the case law of the ECJ, the case law of the Strasbourg Court does not bind the national courts. The willingness of the national courts to apply, and even bow down to, the ECHR jurisprudence is, therefore, based essentially on a confidence in the quality of the leading rulings handed down in Strasbourg. Part of that quality is consistency.

Not surprisingly, therefore, one significant tool that the Strasbourg Court has, from the very beginning of its existence, employed for ensuring coherence of its successive judgements as a corpus of "law", and for avoiding uncertainty and unequal treatment from case to case and country to country, is a practice of precedent. I say "practice" because there is no formal rule of *stare decisis*.[7] This the Strasbourg Court itself spelt out expressly in a 1990 judgement in which it declined, at that moment in time, to go back to an earlier case law holding that the impossibility under British law for a birth certificate to be altered so as to take account of a sex-change surgery did not violate the right to respect for private life:

> *"It is true that ... the Court is not bound by its previous judgements; ... However, [the Court] usually follows and applies its own precedents, such a course being in the interests of legal certainty and the orderly development of the Convention case law."*

The judgement then explains:

> *"Nevertheless, this would not prevent the Court from departing from an earlier decision if it was persuaded that there were cogent reasons for doing so. Such a departure might, for example, be warranted in order to ensure that the interpretation of the Convention reflects societal changes and remains in line with present-day conditions ..."*[8]

---

6   Cited in Mahoney, footnote 3 above, p. 63.
7   Although the rule empowering a chamber to relinquish jurisdiction in favour of the Grand Chamber clearly presupposes at least the desirability of following precedent: Article 30 ECHR, under which relinquishment is possible *"where the resolution of a question before the chamber might have a result inconsistent with a judgement previously delivered by the Court"* (a provision that prior to 1998 figured in the Rules of Court).
8   *Cossey v. UK*, 25 September 1990, Series A, Vol. 184, § 35 – adverting to the principle of interpretation whereby the ECHR is a living instrument to be interpreted in an evolutive way, in the light of changing circumstances in democratic society. As regards the question of birth-certificate recognition – and marriage – for operated transsexuals, departure there indeed was from the *Cossey* judgement itself on this very ground of societal changes twelve years later in the case of *Goodwin v. UK*: ECHR 2002-VI.

The 2000 case *Kudla v. Poland*[9] provides another example of when an existing line of case law authority in relation to the level of human rights protection afforded by the treaty may be reversed, namely for reasons going to the functioning and effectiveness of the ECHR system. In the light of the ever growing volume of applications being lodged in Strasbourg alleging solely or primarily inordinate length of legal proceedings, the Strasbourg Court concluded that the time had come to revise its previous case law and to hold that the Member States had to make available an effective domestic remedy enabling individuals to raise such a complaint at national level.

The establishment of an innovation followed by accumulation of similar precedents may be used to set new directions not only for substantive issues going to the content of the rights and freedoms guaranteed by the ECHR, but also for shaping the procedure for processing cases. The emergence over the past few years of the pilot-case procedure in the Strasbourg Court's procedural armoury is a good example of this phenomenon.[10]

My perception is that it is with some success that the Strasbourg Court has opted for progress through incremental additions to the jurisprudence, on the whole preferring not to frequently impose, through evolutive, dynamic interpretation, radical changes of direction.[11] Relatively few sharp bends in the pathways which are built up through progressive accretion of precedents; mainly gentle curves.

This perception is, I am happy to say, confirmed by informed Swiss scholarship in the person of Professor Luzius Wildhaber, former President of the Strasbourg Court, who has published one of the best accounts published so far of the doctrine of precedent in the practice of the Strasbourg Court. I do not think that I am stealing any of Professor Caflisch's thunder by quoting

---

9   *Kudla v. Poland*, ECHR 2000-XI, especially paras.148–149 and 155.
10 The two Grand Chamber judgements in *Broniowski v. Poland* (ECHR 2004-V (merits), ECHR 2005-IX (just satisfaction)) inaugurated an innovatory interpretation of the treaty obligation of Contracting States to execute judgements (Article 46 ECHR), so as to lay down a blueprint for a procedure whereby, when faced with a systemic problem provoking or liable to provoke multiple applications against one State, one suitable pilot case is taken for hearing, the other pending applications on the same matter are suspended, a pilot judgement is delivered (where appropriate, broadly indicating the kind of remedial measures called for in order to eliminate the systemic problem in the future and to provide redress for all those adversely affected by it in the past) and the remaining applications are thereafter dealt with in a summary manner. Other pilot cases have followed in which this innovatory interpretation of the article in the ECHR on execution of judgements has been acted on, and the new procedure has been applied and refined (e.g. *Hutten-Czapska v. Poland*, ECHR 2006-VIII (merits), ECHR 2008 (just satisfaction)). It is likely that the procedural practice established in these case-precedents will be codified in the Rules of the Court. In this context, precedent, once solidified, will be converted into black-letter law. On the question of the pilot-case procedure, see Renata Degener and Paul Mahoney, The Prospects for a Test Case Procedure in the European Court of Human Rights, in Hanno Hartig, ed., Trente ans de droit européen et des droits de l'homme – Études à la mémoire de Wolfgang Strasser, pp. 173–207 (Bruylant, 2007).
11 As one scholar has written of the American Constitution: *"It is illegitimate ... to break the limits of continuing constitutional traditions in this way very often, because breaks with continuity strain the very idea of law."* (cited in Mahoney, footnote 2 above, p. 77).

Professor Wildhaber's conclusion that *"the doctrine of precedent is well and thriving in the European Court of Human Rights"*.[12]

III. European Court of Justice

Turning now to the other main "European High Court", one interesting particularity of the ECJ, distinguishing it from the Strasbourg Court, is that it has three levels of jurisdiction – not just a Grand Chamber and other kinds of lesser chambers, but three separate courts, each having different competences and in a hierarchical relationship with one another: The Court of Justice itself at the apex; underneath it the General Court; and, at the third level, the Civil Service Tribunal, the first of what will perhaps become a series of specialised tribunals. We can, therefore, look at the operation of precedent up and down the hierarchical ladder of the three courts and not just within the judicial body, the ECJ, as an overall entity.

The Statute of the ECJ expressly provides that when, after deciding a case on appeal on points of law from the General Court, the Court of Justice refers the case back to the General Court, the latter is bound by the points of law settled by the Court of Justice in its appeal decision.[13] Formal binding effect of a legal precedent of the Court of Justice on the General Court is, therefore, limited to the context of a single decided appeal case referred back to the General Court.

Nevertheless, in a recent judgement in a case concerning the freezing of the assets of a person suspected of connections with Al-Qaeda, the General Court has acknowledged that *"the appellate principle itself and the hierarchical judicial structure which is its corollary generally advise against the General Court revisiting points of law which have been decided by the Court of Justice"*, and *"a fortiori in the case when ... the Court of Justice was sitting in Grand Chamber formation and clearly intended to deliver a judgement establishing certain principles"*. The General Court considered that it falls not to it but to the Court of Justice to reverse such precedent. The General Court, therefore, faithfully followed and applied the principles of law as established in the relevant previous judgement by the Court of Justice in an earlier case brought by the same applicant, even

---

12   Luzius Wildhaber, Precedent in the European Court of Human Rights, in: The European Court of Human Rights, 1998–2006 – History, Achievements, Reform, p. 173 (N. P. Engel, 2006). Wildhaber (at pp. 157–158 and 165) describes the practice as follows: *"[P]recedents are followed regularly, but not invariably; ... for the sake of attaining uniformity, consistency and certainty, precedents should normally be observed where they are not plainly unreasonable and inconvenient ...; ... one 'big' case may constitute just as valid a precedent as a line of lesser cases; ... precedents should normally be followed even before the existence of actual customary law can be demonstrated; and ... sound judicial caution requires that the underlying rationale of a case should not be defined so as to be too far detached from the specific facts... Where the facts of a new case are obviously or reasonably different, the Court will in effect (and whether or not it uses this terminology) resort to the technique of 'distinguishing' earlier cases."* He cites with approval (at p. 172) a separate opinion of Judge Pieter van Dijk (now Vice-President of the Dutch Council of State) (in Van Mechlen and Others v. Netherlands, Reports 1997-III): *"Even though the Court is not bound by precedent, legal certainty and legal equality require that the Court's case law be both consistent and transparent as well as reasonably predictable in so far as the facts of the case are comparable to those of earlier cases."*

13   Article 61.

though it did not regard itself as formally bound to do so by the Statute or otherwise and even though it evidently did not feel wholly convinced by the reasoning of the Court of Justice.[14]

The Civil Service Tribunal is doubtless under a similar duty of precedential loyalty,[15] if I can put it like that, to the two courts above it.[16] Nonetheless, it might be surmised that the tendency of specialist judges to give judicial recognition to the specificity of their particular domain of law will occasionally give way to a temptation to wriggle out of unwanted general case law coming from above, by invoking the specialised character of EU staff law. Precedents laid down by the two generalist courts, say in relation to commercial entities, could be distinguished by reference to the particularity of employment rights as laid down in EU law or international standards. It is not for me to opine whether the Civil Service Tribunal has ever succumbed to such a hypothetical temptation in its short life since 2005; I would simply say that this is one aspect where the existence of specialist tribunals within the ECJ may have an effect on the internal operation of the doctrine of precedent. Wait and see – in particular, see how the General Court will react if ever there is an appeal challenging any such "specialist" attempt by the Civil Service Tribunal to distinguish its way out of adherence to "generalist" precedents.

Taking a wider-angled view of precedent as one of the components for understanding the influence of the ECJ on the development of EU law, the first point to note is that EU law is more directly integrated into the national legal orders of the Member States than is the ECHR. The mechanism whereby national courts may request preliminary rulings of the ECJ invests the ECJ's case law with an especially influential harmonising character. Not only is the specific preliminary ruling of the ECJ binding on the particular national court that sought it, for the purposes of the decision to be given in the main national proceedings,[17] but, given the exclusive mission, conferred on the ECJ by the Treaties, of ensuring the unity of interpretation of EU

---

14 *Kadi v. European Commission*, Case T-85/09, judgement of 30 September 2010, especially paras. 112, 121 and 123 (to be reported in [2010] ECR). The judgement of principle of the Court of Justice referred to was that delivered in Joined Cases C-402/05 P and C-415/05 P *Kadi and Al Barakaat International Foundation v. Council and Commission* [2008] ECR I-6351, which was itself delivered on appeal against the judgement of the Court of First Instance (as the General Court was then called) in Case T-315/01 *Kadi v. Council and Commission* [2005] ECR II-3649. The General Court's declaration of precedential loyalty in the second *Kadi* case came after a lengthy critique which queried the wisdom of the reasoning followed by the Court of Justice in its appeal judgement in the first *Kadi* case.
15 NB the Tribunal is subject to a similar provision to Article 61 of the Statute: Annexe I to the Statute ECJ, Article 13 (2).
16 For an example where the Civil Service Tribunal, applying an interpretative approach not dissimilar to that used by the Strasbourg Court in the sex-change cases (see footnote 8 above), cited modernising developments in EU and international standards in order to overturn long established, restrictive case law of the Court of Justice and the General Court on a specific point of EU civil service law, see *Landgren v. European Training Foundation* (Case F-01/05, judgement of 26 October 2006, ECR-SC, p. I-A-1-123 et II-A-1-459), which for the first time recognised the obligation of the EU institutions to give reasons for the dismissal of staff employed on "temporary" contracts of unlimited duration. The Tribunal's judgement was upheld on appeal by the General Court, albeit on narrower, less "evolutive" grounds: *European Training Foundation v. Landgren* (Case T-404/06, judgement of 8 September 2009, to be reported in ECR-SC).
17 See the settled case law to this effect cited in the recent (preliminary ruling) judgement in Case C-173/09 *Elchinov v. Natsionalna zdravnoosiguritelna kasa*, 5 October 2010 – as yet unreported, para. 29.

law,¹⁸ the body of interpretative jurisprudence emanating from the ECJ is binding on national courts throughout the EU.¹⁹

The scope for the ECJ to indulge in lawmaking through interpretation and its use of precedent are thus critical factors for situating its power in relation to the other actors within the EU legal order.

Although not as open-ended as the ECHR, the EU Treaties nonetheless leave wide discretion to the ECJ. What is more, as with the Strasbourg Court, the formal means for reversing the ECJ's interpretation, namely treaty amendment, is so cumbersome to operate that, according to some commentators, the result is a weak system of control over the ECJ's lawmaking activity, *"thereby favouring the on-going dominance of the ECJ over the constitutional evolution of the [EU legal order]"*.²⁰

Most commentators seem to agree on two things:

Firstly, that judicial discretion and precedent at the level of the ECJ have been fundamental to the construction of the EU legal order. Indeed, for many the EU is one of the most striking examples of a legal system built on precedent, a phenomenon that has become ever more pronounced over the years. Statistics have been compiled showing that reliance on citation of previous judgements is increasing every year, not only numerically as one would expect as the corpus of jurisprudence expands organically but also in terms of the formulation of the rulings.²¹

The second consensus is that the ECJ *"has used its lawmaking powers for pro-integrative purposes"*.²² On this analysis the ECJ has become actively involved in policy-making, so that its precedents are not merely of technical value for clarifying doubtful points of law in the pure sense.

---

18 See, notably, Article 19 (1) of the Treaty on the European Union (vesting the ECJ with the mission of ensuring that *"in the interpretation and application of the Treaties the law is observed"*) and Articles 263 and 267 of the Treaty on the Functioning of the European Union (which confer on the ECJ the monopoly for the judicial control of the legality of the acts of the EU institutions).

19 The primacy of EU law over national law, and the monopoly that is given to the ECJ by the treaties to interpret EU law, covering both primary treaty provisions and secondary law in the form of directives and regulations, may well trump the operation of *stare decisis* between higher and lower national courts, allowing a lower court to ignore an otherwise binding precedent of a higher court on the basis of an ECJ preliminary ruling. As recently spelt out, only 10 days ago, in the *Elchinov* case, footnote 17 above, para. 32: *"EU law precludes a national court which is called upon to decide a case referred back to it by a higher court hearing an appeal from being bound, in accordance with national procedural law, by legal rulings of the higher court, if it considers, having regard to the interpretation which it has sought from the [ECJ], that those rulings are inconsistent with [EU] law."*

20 Point made by Stone Sweet and McCown, footnote 2 above, pp. 87–89: *"Compared with most courts in the world, the ECJ operates in a zone of discretion that is unusually large"*, or, as the authors put it in another place, *"in an unusually permissive environment ... when it interprets the Treaty"*. See also Komarek, footnote 5 above, pp. 428–429; *"the [EU] legislature ... is unable to monitor and modify the Court's activity"*, as is traditionally the case in national legal orders.

21 Stone Sweet and McCown, footnote 2 above, pp. 96–97 and 109–111.

22 Ibid., p. 85.

IV. Suggested Strands to Look for in the Speakers' Papers

If I am rash enough to pre-empt Dr. John Temple Lang and Professor Caflisch by attempting a comparison between Strasbourg and Luxembourg. My impression is that the Strasbourg Court is less formal but more transparent in its manipulation of the doctrine of precedent. As Professor Wildhaber puts it, there is nothing mechanical in the Strasbourg Court's methodology.[23] And it is more open about the occasions when it is departing from or varying previous case law, and why. In the ECHR system, the presence of separate opinions attached to the judgement of the Court often allows the precedential value of judgement to be better understood, in that separate opinions to a certain extent lift the veil on the confidentiality of deliberations and thereby illuminate whether and to what extent the existing case law is really being followed or, on the contrary, is being varied in some substantial way or even departed from.[24]

In the ECJ on the other hand, although the independent – and usually comprehensive – opinion delivered by the Advocate General prior to the judges' deliberations often goes a long way to explain the subsequent – and usually shorter – judgement of the Court, the judgements themselves, like those of the EFTA Court, have no illuminating separate opinions by the judges sitting in the case to assist in situating the succeeding precedents one against another. The style of the ECJ judgements is also different – more precise, more concise, less diffuse, but less expansive in the provision of explanations. The ECJ tends to reiterate classic passages from case to case, almost like incantations in religious services, without explicitly acknowledging that, perhaps, the context is materially different or the import of the reasoning not the same. That being so, as national judges from common law countries have sometimes complained, the citation of precedent may sometimes be deceptive as to the orthodoxy of what is being accomplished in that particular judgement – more like a smoke-screen than a transparent explanation of the result arrived at.[25] It may be that these common law reservations are not shared by all, of course.

As to the transparency of the recourse of precedents in EFTA judgements, being under the watchful eye of Professor Carl Baudenbacher, the EFTA Court's President, I take the prudent stance that I am not best qualified to offer any appraisal.

---

23 Wildhaber, footnote 11 above, p. 156.
24 See Paul Mahoney: The Drafting Process of the Judgements of the European Court of Human Rights, in Stefan Vogenauer and Mads Andenas, (eds.), A Matter of Style? The Form of Judgements in the United Kingdom and Abroad (Hart Publishing, forthcoming).
25 See, e.g., Mary Arden (member of the Court of Appeal of England and Wales), Peaceful or Problematic? The Relationship between National Supreme Courts and Supranational Courts in Europe, in Lincoln's Inn Lectures on European Law and Human Rights, pp. 131 at seq., especially at paras. 23 and 65 (Simmonds and Hill Publishing, 2010) and also to appear in 29 The Yearbook of European Law (2010): *"The Luxembourg Court is probably very tired of common law courts making this point but it is an important one. ... Judgements of the Luxembourg Court are often brief and contain little reasoning. ... The Luxembourg Court frequently says that something follows when it does not follow and there is in fact a large and unexplained development in the law. Cases are referred to which are clearly not being followed and it is not distinctly said that they are being overruled. What often prevails is some rather general Community law principle, like effectiveness. ... When the Luxembourg Court fails to issue a judgement that is clear, it is not being transparent, and it does not meet the benchmark ... about the quality of reasoning."* This lack of transparency in the use of precedent *"sometimes [makes it] difficult [for national courts] to understand what exactly has been decided by the supranational court"*.

So much for each court's internal precedents. What about reliance on external case law authorities in the "European High Courts"? This is the judicial dialogue that Dr. John Temple Lang refers to in the title of his paper. In this context, the contribution of Professor Christine Kaddous, looking at the use of ECJ precedents by an "outsider" court, the Swiss Federal Court, will shed an original, and differently instructive, light.

The Strasbourg Court, for its part, not infrequently invokes precedents from other legal orders in support of its evolutive, forward-looking interpretation of the ECHR. Some commentators, in particular from the French-speaking world, accuse the Strasbourg Court of adopting a somewhat dubious pick-and-choose policy in this regard, selecting those few precedents which appear to go in its preferred direction but ignoring all those many others which do not.[26] Professor Caflisch may well tell us whether this is a fair comment or not.

As it is well known, the ECJ has for many years regularly relied on both the text of the ECHR and the case law of the Strasbourg Court when having to resolve issues of fundamental rights under EU law. Now, the accession of the EU to the ECHR will bring another dimension to citation of precedents between the three European Courts across the whole domain of human rights issues. The Strasbourg Court is already citing the EU Charter of Fundamental Rights to justify evolving interpretation of the ECHR, a recent example being to overturn its previous jurisprudence and, in line with the ECJ, to reinterpret the right to a fair trial so as to extend its safeguards also to court proceedings seeking interim measures.[27]

What will be interesting today then will be to hear from our speakers about three broad themes:

– Firstly, about the technical rules or principles governing how each European Court goes about the business of creating precedents, overruling, modifying and clarifying previous case law and so on – which is of direct concern for those who practice before one or other of those courts or for those who are called on to regulate their conduct in the light of that case law. How successful do the speakers consider the operation of the doctrine of precedent to have been, in its own terms, in each system?

– Secondly, what will be as interesting, for me at any rate, are the general lessons that can be learnt as to the role and the behaviour of the judicial branch of government within the legal order concerned. Precedent, it has been said, camouflages active judicial lawmaking while enabling it.[28] The approach to precedent is indicative of how involved in policy-making the judges are trying to be, how activist they are or are not – in short, how much power over the rules governing society they are trying to pull to themselves at the expense of the two other arms of government (the legislature and the executive).

---

26 See, e.g., the regular commentaries of Jean-François Flauss, Actualité de la Convention européenne des droits de l'homme, in the French legal journal Actualité juridique droit administratif (AJDA).
27 *Micallef v. Malta*, 15 October 2009, to be reported in ECHR 2009 – citing *Bernard Denilauler v. SNC Couchet Frères*, Case 125/79, judgement of 21 May 1980, [1980] ECHR 1553, and Article 47 of the EU Charter.
28 Stone Sweet and McCown, footnote 2 above, p. 97.

– And, thirdly, what do the speakers think of the reliance as precedent on external case law, in particular each other's case law, by the European Courts (or such reliance in relation to the European Courts, in the case of the Swiss Federal Court)? Cross-citation, if not transfrontier citation.[29]

---

29 See the paper given at the first panel of this conference by Ilka Klöckner.

Precedent in the Practice of the European Court of Human Rights

LUCIUS CAFLISCH[1]

I. The Respect for Precedent: General Observations

Certainty and foreseeability are pillars of every legal system. A mean for reaching these goals is unified judicial practice. This is achieved by ensuring:

(i) that, within a given court and among its organs, chambers for instance, no contradictory decisions are taken; and

(ii) that there is, at the top of the judicial system, an organ of control verifying the uniform interpretation and application of the system's rules.

Reliance on precedent is often viewed as a factor dividing the world of common law from that of civil law. One may argue that in civil law systems, the bulk of the law is codified, the case law thus consisting mainly of decisions interpreting and applying the codified law. In common law environments this may not be the case. It could further be argued that whereas common law courts are bound by precedent, civil law courts are not. This is not quite true, however.

In civil law countries tribunals of first instance are generally entitled to deviate from precedents established by the highest court of the land. But if they do, they run the risk – a high risk – that their rulings will be reversed on appeal or, subsequently, by the supreme judicial organ. There is, however, an opportunity as well. By eschewing precedent, the tribunal of first instance may become the starting point for setting a *new precedent*. By contrast, in common law systems precedents stand as long as they are not reversed by the supreme judicial organ; but they can be abandoned, and sometimes are, for economic, social, political and other reasons. The above distinctions and divisions are rough and would deserve some refinement.

It may be assumed, however, that in both systems respect for precedent is deemed essential and is guaranteed by a hierarchically structured judiciary. Precedent can be overridden in both, perhaps a trifle more easily in a civil law context than in a common law framework because in civil law systems precedent relates to the *interpretation of existing law*, while precedents may be *part and parcel of the law itself* in a common law setting.

---

1 Prof. (em.), The Graduate Institute of International Studies and Development, Geneva; former judge of the European Court of Human Rights, Strasbourg; member of the United Nations International Law Commission.

A point to be made here is that changes in the case law are only possible if the decisions forming it are adequately reasoned. In the absence of such reasoning, it may be difficult to demonstrate and to understand why a set of given decisions are being and should be overruled.

Another point to be mentioned in this connexion is that any departure from the existing case law seems to lead to a kind of factual discrimination *ratione temporis* between those who have sought justice in the past and those who do so today – what could be gained by the former cannot be obtained by the latter, or vice-versa – on account of the change. Legally, this does not amount to discrimination, however, as a fundamental rule of law requires that existing situations be adjusted to ever-changing realities. To preserve the trust of those going to court, it seems advisable, however, to do so only where absolutely necessary.

II. Precedents in International Courts and Tribunals[2]

Certainty and foreseeability are desirable on the international level as well. But these goals are difficult to attain, because, at that level, there is no centralisation of the judicial function and no hierarchy of courts and tribunals in the absence of special rules to the contrary. This means, at least in theory, that the International Court of Justice (ICJ) can modify its practice at any moment – although it may be reluctant to do so and even more reluctant to admit that it has done so. It further means that arbitral Tribunal A can decide not to follow the practice of Tribunal B.[3] It even means that arbitral tribunals can disregard precedents set by the ICJ, although the latter would find this difficult to concede as Article 92 of the United Nations Charter considers the Court to be the principal judicial organ of the Organisation, which could be taken to mean the highest tribunal of the community of nations. It is true that the ICJ sometimes did play that role when examining the validity of international arbitral awards, but its competence to do so had been accepted by the states concerned.[4] It is equally true that, always with the agreement of those states, an arbitral tribunal could invalidate a judgement of the Court, although this is hardly a realistic hypothesis.

Despite the absence of a hierarchy among the organs of international adjudication – except *within* multi-layered international courts or tribunals, such as the Court of Justice of the European Union and the European Court of Human Rights (ECtHR) –, precedents are considered important. As a rule, these organs and their members seek to discharge their task by offering

---

2 On this issue, see G. Guillaume, Le précédent dans la justice et l'arbitrage international, Journal du droit international (Clunet), 137e année, 2010, pp. 685–703.
3 The Orinoco Steamship Company, *United States v. Venezuela*, US-Venezuela Claims Commission, award of 1903, United Nations Reports of International Arbitral Awards (UNRIAA), Vol. IX, p. 180, and award of the Permanent Court of Arbitration of 25 October 1910, ibid., Vol. XI, p. 227.
4 Delimitation of Maritime Boundary, *Guinea-Bissau v. Senegal*, ad hoc Tribunal, award of 31 July 1989, UNRIAA, Vol. XX, p. 119 and Arbitral Award of 31 July 1989, *Guinea-Bissau v. Senegal*, judgement of 12 November 1991, ICJ Reports 1991, p. 53; arbitral award of the King of Spain of 23 December 1906 on the *Delimitation of the Boundary between Honduras and Nicaragua*, UNRIAA, Vol. XI, p. 101 and case regarding the Arbitral Award Made by the King of Spain on 23 December 1906, *Nicaragua v. Honduras*, judgement of 18 November 1960, ICJ Reports 1960, p. 192.

some degree of consistency and predictability. They will do so by following precedents – except if the latter are considered faulty or at variance with present-day realities. Respect for precedent is important to judges and arbitrators, who are generally reluctant to take unnecessary risks.

Thus, while there is no assurance that international courts and tribunals will invariably be guided by precedent, there is, in practice, a strong trend in that sense.

III. The Respect for Precedent in the Framework of the European Convention on Human Rights

A. Practice Prior to 1998

A first question to be examined is whether the ECtHR as it has emerged from Additional Protocol No. 11[5] has made a completely new start or has endeavoured to build on the case law developed by the "old" Court and by the European Commission of Human Rights (disbanded after 1998).

Recently, Luzius Wildhaber, President of the Court from 1998 to 2007, has pointed out that continuity was among the priorities of the "new" Court:

> *"The 'new' Court followed in its activity the existing case law, except where the doctrine of an evolutive interpretation of the Convention guarantees or societal changes or the novelty or dimensions of some new problem impelled it to tread new paths[6]. I have always felt a strong responsibility to ensure that the achievements of the 'old' Court's first 40 – and the Commission's 45 – years of existence were not lost in the transition to the new system. There is nothing surprising in this. It would not have been very professional if the 'new' Court had behaved differently, and neither Protocol No. 11 nor the Member States gave it a mandate to give an abruptly different content to the Convention guarantees."[7]*

Accordingly, the "new" Court was determined to preserve the heritage left by its predecessor.

B. Internal Consistency of the Court's Case Law

Even more than the classical international bodies of adjudication, those *protecting the fundamental rights and freedoms* of the human person strive for stability and foreseeability, as the ECtHR did and continues to do. This policy has *internal* and *international* aspects.

---

5   European Treaties, No. 155.
6   See *Tyrer v. United Kingdom*, No. 5856/72, judgement of 25 April 1978, para. 31.
7   The Priorities of the "New" Court, in: Ten Years of the "New" European Court of Human Rights 1998-2008: Situation and Outlook. Proceedings of the Seminar (Strasbourg, 2008), p. 73.

On the *internal level*, the respect for precedent by the Court's organs is ensured mainly by two provisions of the European Convention on Human Rights (ECHR).[8] The first is Article 30 on *relinquishment* to the Court's Grand Chamber (GC), which prescribes, *inter alia*, that "*where the resolution of a question ... might have a result inconsistent with a judgement*[9] *previously delivered*", the Chamber of the Court dealing with the application *may*, prior to judgement and in the absence of objections by one or the other party,[10] relinquish jurisdiction over a case to the Court's GC. In other words, when the Chamber feels that the Court's case law could or should move in a new direction, the case *may* be passed on to the GC. The idea behind this provision is that, as the power to modify the Court's practice lies with the GC, relinquishment makes it possible to avoid having a case examined twice, first in a chamber and then by the GC.

The second relevant provision is Article 43 of the Convention which allows the applicant or/and the respondent state to ask for the *referral* of a judgement to the Court's GC. Referral, which implies a full re-examination of the case, must be requested within three months from the date of the Chamber's judgement. The case must be "exceptional" and raise "*a serious question affecting the interpretation or application of the Convention or the Protocols thereto, or a serious issue of general importance*".

What is more, leave to refer must be obtained from a five-member panel of the GC. Such leave is difficult to secure. From 1998 to 2010, referral has been requested in 1810 cases and allowed in 5% of them. What precedes shows that it is the GC, and in particular its five-member panel established by Article 43 of the ECHR, which controls the Court's case law and decides whether it needs a change. It does so by interpreting the Convention, not only in conformity with Articles 31 and 32 of the 1969 Vienna Convention on the Law of Treaties,[11] but also in accordance with the idea that the ECHR is a "living instrument" which must be responsive to social and other changes.[12]

The above description of the two provisions of the ECHR explicitly relating to modification of the case law prompts three observations.

The *first observation* is that generally the essence of the case law of an international organ of adjudication emerges in the first years of that body's existence. The ECtHR perfectly illustrates the point. But lacunae may remain and be discovered much later. This means that some virgin areas may remain for a long time, as it was the case regarding the principle of the separation

---

8   European Treaties, No. 5.
9   The use of the word "judgement" suggests that relinquishment may take place *after* the decision on admissibility.
10 It would appear preferable to drop this requirement which enables a party, all by itself, to force the Court to examine the same case twice. On this point, see L. Caflisch/M. Keller, Le Protocole additionnel n° 15 à la Convention européenne des droits de l'homme, in: Human Rights – Strasbourg Views. Liber Amicorum Luzius Wildhaber, Kehl, N.P. Engel, 2007, pp. 91–113, at p. 109.
11 Convention of 31 May 1969, United Nations Treaty Series, Vol. 1155, p. 331.
12 See the *Tyrer* judgement cited in footnote 6, para. 31.

of powers in the context of the ECHR.¹³ It also means that some of the existing case law may have aged and require adjustment.

The *second observation* is that case law can only emerge or be modified if decisions and judgements are *reasoned*. There may be, today, a general principle of law pursuant to which rulings must be reasoned, although that principle may not always be respected. Thus, regarding the admissibility of applications, Article 7 of Additional Protocol No. 14 to the ECHR, entered into force on 1 July 2010[14] and adding a new Article 27 to the Convention, prescribes that from now on single judges will decide issues of admissibility *"where such a decision can be taken without further examination"*. The inadmissibility decisions that may be made pursuant to new Article 27 will be summarily reasoned and, therefore, hardly contribute much to the formation of case law.

Always in connexion with new Protocol No. 14, attention must be drawn to its Article 8 amending Article 28 of the Convention. The new provision prescribes that, if a three-member committee of the Court receives an application from a single judge, it may decide unanimously[15] on both the admissibility of the application and its substance, provided that the question underlying the case, *"concerning the interpretation or the application of the Convention or the Protocols thereto, **is already the subject of well-established case law of the Court**"* (author's emphasis). If this condition is not met, the case will have to come before a chamber. This rule calls for two comments. Firstly, the Committee's decision or judgement is likely to a be summary; as it will have to conform to "well-established case law", it will have no significant impact on that law, apart from enhancing the effect of accumulation. Secondly, the very reference to "well-established case law" in new Article 28, which is the criterion for deciding whether cases go before a committee or a chamber, shows how important the case law is for the functioning of the Court.

The *third observation* concerns the "pilot-case" procedure[16] introduced by the Court a few years ago[17] with the blessing of the Council of Ministers of the Council of Europe.[18] In that procedure the Court delivers a "pilot judgement" in one of a series of cases triggered, or susceptible of being triggered, by the same event or situation. Such a "model judgement" will be followed by a succession of summary rulings following the same lines unless the Court, the Council of Ministers and the State concerned decide, under Article 46 of the ECHR,[19] to follow anoth-

---

13 Marković v. Italy, No. 1398/03, judgement of 14 December 2006, commented by the present writer: Actes de gouvernement et droits de l'homme: L'affaire Marković, in: International Law – Conflict and Development: The Emergence of a Holistic Approach in International Affairs, Leyden (Brill, 2010), pp. 135–167.
14 Protocol of 13 May 2004, European Treaties, No. 194.
15 What if there is no unanimity? The solution must be that in this event the case goes before a chamber.
16 A description and analysis of the pilot-case procedure will be found in the present writer's article: New Practice Regarding the Implementation of the Judgments of the Strasbourg Court, Italian Yearbook of International Law, Vol. XV, 2005, pp. 3–23 at pp. 11–22.
17 See the case of Broniowski v. Poland, No. 31443/96, judgement of 22 June 2004.
18 Resolution DH (3004)3 of 12 May 2004.
19 Article 46 provides: " 1. *The High Contracting Parties undertake to abide by the final judgement of the Court in any case to which they are Parties.*
    2. *The final judgement of the Court shall be transmitted to the Committee of Ministers, which shall supervise its execution*".

er course.[20] Pilot judgements evidently are important elements in the formation of the Court's case law, first in and of themselves and, second, on account of the many summary judgements they will generate.

Having dealt with the statutory provisions on the handling of precedents by the Court, something must now be said about the *organisation* of the Court and its incidence on the issue of precedents. It may be recalled that today the Court is one of the world's largest judicial institutions, consisting of 47 judges organised into five sections, and a registry of about 650 individuals; its potential "clientele" comprises about 800 million human beings; and more than 150'000 applications are currently pending before it. As pointed out above, its structures and procedures have recently been overhauled and changes have been made by the Additional Protocol No. 14 to improve the Court's performance. Other changes will occur as the further work decided by the Interlaken Conference progresses.[21] Despite its wish to abide by its case law, the ECtHR is and will remain a slow-moving mechanism where one hand, often, is unaware of what is done by the other. To ensure consistency between the rulings of the Court's organs, the Court's jurisconsult, a senior member of the Registry, and the Court's Research Division examine the decisions and judgements prepared for the chambers from the angle of existing case law and inform them of possible deviations. While this mechanism may be inadequate, it does attest to the Court's will to follow the precedents established by it.

So much for the ways and means by which the Strasbourg Court induces the GC, its chambers and its other organs to conform to the existing case law and encourages national judicial organs adequately to explain reversals of the existing case law.

Before concluding this sub-heading, the recent case of *Atanasovski v. Macedonia*[22] may be mentioned briefly. That case deals with the question of whether Article 6.1 of the ECHR and the principle of fair trial it embodies make it mandatory for national courts, especially courts of last resort, to provide a substantial explanation to claimants if and when they decide their case contrary to their practice. In the present instance, the Court found that the claim had been decided, on the national level,

> "*contrary to already established case law on the matter. In this connection the Court notes that case law development is not, in itself, contrary to the proper administration of justice since a failure to maintain a dynamic and evolutive approach would risk rendering it a bar to reform or improvement. However, it recalls that the existence of an established judicial practice should be taken into account in assessing the extent of the reasoning to be given ... In the present case, the Supreme Court deviated from both the lower courts' and its own jurisprudence on the matter. In this connection, the Court recalls that the requirement of judicial certainty*

---

20   As was done in the *Broniowski* case cited in footnote 17.
21   The "High Level Conference on the Future of the European Court of Human Rights", organised by the Swiss Government at Interlaken on 18–19 February 2010, adopted a declaration containing the road map for a new reform of the Court and for upgrading its performance. For the text of the Declaration and participants' interventions, see Council of Europe, Proceedings of the High Level Conference, document H/INF (2010)5.
22   No. 26815/03 judgement of 14 January 2010, para. 38.

and the protection of legitimate expectations do not involve the right to an established jurisprudence ... However, given the specific circumstances of the case, the Court considers that the well-established jurisprudence imposed a duty on the Supreme Court to make a more substantial statement of reasons justifying the departure. That court was called upon to provide the applicant with a more detailed explanation as to why his case had been decided contrary to the already existing case law."

C. The Practice of Other Bodies

Unlike some international courts and tribunals, the ECtHR has no scruples to invoke decisions taken by other entities. In the inter-state case of *Cyprus v. Turkey*,[23] for instance, the Court's GC abundantly referred to the ICJ's advisory opinion of 21 June 1971 on *Namibia*[24] when examining the status of the TRNC (Turkish Republic of Northern Cyprus). Its judgement shows that the GC considered the opinion of the ICJ to be relevant.[25]

In its rulings, the ECtHR has again and again cited all kinds of decisions and texts of other international institutions such as the UN Human Rights Committee[26] and the Inter-American Committee of Human Rights or the Inter-American Court of Human Rights.[27] This is hardly surprising, for the treaties establishing these organs are, in many aspects, modelled after their European forerunners. The Strasbourg Court has also made use of texts prepared by the European Union and invoked the case law of the Court of Justice of the European Union.[28]

In addition, the ECtHR frequently quotes decisions of national courts to confirm, illustrate or explain a viewpoint, including those emanating from countries which are not Parties to the ECHR such as the United States or Canada.[29] Evidently, the Court's task is to make sure that the Convention and its Protocols have been respected on the domestic level, rather than to *rely* on domestic decisions. But the practice – especially the case law of the courts of member or non-member countries – may make it possible to identify trends in the area of human rights, and, as is well known, the sources of international law listed in Article 38.1 of the Statute of the ICJ include judicial decisions among the *"subsidiary means for the determination of rules of law"*, a category which comprises decisions of domestic tribunals.

---

23 No. 25781/94, GC, judgement of 10 May 2001, paras. 90–102.
24 ICJ Reports 1971, p. 16.
25 See the judgement cited in footnote 23, paras. 92–97.
26 For an example, see *Varnava and Others* v. *Turkey*, Nos 16064-16066/90 and 16068-16073/90, GC, judgement of 18 September 2009, paras. 99–107.
27 For an example, see the *Varnava* judgement cited in the preceding footnote, paras. 93–98.
28 See for instance *Pellegrin* v. *France*, No. 28541/95, GC, judgement of 8 December 1999, paras. 37–41 and 65.
29 Cf., for example, *Hirst* v. *United Kingdom*, No. 74025/01, GC, judgement of 6 October 2005.

D. Conclusions

One cannot deny that the Strasbourg organs have proved sensitive, when making decisions, to the need of taking into account the precedents established by themselves, by other international judicial bodies and even by domestic courts, except where circumstances suggested a need for change. In a study published in 2000, Luzius Wildhaber, President of the ECtHR examines the cases in which, in his view, the "old" Court modified the existing case law.[30]

It would be difficult to repeat that exercise in the framework of the present study for the numerous cases decided between 1998 and 2010. The relevant judgements and decisions would be difficult to identify since neither lists nor statistical data are available; and the Court's rulings, unlike those of some national authorities – such as the Swiss Federal Court –, do not always indicate explicitly whether a modification ("revirement de jurisprudence") has occurred. Another difficulty is that of determining what "modification" means. Is it possible to speak of a "change" when a precedent is not applied because the Court thinks that the factual situation is different?[31] What if the existing case law is amplified to cover other situations, or if it remains untouched but is explained more completely or in a different way?

Despite these difficulties, one may conclude that the ECtHR, when it had to reconsider its case law, has done so reasonably and in moderation. In some instances, though, it may have gone overboard, as is shown by two cases to be discussed now.

IV. Changing the Case Law: Two Extreme Cases

A. *Eskelinen and Others v. Finland*[32]

A problem often encountered by the Court is whether the guarantee of a fair trial in civil matters found in Article 6.1 of the ECHR covers civil servants who are in conflict with the state, their employer. In the days of the European Commission of Human Rights, such trials had been removed from the purview of Article 6.1, except where "pecuniary interests" were involved: Matters relating to salaries and ancillary benefits were regarded as "civil", whereas issues such as conditions of engagement, advancement or dismissal were not. The criterion of "pecuniary interests" proved unworkable, however: While it is true that the non-promotion or dismissal of a state employee is a question of public law, how can it be argued seriously that they have no direct bearing on the employee's "pecuniary interests"?

---

30   L. Wildhaber, Precedent in the European Court of Human Rights, in: P. Mahoney et al. (ed.), Protecting Human Rights: The European Perspective. Studies in Memory of Rolv Ryssdal, Cologne, Carl Heymann, 2000, pp. 1529–1545 at. pp. 1532–1533).
31   Ibid., pp. 1538–1545.
32   *Eskelinen and Others* v. *Finland*, No. 63235/00, GC, judgement of 19 April 2007.

Practice evolved with the GC's judgement in *Pellegrin v. France*,[33] a case relating to the dismissal of an employee of the French Foreign Ministry who had been seconded to the authorities of Equatorial Guinea, and later to those of Gabon, as a high-ranking economic adviser. Borrowing from the international law rules on sovereign immunity the well-known distinction between acts accomplished *jure imperii* and *jure gestionis*, the GC held that the protection of Article 6.1 was not available to employees exercising part of their employer's sovereign powers, acting *jure imperii*, but that the provision did protect individuals not involved in the exercise of such powers, such as doctors and nurses in public hospitals, university and other teachers, garbage collectors, and pensioners *no longer* working for the state. One of the basic ideas behind this distinction was that individuals performing state functions owe a special duty of loyalty to the state and should not, therefore, engage in litigation against it.

While this new criterion seems to have worked reasonably well, there was considerable opposition to it by those who thought that Article 6.1 should apply, across the board, to each and every state employee. In 2007, they succeeded in reversing *Pellegrin*. The issue before the Court's GC in *Eskelinen v. Finland* were claims of Finnish police officers to hardship allowances which they had been promised for serving on remote posts. These claims having been rejected by the domestic courts, the police officers turned to Strasbourg alleging violations of Article 6.1 (reasonable-time requirement, absence of a public hearing).

Asserting that the *Pellegrin* doctrine had proved difficult to apply (judgements, paras. 51–56),[34] that it had resulted in discriminatory treatment (ibid., paras. 58–59) and that in most countries the due-process rules now tended to cover everyone (ibid., para. 58), the GC resolved to broaden the scope of Article 6.1. For that provision *not* to apply, the respondent state now has to show:

(i) that its own law explicitly rules out access to courts for the kind of post held by the employee claiming the protection of Article 6.1; and

(ii) that "*the subject matter of the dispute is related to the exercise of state sovereignty*" (ibid., para. 62).

How these two criteria will work is unclear. One wonders, for instance, how often states' laws *expressly* exclude access to courts for the category of persons to which the applicant belongs, and what happens if such access is excluded *implicitly* by the law or the case law of the domestic courts. These doubts did not seem to trouble the GC overmuch, witness its assertion that "*[t]here will be, in effect, a presumption that Article 6 applies*" (ibid., para. 62), and, since that presumption will be most difficult to reverse, it will in fact become the rule.

Objectively, the change brought about by the GC is unwelcome. It would have been simpler and more straightforward to go all the way and to extend the scope of Article 6.1 to each and

---

33 See footnote 28. Cf. equally *Frydlender v. France*, No. 30979/96, GC, judgement of 27 June 2000.
34 See, on this point, the joint dissenting opinion of judges Costa, Wildhaber, Türmen, Borrego and Jociene, para. 6.

every case involving state employees. Alternatively, it would also have been preferable to do nothing and to maintain the *Pellegrin* ruling. Now the situation is more confused than ever.[35]

B. The *Mamatkulov* Case

The case of *Mamatkulov and Askarov v. Turkey*[36] pertains to the "indication" of interim measures of protection by the ECtHR. To deal with this issue, it may be useful to begin by consulting Article 41 of the Statute of the ICJ which provides that that Court has *"the power to indicate, if it considers that circumstances so require, any provisional measures which ought to be taken to preserve the respective rights of either party to the dispute"*.

The question of whether such measures can be binding on the States concerned has, after years of hesitation, been answered in the affirmative by the International Court in the *LaGrand* case (*Germany v. United States*)[37]: The verb "indicate" used in Article 41 of the Court's Statute, *i.e.* a treaty accepted by the states parties to it, will from now on be interpreted by the Court as meaning "prescribe".

The ECHR, by contrast, is entirely silent on interim measures, but Article 39 of the Rules of Court[38] provides that Chambers or their Presidents

> *"may, at the request of a party or of any other person concerned, or of [their] own motion, indicate to the parties any interim measure which [they consider] should be adopted in the interests of the parties or of the proper conduct of proceedings"*.

This text, like that of Article 41 of the ICJ's Statute, uses the verb "indicate", which may denote both optional *or* prescriptive character. The difference between the two texts is that, whereas in the case of the ICJ the right to "indicate" interim measures is provided for in a treaty binding on all States Parties, this is not the case of the ECtHR: The power to "indicate" provisional measures merely results from the *Rules of Court*, drawn up and approved by the Court and no one else.

This situation led the ECtHR (*Cruz Varas v. Sweden*;[39] *Čonka v. Slovakia*[40]) to hold that provisional measures should not be viewed as binding. That view prevailed at least until 2001, when the ICJ broke its silence and decided, in *LaGrand*, that Article 41 of its Statute had to

---

35 In para. 6 of their joint dissenting opinion, judges Costa, Wildhaber, Türmen, Borrego and Jociene point out that the judgement in: *Eskelinen* "*encourages a dependent and variable, not to say uncertain, interpretation, in other words an arbitrary one. In our opinion, this is an inappropriate step back*".
36 No. 46827/99 and No. 46951/99, GC, judgement of 4 February 2005. For a recent commentary of the case, see M. J. Bossuyt, Strasbourg et les demandeurs d'asile: des juges sur un terrain glissant (Bruylant, Brussels , 2010), pp. 107–113.
37 *Germany v. United States*, judgement of 27 June 2001, ICJ Reports 2001, p. 466.
38 Rules of Court (1 April 2011).
39 GC, No. 15576/89, judgement of 20 March 1991.
40 No. 51564/99, unpublished decision of 13 March 2001, delivered by a chamber of the Court's Third Section.

be interpreted as enabling it to *impose* such measures. In 2005, in the framework of *Mamatkulov and Askarov v. Turkey*, a case relating to the extradition of two Uzbek nationals accused of criminal activities in a political context by Turkey to Uzbekistan, the President of the Chamber concerned asked Turkey, as an interim measure, to refrain from extraditing the two individuals. But, after having sought and received diplomatic assurances from Uzbekistan about the treatment they would receive if extradited, Turkey handed them over to the Uzbek authorities. The Court's GC subsequently found that the interim measure indicated by the Chamber concerned was binding on Turkey. One of the reasons for this decision was undoubtedly the increasing tendency on the part of international courts and tribunals to regard their provisional measures as compulsory. The argument that interim measures were not even mentioned by the ECHR was brushed aside by pointing out that a refusal to attribute binding force to such measures would prevent the Court *"from effectively examining the applicant's complaint"* and thus result in a breach of Article 34 of the Convention establishing the right of individual application (judgement, paras. 108–127).

This explanation is wholly unconvincing. Article 34 of the ECHR provides that

> "[t]he court may receive applications from any person ... or group of individuals claiming to be the victim of a violation by one of the High Contracting Parties of the rights set forth in the Convention or the Protocols thereto. The High Contracting Parties undertake not to hinder in any way the effective exercise of this right."

It is difficult to see how the Court's right to receive applications from individuals could be impaired by the optional nature of its interim measures; nor is it evident that this circumstance could prevent the Court from effectively examining complaints. Indeed, what Article 34 does *not* say and should have said to lend weight to the Court's argument is that the ECtHR must be in a position to protect the substance of claims before deciding them. And even if it did say so, provisional measures should be binding only where it is established, *in concreto*, that in their obsence the Court would be deprived of the possibility of properly examining the application.[41] In addition, one will note that a proposal made by a State Party to the ECHR to allow for binding interim measures *in the Convention* was not accepted.[42]

These considerations point to the conclusion that while binding provisional measures may appear desirable, the course chosen by the Court in *Mamatkulov* was *ultra vires*, that is, the exercise of a power the Court simply does not have under its constitutive treaty. One will note with interest, however, that the Contracting Parties appear to have acquiesced in the Court's construction. So, from now on, provisional measures enacted by the Court can be binding even in the absence of any treaty basis to that effect. The manner in which the ECtHR, here, has disregarded its own case law and the acceptance of the Court's construction by states has wider implications as well: It is an open invitation for the Court to go forth and do likewise in other areas.

---

41 Concurring Opinion of judge Cabral Barreto.
42 Joint partly dissenting opinion of judges Caflisch, Türmen and Kovler, para. 18.

V. Conclusion

Precedent is of critical importance to the ECtHR. It provides the certainty and foreseeability rendering the Court credible and reliable. But continuity is not everything. Life goes on, circumstances change; and the ECHR has been, and must be, regarded as a "living instrument" which may require new interpretations. By and large, the Court has handled this issue wisely; occasionally, however, it seems to have done too much (*Eskelinen*) or to have disregarded the limits of its competence (*Mamatkulov*).

The Significance of "Precedent" in the Bilateral Agreements between Switzerland and the European Union

CHRISTINE KADDOUS[1]

The Swiss Confederation, located in the very heart of the European continent, is not a member of the European Union, nor indeed of the European Economic Area. Even so, Switzerland's relations with the European Union are dense, intense and in constant evolution. They have been developed in an ad hoc way and are founded on specific institutional mechanisms. Some twenty agreements of primary importance together with one hundred or so secondary agreements are linking Switzerland with the European Union today.[2]

The aim of this contribution is to examine the question of "precedent" in the relations between Switzerland and the European Union, which comes up in specific terms due to the content of the agreements concluded between the Contracting Parties. After a brief look at the history of these bilateral relations, which should help to better understand their specificity (I), the characteristics and the institutional framework of the Bilateral Agreements I and II will be studied in order to determine the way they function and the link which is established with the concept of "precedent" (II). The position of the Swiss Federal Court[3] will be scrutinised with respect to the case law rendered by the European Court of Justice in relation to the Bilateral Agreements. The Agreement on the Free Movement of Persons (FMP Agreement) will be specifically addressed, as it makes express reference to the case law of the European Court of Justice; this case law being considered as "precedents" for Swiss tribunals. Three examples of situations will be given in order to illustrate the main issues which are at stake (III).

I. Introductory Remarks on the Bilateral Agreements

After the rejection of the European Economic Area Agreement (EEA Agreement) in 1992 by referendum,[4] which was mainly due to certain institutional features perceived as a limitation on the sovereignty of the people, in particular in relation to the principle of direct democra-

---

1   Christine Kaddous, Professor of European Law, Jean Monnet Chair, University of Geneva, Director of the Centre for European Legal Studies (Centre d'études juridiques européennes).
2   For a list of these agreements, see C. Kaddous and M. Jametti Greiner (eds.), Accords bilatéraux II Suisse – UE et autres Accords récents, Dossier de droit européen n° 16 (Basel-Brussels-Paris: Helbing-LGDJ-Bruylant, 2006), pp. 929–946.
3   "Das Bundesgericht", "le Tribunal fédéral".
4   The EEA Agreement of 2 May 1992, OJ 1994 L 1/3, was defeated because it only received 49.7 per cent of the votes with seven cantons voting in favour.

cy, Switzerland froze the application for European Union membership that it had submitted in May 1992. It then adopted the approach of conducting bilateral negotiations with the European Union in key sectors. After lengthy negotiations, seven agreements were signed in 1999 – the Bilateral Agreements I or *Bilaterals I* – and approved by a large majority in a referendum in May 2000.[5] These Agreements cover Free Movement of Persons, Overland Transport, Air Transport, Agriculture, Research, Technical Barriers to Trade and Public Procurement,[6] and came into force on 1 June 2002. The Agreement on Free Movement of Persons (FMP Agreement) is implemented in stages, with a transitional period in which the Swiss labour market is opened to nationals of the European Union Member States on a gradual basis subject to strict controls.[7] Time has shown that these seven agreements are beneficial to both the European Union Member States and Switzerland.

A further round of negotiations – the so-called *Bilaterals II* – were completed at the political level on 19 May 2004. This produced new agreements in eight other sectors: Cooperation in the fields of Police, Justice, Asylum and Migration (Schengen and Dublin), Taxation of Savings, Fight against Fraud, Processed Agricultural Products, Environment, Statistics, Media, Ed-

---

5   On 21 May 2000, the Swiss people approved the agreements by 67.2 per cent.
6   They are published in the OJ 2002 L 114/1, and in the systematic collection (SC) under different numbers according to their context. Agreement on the Free Movement of Persons between the European Community and its Member States on the one part, and the Swiss Confederation, on the other part, of 21 June 1999, OJ 2002 L 114/6, SC 0.142.112.681; Agreement between the European Community and the Swiss Confederation on the Carriage of Goods and Passengers by Rail and Road of 21 June 1999, OJ 2002 L 114/91, SC 0.740.72; Agreement between the European Community and the Swiss Confederation on Air Transport of 21 June 1999, OJ 2002 L 114/73; SC 0.748.127.192.68; Agreement between the European Community and the Swiss Confederation on Trade in Agricultural Products of 21 June 1999, OJ 2002 L 114/132, SC 0.916.026.81; Agreement on Scientific and Technological Cooperation between the European Community and the Swiss Confederation of 21 June 1999, OJ 2002 L 114/468, SC 0.420.513.1; Agreement between the European Community and the Swiss Confederation on Mutual Recognition in relation to Conformity Assessment of 21 June 1999, OJ 2002 L 114/369, SC 0.946.526.81; Agreement between the European Community and the Swiss Confederation on Certain Aspects of Government procurement of 21 June 1999, OJ 2002 L 114/430, SC 0.172.052.68. See also the Message of the Federal Council, which is the Swiss Government, to the Parliament of 23 June 1999, Federal Journal (FJ) 1999, 6128 et seq. that gives details of explanatory report for each agreement.
7   Article 10 FMP Agreement.

ucation, Vocational Training, Youth and Pensions.⁸ They have had the effect of extending and systematising the conventional framework of the relations with the European Union, and of developing the cooperation beyond purely economic aspects in fields such as internal security, asylum, environment, statistics and culture. These agreements were endorsed by the Swiss Parliament in December 2004. At the instigation of some 50,000 petitioners opposing Switzerland's participation in the Schengen and Dublin cooperation, a referendum was mounted but on 5 June 2005 the electorate voted in favour of Swiss participation in Schengen and Dublin.⁹ All of these agreements are now in force, except the one on the fight against fraud. Since it is of a mixed nature, i.e. concluded in 2004 by the European Community and its Member States, it requires *today* ratification by the European Union and by all the Member States individually. The process of ratification is still pending; however, the Agreement is provisionally applied.

The enlargement of the European Union in 2004 only necessitated amendments to one of the Bilateral Agreements I, i.e. the FMP Agreement because it was a mixed one concluded on the part of the European Union by the European Community and its Member States. On 25 September 2005, Swiss voters approved the extension of that Agreement to include the ten new European Union Member States.¹⁰ The other six agreements of 1999 were automatically extended as they fell fully within the exclusive competence of the European Community. Since 1 January 2007, the European Union has enlarged with Romania and Bulgaria and now comprises twenty-seven Member States. New negotiations have been launched with Switzerland in order to extend the FMP Agreement to the two new European Union members, which are now also parties to this Agreement. The extension to these two states as well as the continu-

---

8   The Bilateral Agreements II were signed on 26 October 2004. All of them are in force, except the Agreement on Fight against Fraud. For the references of publications, see Agreement between the European Community and the Swiss Confederation amending the Agreement between the European Economic Community and the Swiss Confederation of 22 July 1972 as regards the provisions applicable to processed agricultural products, OJ 2005 L 23/19; SC 0.632.401.23; see Message of the Federal Council of 1 October 2004, FJ 2004, 5927 et seq.; Agreement between the EC and the Swiss Confederation on cooperation in the field of statistics, OJ 2006 L 90/2, SC 0.431.026.81; see also the Message of the Federal Council of 1 October 2004, FJ 2004, 5973 et seq.; Agreement between the European Community and the Swiss Confederation concerning the participation of Switzerland in the European Environment Agency and the European Environment Information and Observation Network, OJ 2006 L 90/37, SC O.814.092.68; see the Message of the Federal Council, FJ 2004, 6001 et seq.; Agreement between the European Community and the Swiss Confederation in the audiovisual field, establishing the terms and conditions for the participation of the Swiss Confederation in the Community programmes MEDIA Training, OJ 2006 L 90/23, SC 0.784.405.226.8; see also Message of the Federal Council 2004, 6021 et seq; Agreement between the European Union, the European Community and the Swiss Confederation concerning the latter's association with the implementation, application and development of the Schengen acquis, OJ 2008 L53/52; Agreement between the European Community and Switzerland concerning the criteria and mechanisms for establishing the state responsible for examining a request for asylum lodged in a Member State or in Switzerland, OJ 2008 L 53/5; Cooperation Agreement between the European Community and its Member States, on the one part, and the Swiss Confederation, on the other part, to counter fraud and all other illegal activities affecting their financial interests, OJ 2009 L 146/8; see also Message of the Federal Council 2004, 6127 et seq.; Agreement between the European Community and the Swiss Confederation providing for measures equivalent to those laid down in Council Directive 2003/48/EC on taxation of savings income in the form of interest payments – Memorandum of Understanding, OJ 2004 L 385/30, SC 0.642.026.81; see also Message of the Federal Council of 1 October 2004, FJ 2004, 6163 et seq.
9   The Swiss people approved the Schengen and Dublin Association Agreements by 54.6 per cent.
10 The extension of the FMP Agreement and the revision of accompanying measures were approved by the Swiss population by 56 per cent.

ation of the FMP Agreement were submitted to the Swiss people and accepted by them on 8 February 2009. The modifications came into effect on 1 June 2009.

The relations between Switzerland and the European Union are developing continually. New negotiations are currently taking place in different fields but it is not yet decided if these future agreements will form a "third package" of Bilateral Agreements. The fields concerned are mainly Agriculture, Food Safety, Product Safety, Public Health, Electricity, Emission Trading, Satellite Navigation, Reach and Cooperation between Competition Authorities.

Apart from these Bilateral Agreements containing international obligations for Switzerland in relation to European Union law, the Federal Council decided *unilaterally* in 1988,[11] to bring Swiss legislation with international implications in line with European standards in order to reduce the differences between the Swiss legal order and that of the European Union. Since then, the "autonomous adaptation" of Swiss legislation to European Union regulations and standards, without any treaty obligation, is often reverted to and will remain important in the future for those matters not covered by the Bilateral Agreements I and II.[12]

II. The Characteristics of the Bilateral Agreements and their Institutional Framework

This part of the contribution deals with the nature and the characteristics of the Bilateral Agreements (A) and their institutional framework (B). It provides an overview of the principles that govern the functioning of these agreements in the development of the law (C), the issues of "equivalence of legislation" (D) and of the "*acceptance of the acquis*"(E), as well as the reference to the case law of the European Court of Justice (F).

A. The Nature of the Bilateral Agreements

The Bilateral Agreements concluded between Switzerland and the European Union fall into three different categories, each of them presenting specific characteristics.[13]

The "integration agreements" provide for the adoption of the European Union "*acquis*", as defined in the annexes of the agreements. They also allow the contracting party Switzerland certain rights of decision-shaping in the preparation of the future developments of these Agree-

---

11   FJ 1988 III 388.
12   On this question, see C. Kaddous, L'influence du droit communautaire sur l'ordre juridique suisse, in: Mélanges en l'honneur de M. l'Avocat Général Léger. Le droit à la mesure de l'homme (Paris: Pédone, 2006), pp. 407–423; W. Wiegand and M. Brülhart, Die Auslegung von autonom nachvollzogenem Recht der Europäischen Gemeinschaft, Swiss Papers on European Integration (1999), Vol. 23, pp. 29.
13   For further information on the main content of each of the Bilateral Agreements, see C. Kaddous, The Relations between the European Union and Switzerland, in: Recent Trends in the EU External Relations, Alan Dashwood and Marc Maresceau (Cambridge University Press: 2008), pp. 227–270.

ments. Only three main agreements belong to this category: The 1999 Agreement on Air Transport and the 2004 Schengen and Dublin Association Agreements.

The "cooperation agreements", as it flows from their name, are based on a classical cooperation between the contracting parties. This category covers the 1999 Agreement on Scientific and Technological Cooperation as well as those on Statistics, Fight against Fraud, Taxation of Savings, MEDIA programmes, Environment and Pensions. It includes also the 1999 and 2004 Research Agreements.[14]

Most of the Bilateral Agreements are "liberalisation agreements" providing for the application of the *"equivalence of legislation"* principle in the contracting parties. These agreements take into account the law as it stood at the date of signature of the agreements. In this regard, they are described as having a static dimension.[15] However, they need to be regularly adapted in order to consider the evolution of law in the contracting parties and to maintain the proper functioning of the agreements.[16] To this category belong: The FMP Agreement, the Agreement on the Carriage of Goods and Passengers by Rail, the Agreement on Mutual Recognition in relation to Conformity Assessment, the Agreement on Trade in Agricultural Products, the Agreement on Certain Aspects of Government Procurement as well as the Agreement on Processed Agricultural Products which modifies the 1972 Free Trade Agreement between Switzerland and the European Community.[17]

B. The Institutional Framework of the Bilateral Agreements

Unlike the EEA Agreement[18] and other association agreements concluded by the European Union with third countries, the institutional framework of the Bilateral Agreements is limited. Based on classical intergovernmentalism (except for the Air Transport Agreement and for the Schengen and Dublin Association Agreements), cooperation within the Agreements is

---

14 These two agreements are not formally part of the series of Bilateral Agreements. They are published at SC 0.420.513.1. For further information, see P.-E. Zinsli, in: C. Kaddous and M. Jametti Greiner (eds.), footnote. 1, pp. 901–910.
15 On the static character, see notably D. Felder, Appréciation juridique et politique du cadre institutionnel et des dispositions générales des accords sectoriels, in: D. Felder and C. Kaddous (eds.), Accords bilatéraux Suisse – EU (*Commentaires*), Dossier de droit européen n° 8 (Basel-Brussels: Helbing & Lichtenhahn-Bruylant, 2001), p. 128; T. Jaag, Institutionen und Verfahren, in: D. Thürer, R. Weber and R. Zäch (eds.), Bilaterale Verträge Schweiz-EG (Zurich: Schulthess, 2002), pp. 39–65.
16 See infra Section II. C. "Development of the law".
17 Agreement of 22 July 1972 between the Swiss Confederation and the European Economic Community, OJ 1972 L 300/189; also published in the SC of Swiss Law under 0.632.401.
18 On the EEA Agreement, see *e.g.* O. Jacot-Guillarmod (ed.), Accord EEE. Commentaires et réflexions. EWR-Abkommen. Erste Analysen. EEA Agreement. Comments and reflexions (Zürich: Schulthess/Stämpfli 1992), pp. 49–75, at p. 55; S. Norberg, K. Hökborg et al. (eds.), EEA Law. A Commentary on the EEA Agreement (Stockholm: Fritzes, 1993); S. Norberg, The Agreement on the European Economic Area, 29 CMLRev. (1992), pp. 1171–1198; R. Zach, D. Thürer and R. Weber (eds.), Das Abkommen über den Europäischen Wirtschaftsraum – Eine Orientierung (Zürich: Schulthess, 1992); P.-C. Müller-Graff and E. Selving (eds.), EEA-EU Relations (Berlin: Verlag Arno Spitz, 1999); C. Baudenbacher, P. Tresselt and T. Örlygsson (eds.), The EFTA Court. Ten Years on (Cambridge: Hart Publishing, 2005); M. Johansson, U. Wahl and U. Bernitz (eds.), Liber Amicorum in Honour of Sven Norberg. A European for all Seasons (Brussels: Bruylant, 2006).

made through Joint Committees, in charge of the administration and surveillance of their application.[19]

A Joint Committee is set up for every agreement; it is composed of representatives of the contracting parties and the decisions are taken by consensus. The Committee is the forum for the exchange of views and information between the contracting parties. It shall make recommendations and, in specific cases provided for in the agreements, it disposes of a decision-making power. For example, in the FMP Agreement, the Joint Committee is authorised to modify the Annexes II and III of the Agreement but it has no competence to change the main text of the Agreement or Annex I.[20] In the Schengen and Dublin Association Agreements, the Joint Committees have a specific structure and benefit special competences.[21]

The Joint Committees are also competent to settle disputes between the contracting parties.[22] There is no joint judicial body or tribunal to supervise the correct application and uniform interpretation of the Bilateral Agreements.[23] Consequently, it is possible that courts in the contracting parties, which are institutionally independent, take divergent decisions within their own legal system.[24] However, national courts in the European Union may submit a question for preliminary ruling to the European Court of Justice in accordance with Article 267 FEU Treaty. In that respect, uniformity in the application of the Bilateral Agreements is guaranteed within the European Union through the role played by the European Court of Justice.[25] Such a mechanism of preliminary ruling is not provided for in the Bilateral Agreements and no direct dialogue is foreseen between the Swiss judges and the European Court of Justice.

---

19   It must be mentioned that the Taxation of Savings and Pensions Agreements are exceptions; they do not set up joint committees.
20   Article 18 FMP Agreement.
21   Their meetings take place at different levels: Ministers, senior officials or experts, see Article 3 (1) and (5). For further details on this question, see the contribution of S. Gutzwiller, Komitologie und Gemischte Ausschüsse im Rahmen der Assoziierung der Schweiz an Schengen/Dublin, in: C. Kaddous and M. Jametti Greiner (eds.), footnote 1, pp. 245–266. These Committees constantly review the evolution of the case law of both the European Court of Justice and the Swiss courts relating to the provisions of the Agreements, see Article 8 (1) Schengen Association Agreement and with a formulation a bit different without incidence however on the substance, Article 5 (1) of the Dublin Association Agreement. These Committees have an important power, particularly where new acts have not been incorporated into the Swiss internal legal order, see Article 7 (4) and (10) Schengen Association Agreement and Article 4 (7) Dublin Association Agreement.
22   See, for example, Article 40 Agreement concerning the Fight against Fraud.
23   Exceptionally, in the Agreement on Air Transport the provisions on competition shall be applied and controlled by the European Union institutions in accordance with European Union rules. A first case has to be mentioned, which opposed Switzerland to the Commission before the General Court in relation to the Agreement on Air Transport concerning Zurich Airport. See Case T-319/05 (originally C-70/4) *Swiss Confederation v. Commission*. The judgement was rendered on 9 September 2010 and an appeal has been lodged before the European Court of Justice, still pending.
24   B. Spinner, Rechtliche Grundlagen und Grenzen für bilaterale Abkommen, in: D. Felder and C. Kaddous, footnote 15, p. 15; also T. Jaag, Institutionen und Verfahren, in: D. Thürer et al., Bilaterale Verträge Schweiz-EG, Ein Handbuch (Zurich: Schulthess, 2002), pp. 39–64, p. 45; S. Breitenmoser, Sectoral Agreements between the EC and Switzerland: Contents and Context, 40 CMLRev. (2003), pp. 1137–1186.
25   See Case 181/73 *Haegeman* [1974] ECR 449; see also Case 12/86 *Demirel* [1987] ECR 3719.

C. Development of the Law

By contrast to the EEA Agreement which has a dynamic character, since the EEA-EFTA states accepted the obligation to adopt the future *acquis* of the European Union,[26] the Bilateral Agreements are almost all of static character and only refer to the mutual recognition of equivalent legal provisions.[27] Only the *acquis* as it stood prior to the date of their signature and to which reference is made, will be applied in the relations between the contracting parties. For example, in the FMP Agreement, the case law of the European Court of Justice as established after 21 June 1999 must only be brought to Switzerland's attention through the Joint Committee.[28] It is then for the Committee to determine the implications of such case law. Similarly, if one of the contracting parties initiates new legislation it shall inform the other party through the Joint Committee, which shall hold an exchange of views on the implications of such an amendment for the proper functioning of the Agreement.[29] Since the references in the Bilateral Agreements are static, a change in European Union legislation does not automatically bring about a change in the Bilateral Agreements. Amendments to the Agreements only enter into force after the respective internal ratification procedures have been completed on both sides. Merely technical adjustments and amendments to the *acquis* (such as acts listed in the annexes) may nevertheless be adopted by decision of the Joint Committee and enter into force immediately thereafter.[30]

However, two main agreements of the *Bilaterals II* constitute an exception to the equivalence of legislation principle. The Schengen and Dublin Association Agreements provide that Switzerland accept the Schengen and Dublin *acquis* as well as their future developments.[31]

Thus, the Bilateral Agreements are based either on the principle of "equivalence of legislation" or on the principle of "acceptance of the *acquis*".[32] These issues should then be addressed in more details.

---

26 On the homogenous character of the EEA Agreement, see e.g. O. Jacot-Guillarmod, Préambule, objectifs et principes (articles 1–7 EEE), in: Accord EEE. Commentaires et réflexions. EWR-Abkommen. Erste Analysen. EEA Agreement. Comments and reflexions (Zürich: Schulthess/Stämpfli, 1992), p. 55; M. Cremona, The Dynamic and Homogeneous EEA: Byzantine Structures and Variable Geometry, 19 ELRev. 1994, pp. 508–526; C. Baudenbacher, Between Homogeneity and Independence. The Legal Position of the EFTA Court in the European Economic Area, Columbia Journal of European Law (1997), pp. 169–227.
27 The Schengen and Dublin Association Agreements as well as the Air Transport Agreement are exceptions. They are based on the "acceptance of the Acquis". See *infra* Section II. D. and E. on the principles of "Equivalence of legislation" and "Acceptance of the *acquis*".
28 Article 16 (2) FMP Agreement.
29 Article 17 (2) FMP Agreement.
30 Article 18 FMP Agreement.
31 On the acceptance of the *acquis*, see infra Section II. E.
32 Other bilateral agreements refer to a classic cooperation between the Contracting Parties.

D. Principle of "Equivalence of Legislation"

The principle of "equivalence of legislation" of the contracting parties is fundamental to the proper functioning of numerous Bilateral Agreements. It is worth recalling that one of the main reasons for the rejection of the EEA Agreement by the Swiss people was its dynamic character, i.e. the obligation to adopt the future acquis. Therefore, most of the Bilateral Agreements only refer to the mutual recognition of equivalent legal provisions.[33]

By this means, both contracting parties safeguarded their legislative autonomy with the requirement of maintaining the equivalence of their legislation. This task of safeguarding the equivalence is facilitated by the introduction of reciprocal information procedures and, in certain cases, of consultation when one of the contracting parties envisages amending its legislation on a point regulated by the agreements.[34] Consequently, the evolution of legislation in a contracting party has to be taken into account regularly in such a way as to avoid any divergence between Swiss law and the law of the European Union in the fields regulated by the agreements. Otherwise, the proper functioning and the efficiency of these texts would seriously be jeopardised.

E. Principle of the "Acceptance of the *Acquis*"

As mentioned above, the principle of the "acceptance of the *acquis*" is rather an exception in the Bilateral Agreements. Only two examples are given in the *Bilaterals II*: the Schengen and Dublin Association Agreements. In these fields Switzerland shall accept the *acquis* as it stood at the moment of the signature of the agreements (26 October 2004)[35] as well as their future developments. However, it managed to safeguard a measure of autonomy insofar as it may decide independently whether it will accept or refuse new developments of the Schengen or Dublin *acquis*. The refusal to accept may lead, in certain circumstances, to the termination of the agreements.

F. Reference to the Case Law of the European Court of Justice

The objective of "equivalence of legislation" or "homogeneity" (as far as the Air Transport Agreement is concerned) is very important for the proper functioning of the Bilateral Agreements. However, only two of them contain express provisions on taking into account the European Court of Justice case law: the FMP and the Air Transport Agreements.

Article 16 (2) of the FMP Agreement provides that, insofar as the application of the Agreement involves concepts of European Union law, account shall be taken of the relevant European Court of Justice case law rendered prior to the date of its signature. Case law after that

---

33 See supra Section II. C. "Development of the law".
34 See, for example, Article 4 of the Agreement in the field of Statistics.
35 The relevant acts and measures are enumerated in Annexes A and B Schengen Association Agreement and in Article 1 (1) Dublin Association Agreement.

date shall be brought to Switzerland's attention. At the request of a contracting party, the Joint Committee shall determine the implications of such case law. A similar system is provided for in the Air Transport Agreement.[36]

The obligation of taking into account the case law of the European Court of Justice has not been extended in these two agreements to the one rendered after the date of signature, since it would have meant that Switzerland submits to "foreign judges".

Unlike the FMP and the Air Transport Agreements, the Schengen and Dublin Agreements do not take into account any case law of the European Court of Justice rendered prior or after to the date of signature of the agreements, but provide for another system. The contracting parties clearly indicate in these two agreements their objective of ensuring the most uniform possible application and interpretation of the *acquis* provisions.[37] With this aim in mind, the Joint Committees shall keep under constant review developments in the European Court of Justice and Swiss case law. A mechanism of regular mutual transmission of such case law is set up. Furthermore, Switzerland shall report each year to the Joint Committee on the way in which its administrative authorities and courts have applied and interpreted the provisions of the Schengen and Dublin Association Agreements.[38] In case of a substantial divergence between the European Court of Justice case law and that of Swiss courts or a substantial divergence in the application of the Agreements' provisions between the authorities of the Member States concerned and the Swiss authorities, the Joint Committees must resolve the problem. They have two months to ensure a uniform application and interpretation by the contracting parties.[39] If they are unable to do so, the dispute settlement procedure is triggered, with all that this implies, potentially even leading to the termination of the Agreement.[40]

Except the situation of these aforementioned agreements, the other Bilateral Agreements do not contain references to the case law of the European Court of Justice. However, it must be stressed that in order to preserve the *effet utile* of these Agreements, the administrative and judicial authorities designed in Switzerland to apply these texts are encouraged to ensure as uniform an interpretation and application of the rules as possible, the content of which is substantially equivalent to provisions of European Union law. This should also be encouraged in cases of interpretation of Swiss law which was subject to an autonomous adaptation to European Union law.

This position may be defended on the basis of an extensive interpretation of the rules on implementation contained in the agreements themselves in order to ensure the proper functioning of the bilateral relations decided between Switzerland and the European Union. According to the agreements, the contracting parties shall take all appropriate measures to ensure the

---

36 For the Air Transport Agreement, the system of reference to Community law for today (after the entry into force of the Lisbon treaty) to European Union law is provided in Article 1 (2).
37 Article 8 Schengen Association Agreement and Article 5 Dublin Association Agreement.
38 Article 9 Schengen Association Agreement and Article 6 Dublin Association Agreement.
39 Article 9 (2) Schengen Association Agreement and Article 6 (2) Dublin Association Agreement.
40 Article 10 Schengen Association Agreement and Article 7 Dublin Association Agreement.

fulfilment of the obligations arising out of the Agreements and shall refrain from any measures which would jeopardise attainment of the objectives of the Agreements.[41] This formula, which differs from one agreement to another,[42] but which keeps the general substance, takes up the general application of the principle *pacta sunt servanda* according to which every treaty in force is binding upon the parties to it and must be performed by them in good faith (Article 26 Vienna Convention of 1969 and of 1986).[43]

The case law of the European Court of Justice referred to in some of the Bilateral Agreements constitute "precedents" in the way that the Swiss national judges are required to follow decisions rendered by the European Court of Justice even so they might prefer not to do so.[44] This duty exists in the FMP and the Air Transport Agreements as to the case law rendered before the date of signature of the Agreements.

III. The Concept of "Precedent" in the Bilateral Agreements

The purpose of this part of the contribution is neither to examine whether the Swiss Federal Court applies a doctrine of precedent in reaching its decisions. Nor is it aimed at analysing whether the Swiss judge is required to follow a decision given in a previous case, but rather to scrutinize its duty to consider the case law rendered by the European Court of Justice on concepts of European Union law which appear in the Bilateral Agreements concluded between Switzerland and the European Union in which reference is made expressly to European Union's case law. The FMP Agreement belongs to this category of Bilateral Agreements and will be addressed hereafter. After giving an overview of the aim and main content of this agreement (A), three examples may illustrate the questions of "precedent" in relation to the case law of the European Court of Justice (B).

A. Aim and Main Content of the FMP Agreement

The aim of the FMP Agreement is to accord to Swiss nationals and nationals of the European Union Member States the rights of entry, residence and access to work as employed persons, establishment on a self-employed basis and the right to stay in the territory of the contracting parties. The Agreement also facilitates the provision of services in the territory of the Contracting States, and in particular liberalises those of brief duration (for a maximum period of 90

---

41 See Article 10 Agreement on Cooperation in the area of Statistics and Article 15 of the Agreement in the field of Environment.
42 In the FMP Agreement, Article 16 (1) stipulates : *"In order to attain the objectives pursued by this Agreement, the Contracting Parties shall take all measures necessary to ensure that rights and obligations equivalent to those contained in the legal acts of the European Community to which reference is made are applied in relations between them"*.
43 More details have been brought in the Bilateral Agreements II, particularly in the Taxation of Savings Agreement which expressly mentions that Switzerland shall take the measures necessary to ensure that the tasks required for the implementation of the Agreement are carried out by paying agents established within the territory of Switzerland and which specifically provides for provisions on procedures and penalties, see Article 1 (5) Agreement.
44 See infra footnote. 52.

days per calendar year). It also guarantees the right of entry into and residence in the territory of the contracting parties to persons not exercising an economic activity in the host country. Finally, it affords the same living, employment and working conditions as those accorded to nationals. All these rights are provided on the basis of the non-discrimination principle on grounds of nationality. However, one of the essential characteristics of the Agreement is that the free movement of persons is liberalised progressively, in stages, over transitional periods.[45]

The Agreement also provides for the coordination of social security systems[46] and contains the same principles as those in force within the European Union concerning mutual matters for recognition of diplomas so as to make it easier for Swiss and European Union nationals in the partner territories to access and pursue activities as employed and self-employed persons, as well as to provide services.[47] The Agreement also makes provision for the acquisition of immovable property insofar as it is linked to the exercise of other rights conferred by the Agreement itself.[48]

The FMP Agreement is one of liberalisation based on the equivalence of legislation, in which the contracting parties have expressed in the preamble of the Agreement their desire to bring about free movement of persons on the basis of the rules applying within the European Union.[49] The Agreement was extended in 2004 and in 2008. The first additional protocol concerns the extension of the agreement to the new ten European Union Member States,[50] and the second one to Bulgaria and Romania.[51]

B. Examples of "Precedents"

Three examples may illustrate the question of "precedents" in relation to the FMP Agreement and to the case law rendered by the European Court of Justice and by the Swiss Federal Court. The examples chosen relate to different situations. They relate to different situations in which the concept of "precedent" is applied. The first situation gives details on the general rules applicable to the duty to take into consideration the case law rendered by the European Court of Justice (1), the second situation relates to a rare example of the application by the Swiss Federal Court of a reversal of a precedent rendered by the European Court (2), and the third one concerns the effects of the case law of the European Court of Justice on the interpretation and application of the FMP Agreement itself (3).

---

45 Article 10 FMP Agreement, see D. Grossen, P. Gasser and D. Veuve, in: D. Felder and C. Kaddous (eds.), Accords bilatéraux Suisse – EU (Commentaires), Dossier de droit européen n° 8 (Basel-Brussels: Helbing & Lichtenhahn-Bruylant, 2001), pp. 259–311.
46 Article 8 FMP Agreement and Annex II, under which the contracting parties apply between each other the coordination system applicable in the EU Member States or equivalent rules.
47 Article 9 FMP Agreement and Annex III.
48 Article 25 of Annex I, see F. Schobi, in: D. Felder and C. Kaddous (eds.), footnote 15, pp. 417–434.
49 See also the Joint Declaration on the application of the Agreement, according to which the parties will undertake to apply to nationals of the other contracting party the *acquis*, as provided in the Agreement.
50 Additional Protocol, signed 26 October 2006, OJ 2006 L 89/30; OC (Swiss Official Collection) 2006 995.
51 SC 0.142.112.681.1.

1. General Rules on the Duty to Take Into Consideration the Case Law Rendered by the European Court of Justice

As mentioned above, the duty for Swiss courts to take into account the case law of the European Court of Justice in relation to the FMP Agreement exists only as to the judgements rendered prior to the date of signature of the agreement (21 June 1999). According to this rule, the Swiss Federal Court followed regularly the case law rendered by the European Court, except in the field regarding health care as the free movement of services in the Bilateral Agreement is not identical in substance to the one granted in the European Union Member States under the EU treaties.[52]

However, it is worth pointing out that the Swiss Federal Court does not hesitate to take inspiration from judgements issued after the signing date of the FMP Agreement, when these confirm or specify prior case law.[53]

Despite this approach, it is not easy to define the effects of this delimitation. First, very often the Federal Court refers to the case law rendered after the date of the FMP Agreement's signature but without specifically mentioning their subsequent character.[54] At the same time, the Swiss Supreme Court never extended its obligation under the Agreement in order to cover also the case law rendered after the date of signature. It simply stated that these subsequent judgements may only "inspire" the Swiss judge.

This distinction made by the Swiss Federal Court is quite logical since the "new" case law does not necessarily concern the FMP Agreement as it stood at the date of its signature. To illustrate this approach, one may consider the case law related to the Directive 2004/38 on the rights of the citizens in the European Union,[55] which is not applicable within the framework of the FMP Agreement. An illustration of such an exclusion could be the definition of the family members, which is based in the Bilateral Agreement on the former definition which was provided for in the former Article 10 of Regulation No 1612/68.

---

[52] According to the Swiss Federal Court, the free movement of services, as provided for in the EC treaty and in the case law rendered by the European Court of Justice does not form integral part of the *"acquis"* Switzerland accepted under the FMP Agreement. The Bilateral Agreement allows only for a partial liberalisation of services, see ATF 133 V 624, cons. 4.2–4.3.7. For a more recent case law, see Judgements of Federal Court of 30 December 2008, Case 9C_479/2008; of 12 March 2008, Case I 601/06; of 24 June 2008, Case 9C_310/2007, published ATF 134 V 330; of 14 October 2010, Case 9C_630/2010.
[53] See, for example, ATF 130 II 1, ATF 130 II 113 cons. 5.2 Case 2 I.753/2004 of 29 April 2005.
[54] ATF 134 V 235, cons. 5.2.1; ATF 131 V 390, cons. 3.2, ATF 130 V 247, cons. 4.1.
[55] Directive 2004/38/EC of the European Parliament and of the Council of 29 April 2004, on the right of citizens of the Union and their family members to move and reside freely within the territory of the Member States amending Regulation (EEC) No. 1612/68 and repealing Directives 64/221/EEC, 68/360/EEC, 72/194/EEC, 73/148/EEC, 75/34/EEC, 75/35/EEC, 90/364/EEC, 90/365/EEC and 93/96/EEC, OJ L 158 of 30.4.2004. It is still the directive 64/221/EEC of 25 February 1964 on the coordination of special measures concerning the movement and residence of foreign nationals which are justified on grounds of public policy, public security or public health, which is applicable within the framework of the Agreement, OJ L 56 of 4.4.1964.

However, this distinction made in the Swiss case law does not help much in practice. It has to be one thing or the other. If the subsequent case law introduces new principles, the Swiss judge has no obligation under international law in this regard, but it may use it as an inspiration. If, on the other hand, the subsequent case law only confirms a prior judgement (rendered before the date of signature), the Swiss judge is already bound by the former case law and the consequences of this situation simply lies in the fact that, with or without subsequent case law, the "solution" of the dispute should be based on the principles developed in the former case law. These are the two extreme situations. There may also be an intermediate situation, in which the new judgement rendered by the European Court of Justice confirms a prior decision but, at the same time, introduces new elements, which cannot be considered as being part of the Bilateral Agreement. This would be for example the case of judgements rendered by the Court of Justice in relation to the Directive 2004/38 which is not mentioned in the FMP Agreement, but which replaces in some parts secondary legislations which are provided for in the Bilateral Agreement. In this regard, the part of the directive concerning "citizenship", which is not listed in the annexes of the FMP Agreement, should have no influence on the judge of the Federal Court as long as the Agreement has not been modified. This limit has been fixed by the Swiss Federal Court itself.[56]

It appears that the tasks of the Swiss judges are not easy, since the FMP Agreement does not contain clear guidelines in relation to subsequent case law. The taking into account of the judgements rendered after the date of signature remains a question of appraisal decided on a case by case basis.

2. Application of a Reversal of a Precedent in the Case Law of the Swiss Federal Court

The Swiss Federal Court made a reversal of precedent in its case law on the basis of a reversal decided earlier by the European Court of Justice which has departed from its previous decisions. In a judgement rendered in September 2009,[57] the Swiss Federal Court had to decide on a question of family reunification. It concerned a Palestinian, whose application for asylum had been rejected. He was also condemned to more than two years of imprisonment and was subject to an expulsion measure. In 2007, he got married to a Spanish citizen, holder of a Swiss permanent residence permit. His demand to obtain a stay permit to remain with her in Switzerland was refused. In that case, the Swiss Federal Court decided to abandon the former *Akrich* judgement,[58] which was rendered by the European Court of Justice in 2003 and to take into account the *Metock* case rendered in 2008.[59]

---

56 ATF 130 II 113 (6).
57 ATF 136 II 5.
58 Case C-109/01 *Akrich* [2003] ECR I-9607.
59 Case C-127/08 *Metock* [2008] ECR I-6241.

In the *Akrich* case, the Court of Justice decided that a national of a non-Member State married to a citizen of the European Union must be lawfully resident in a Member State before moving to another Member State to which the citizen of the Union is migrating or has migrated.[60] Less than one month later the Federal Court aligned its case law with the *Akrich* case.[61] The judgement of the European Court was very much criticized by the scholars since it reduced considerably the right of the family reunification in the European Union and five years later, on 25 July 2008, the European Court of Justice changed its position and admitted that the *Akrich* judgement should be reconsidered. It concluded that the benefit of such residence rights cannot depend on the prior lawful residence of a spouse in another Member State.[62] By contrast to what has been held in *Akrich*, the Court decided in *Metock*, that it cannot be required that, in order to benefit from the rights provided for in Article 10 of Regulation No 1612/68 on the freedom of movement for workers within the Union, the national of a non-Member State who is the spouse of a Union citizen must be lawfully resident in a Member State when he moves to another Member State to which the citizen of the Union is migrating or has migrated. In September 2009, the Swiss Federal Court decided to align with the *Metock* judgement. The reasoning of the Swiss judges was based on the fact that it was important not to jeopardise the FMP Agreement's aim of developing parallel legal situations in the contracting parties. Very interestingly in this example, the Swiss Federal Court accepted first to take into account the *Akrich* case of 2003, rendered obviously after the date of signature of the FMP Agreement and admitted secondly, to reverse its own case law on the basis of a reversal case law made by the European Court of Justice in 2008. Thus, the Swiss Federal Court followed twice the case law of the European Court of Justice in situations where it had no obligation to do so under the Bilateral Agreement.[63]

3. Effects of the Case Law Rendered on the Interpretation and Application of the FMP Agreement

The third example relates to the potential effects of the case law rendered by the European Court of Justice on the interpretation and application of the FMP Agreement itself. This situation is quite different from the two former situations.

The rule in Article 16 (2) of the FMP Agreement relates to the case law rendered by the European Court on concepts of European Union law which are included in the Agreement (i.e. concepts of "worker" or of "public order"). These are notions and concepts that have to be interpreted in a similar way in the legal orders of the Contracting Parties in order to guaranty parallel evolution of the legal definitions.

---

60 Case C-109/01 *Akrich* [2003] ECR I-9607, paras. 50-51.
61 ATF 130 II 1, of 4 November 2003.
62 Case C-127/08 *Metock* [2008] ECR I-6241, para. 58. The ECJ referred as well to the Case C-459/99 *MRAX* [2002] ECR I-6591, para. 59 and to the Case C- 157/03 *Commission v. Spain* [2005 ECR I-2911, para. 28.
63 On the motivation given by the Swiss Federal Court in relation to the *Akrich* and *Metock* cases, see C. Kaddous and C. Tobler, "Droit européen : Suisse-Union européenne", Revue suisse de droit international et européen (RS-DIE/SZIER) 4/2010, pp. 597–636, sp. pp. 609–613.

The case law of the European Court of Justice interpreting the FMP agreement itself should be differentiated from the above mentioned case law. There are by now four cases which were introduced by jurisdictions of the Member States on the basis of the preliminary ruling procedure (Article 267 FEU Treaty) in relation to the FMP Agreement.[64] The first judgement, the *Stamm and Hauser* case, rendered in December 2008[65] concerning the notion of "self-employed frontier workers" and the application of the equal treatment principle, had already been mentioned by the Federal Swiss Court in a judgement, however without underlining its specific character.[66] The *Grimme* judgement of November 2009[67] examines the question of the compulsory membership of a pension insurance scheme for a member of a managing board of a limited company by shares governed by Swiss law, who is a director in Germany, of a branch of the company. The *Fokus Invest* case of February 2010[68] deals with the free movement of capital and the conditions governing the acquisition, by a company established under Austrian law, the shares of which are held by a company established under Swiss law, of immovable property situated on Austrian territory. The *Hengartner and Gasser* judgement of July 2010[69] examines the provisions on services and on freedom for establishment in the FMP Agreement in order to consider whether a charging of a hunting tax with a higher rate of tax for Swiss nationals than for nationals of the European Union is compatible with the Agreement.

Very formally, all these cases are obviously rendered after the date of signature of the FMP Agreement and do not all refer to concepts of European Union law as it is classically understood under Article 16 (2). One case relates to the conditions of applicability of a rule mentioned in the Agreement (*Stamm and Hauser* case) and the others relate to rules which have a common source of inspiration but the scope of which is different because the objectives of the Bilateral Agreement are not identical to the ones governing the single market (*Grimme, Fokus Invest and Hengartner and Gasser* cases). The consequence of this is that the interpretation given to the provisions of European Union law cannot automatically be applied by analogy to the interpretation of the Agreement.

The Swiss judges have no obligation to take into consideration this case law, but one may be convinced that they will naturally consider it as a source of inspiration. The same interpretations will presumably be given, pointing out the differences of objectives between the internal market and the FMP Agreement as far as the free movement of services and the freedom of establishment are concerned. In that respect, the parallel development of the rules enshrined in the FMP Agreement will thereby be safeguarded in Switzerland and on the territory of the Member States of the European Union.

---

64 For a comment of these judgements, see C. Kaddous, Stamm et Hauser, Grimme, Fokus Invest AG, Hengartner et Gasser ou les accords bilatéraux ne créent pas un marché intérieur, Revue suisse de droit international et européen (RSDIE/SZIER) 2/2010, pp. 1–9.
65 Case C-13/08 *Stamm et Hauser* [2008] ECR I-11087.
66 ATF 135 II 128, cons. 2.2.
67 Case C-351/08 *Grimme* [2009] ECR I-10177.
68 Case C-541/08 *Fokus Invest AG* [2010] not yet reported.
69 Case C-70/09 *Hengartner and Gasser* [2010] not yet reported.

Despite the fact that the FMP Agreement does not provide for any mechanism in order to ensure homogeneity, it is up to the judicial authorities to guarantee as much as possible this uniform interpretation and application of the FMP Agreement.

IV. Conclusions

Firstly, it should be noted that the solutions negotiated between Switzerland and the European Union as to the duty of taking into consideration the case law of the European Court of Justice are not legally satisfactory insofar as they only contribute partially to avoid divergent interpretations and applications of concepts of European Union law enshrined in the Agreement without guaranteeing "full" homogeneity.

Despite the advantage of respecting of the independence of the administrative and judicial authorities of both contracting parties, the present situation brings many uncertainties as to the legal meaning of the provisions of the FMP Agreement, which at the very end runs counter the effective protection of the individuals. In that regard, the proper functioning of the Bilateral Agreement depends notably on the decision of the Swiss administrative and judicial authorities to accept or reject the relevant case law of the European Court of Justice.

The FMP Agreement aims at guaranteeing rights to the ones existing in the European Union, but with differences as stressed by the European Court of Justice in the recent case law. These noted differences correspond to the political will of the Contracting Parties, in that they decided to depart at least partially from the rules governing the free movement of persons in the internal market. This political choice has not to be discussed in the present contribution, but the most important from a practitioner's point of view is for the judicial authorities take all the appropriate measures in order to guarantee legal certainty in the application of the Bilateral Agreements.

Precedents and Judicial Dialogue in European Union Law, Present and Future

JOHN TEMPLE LANG[1]

In any legal system, the judgements of courts should be as far as possible consistent and clear, so that lawyers can say with confidence what the law is, so that controversy and litigation can be minimised.[2] This is particularly important in a relatively young legal system such as the European Union law. It is also particularly important in a decentralised legal system in which many national courts are obliged to follow the guidance given by the European Court of Justice (here „the Court"), and in which the law is applied primarily by national authorities and courts. For many of the national courts, European Union law is less familiar than their national law. So, it is both desirable and necessary that the Court should normally follow its previous judgements, and that the law should be as clear as possible.

However, it is sometimes necessary for the Court to depart from this principle, or at least to appear to do so. In part I, this paper discusses examples of several situations in which this has happened:

– where the Court considers it necessary to alter or correct a previous judgement;

– where the Court needs to choose between two divergent lines of cases in its own case law; and

– where the Court clarifies, explains, or alters the reasons for conclusions that it previously reached.

---

1   Cleary Gottlieb Steen and Hamilton LLP, Brussels and London; Professor, Trinity College, Dublin; Visiting Senior Research Fellow, Oxford.
2   "As the Court has consistently held, it is particularly important, in order to satisfy the requirement of legal certainty, that individuals should have the benefit of a clear and precise legal situation enabling them to ascertain the full extent of their rights and, where appropriate, to rely on them before national courts (see Case 29/84 Commission v. Germany [1985] ECR 1661 para. 23; Case 363/85 Commission v. Italy [1987] ECR 1733 para. 7; Case C-59/89 Commission v. Germany [1991] ECR I-2607 para. 18 and Case C-236/95 Commission v. Greece [1996] ECR I-4459 para. 13)"; Case C-280/00 Altmark Trans [2003] ECR-I-7747 para. 39. These comments concern the need for clarity in national legislation in the sphere of EU law, but they also are appropriate to EU law itself. See also Case C-63/93 Duff and others [1996] ECR I-569 para. 20; Case T-446/05 Amann & Söhne [2010] paras. 124–129 (citing judgements of the European Court of Human Rights).
    In the U.K., Law Lords' Statement on Precedent in 1966 [1966], 1 Weekly Law Reports 1234 they said that „too rigid adherence to precedent may lead to injustice in a particular case and also unduly restrict the proper development of the law": See Paterson, The Law Lords, (1982) ch. 6, The Role of a Law Lord: conflict and change.

The examples chosen are not exhaustive. Many cases under Article 267 TFEU could be regarded as involving clarifications and explanations.

In part II, this paper then discusses the circumstances in which the Court *should* reconsider its case law. The most important of these is when the Court thinks it is appropriate to take into account judgements of other Courts, in particular the EFTA Court and the European Court of Human Rights.

This paper is a practising lawyer's view of precedent. It is not based on any confidential or "inside" information, but merely on experience before various courts, and careful reading of many judgements, some of them clearer than others. For a practitioner, judgements that are not clear may be at least as inconvenient as judgements that are clear but seem wrong. But courts are not legislators, and when they state principles they cannot be expected to anticipate every situation to which the principles might be thought to apply. A lawyer must be ready when necessary to advise that his case is genuinely different.

It should be accepted that any court, no matter how wise or careful, may need from time to time to alter or overrule its previous case law. Circumstances may have altered, new considerations may have arisen or become more important, discrepancies or ambiguities may have arisen, new implications may have become apparent and sometimes as errors of judgement may have been made. Exceptional situations may have arisen that were not envisaged when general rules were stated. An earlier judgement may have been adopted hurriedly, or may have contained a paragraph that implications of which were not fully considered. Similarly, there may be circumstances when it is in the interests of justice to alter „prospectively" a principle of law, so that it does not apply to the parties at issue, who may suffer an injustice if the rule were changed for them as well as for future cases. There is nothing undignified or inappropriate in a court adjusting, clarifying or correcting its own case law. It is much better to do so than to continue to perpetuate an unclear judgement.[3] It is certainly better to correct a judgement that seems to be in conflict with a judgement of another European Court. All of this is particularly true in a developing legal system dealing with questions that have never arisen before, and in which the original Treaties, though *traités cadres*, were not written as a constitution.

I. Overruling a Previous Judgement

Probably the most instructive examples of cases in which the Court overruled its previous judgements are *Keck*[4] and *HAG II*[5].

---

[3] The European Court of Human Rights has modified its case law in response to criticism from English Courts: *Osman v. U.K.* [1998] 29 EHRR 245 and *Z v. U.K.* [2001] 34 EHRR 97; *Morris v. U.K.* [2002] EHRR 38784/97 and *Cooper v. U.K.* [2003] EHRR 48843/99; *Wynne v. U.K.* [1994] 19 EHRR 333 and *Strafford v. U.K.* [2002] 35 EHRR 1121. This is an interesting example of judicial dialogue, because there is nothing in the Convention on Human Rights corresponding to Article 267 TFEU, which establishes a continuing dialogue between national courts and the Court of Justice.
[4] Cases C-267/91 and 268/91 *Keck* [1993] ECR I-6097.
[5] Case C-10/89 *Hag II* [1990] ECR I-3711.

Both cases show how this should be done, when it is necessary to do it.

In *Keck*, the question was whether a law prohibiting sales at less than the cost to the trader was a measure having effect equivalent to a quantitative restriction. This law prohibited selling arrangements, but did not impose requirements to be met by any particular goods.

The question came before the Second Chamber, and the first of two Opinions was given by Advocate General van Gerven. He advised, on the basis of the Court's case law in the *Dassonville* and *Oostboek* judgements, and on the basis of judgements concerned with trading on Sundays, that the legislation was equivalent to a quantitative restriction. The Second Chamber then referred the case to the Full Court. The parties were asked three questions, about the economic effects of resale at a loss, whether the prohibition impeded sales of imports more than domestic goods, whether the prohibition constituted suppression of a sales promotion method, or whether it was part of a national price control system. The Advocate General said that if the *Dassonville* formula remained the cornerstone of the case law, *"In order to avoid any confusion, I think the Court owes a duty to the national courts to make this quite clear"* (p. 6121).

The Court said:

> *"In view of the increasing tendency of traders to invoke Article 30 of the Treaty as a means of challenging any rules that limit their commercial freedom even where such rules are not aimed at products from other Member States, the Court considers it necessary to re-examine and clarify its case law on this matter. Legislation imposing requirements to be met by imported goods themselves are measures of equivalent effect, even if they apply without distinction to all products, unless justified by a public interest objective."*

The Court went on:

> *"By contrast, contrary to what has previously been decided, the application to products from other Member States of national provisions restricting or prohibiting certain selling arrangements is not such as to hinder directly or indirectly, actually or potentially, trade between Member States ... so long as those provisions apply to all relevant traders operating within the national territory and so long as they affect in the same manner, in law and in fact, the marketing of domestic products and of those from other Member States"* (para. 16).

Several points should be made:

- The Court needed to clarify the law because traders were challenging more and more rules regulating their commercial freedom and practices.

- Most of the previous cases had come by references from national courts, and the Court had not needed to establish the facts in detail.

- When the Court asked the parties the three questions, the economic situation became much clearer, and the appropriate legal solution more apparent.

- The Full Court had been asked by the Second Chamber to clarify or alter the Court's case law.

- The Court was able to draw a clear and important distinction between selling arrangements for traders and requirements to be complied with by the goods themselves, which essentially overruled the previous case law casting doubt on the lawfulness of bans on Sunday trading.

- The Court overruled a number of its own previous judgements.

- Two Member States intervened.

- The Court disagreed with the Commission.

In *HAG II*[6] the question was whether the Court would reverse or overrule a single earlier judgement. That judgement had concluded that national law should not allow a company to use a trademark to oppose importation from another Member State of goods that lawfully bear a corresponding mark there, when the two trademarks had originally belonged to companies in the same group (the „common origin" rule).

Advocate General Jacobs pointed out that the „common origin" rule raised a fundamental question that neither of the litigants had any reason to discuss. The reasons given for the rule in the previous *HAG* judgement were brief, unconvincing, and seemed inconsistent with other case law. The reasons given by the Court in *Terrapin v. Terranova* for explaining the "common origin" rule confused the origin of the trademarks with the origin of the goods bearing the marks. There was no rational basis for the "common origin" rule.

He, therefore, advised that, if the Court decided that the common origin rule was incorrect:

"... *then the Court should make it clear, in the interests of legal certainty, that it is abandoning the doctrine of common origin laid down in HAG I. The Court has consistently recog-*

---

6   Case C-10/89 *Hag II* [1990] ECR I-3711.

nised its power to depart from previous decisions, as for example by making it clear that national courts may refer again questions on which the Court has already ruled: see Joined Cases 28/62, 29/62, and 30/62 Da Costa & Schaake [1963] ECR 31 where the Court accepted that a 'materially identical question' could be referred again, and Case 283/81 Cilfit v. Ministry of Health [1982] ECR 3415 para. 15; see also Case 28/67 Molkerei-Zentrale [1968] ECR 143 pp. 152–155 where the Court expressly reconsidered a previous ruling. That the Court should in an appropriate case expressly overrule an earlier decision is I think an inescapable duty, even if the Court has never before expressly done so. In the present case the arguments for expressly abandoning the doctrine of common origin are exceptionally strong; moreover, the validity of that doctrine is already, as I have suggested, in doubt as a result of the intervening case law. To answer [the question asked by the national court] in the affirmative without abandoning the doctrine, or to seek to rationalise such an answer on some other ground, would be a recipe for confusion."

The Court said (para.10):

"... it should be stated at the outset that the Court believes it necessary to reconsider the interpretation given [in HAG I] in the light of the case-law which has developed with regard to the relationship between industrial and commercial property and the general rules of the Treaty ..."

Later the Court went on (paras.16–17):

"... the essential function of the trademark would be jeopardised if the proprietor of the trademark could not exercise the right conferred on him by national legislation to oppose the importation of similar goods bearing a designation lable to be confused with his own trademark, because in such a situation, consumers would no longer be able to identify for certain the origin of the marked goods and the proprietor of the trademark could be held responsible for the poor quality of goods for which he was in no way accountable."

This analysis is not altered by the fact that the mark protected by national legislation and the similar mark borne by the imported goods by virtue of the legislation of their Member State of origin originally belonged to the same proprietor, who was divested of one of them following expropriation by one of the states prior to the establishment of the Community.

Several points should be made:

- The Court considered that there was a conflict between the *HAG I* judgement and its other case law, which needed to be resolved.

- The Advocate General had made an extremely strong and forceful argument, and had said that the conflict could be resolved only by expressly overruling *HAG I*.

- *HAG I* had always been criticised on both legal and commercial grounds.

- Although the circumstances of *HAG I* were unusual (since they involved expropriation), corresponding trademarks in different Member States which have a common origin often come into the hands of unrelated companies, so the broader issue was an important one.

- There was no doubt that the case law cited by the Advocate General expressly envisaged the possibility that the Court might overrule one of its own judgements.

- The Advocate General's view was supported by four Member States.

- As in *Keck*, the Court was frank and very clear that it was overruling the previous judgement, as it is clearly desirable for legal certainty.

A. Social Welfare Precedent Limited

In *Cabannis-Issarte*[7], a more technical case, the Court had to consider the validity of a distinction drawn in earlier judgements between rights to social welfare payments acquired by individuals themselves and rights acquired merely as members of the family of an individual with such rights. The Court had re-opened the oral stage of the procedure, and in his second opinion the Advocate General said that the case law was *"not entirely consistent"*, and that the distinction would lead to *"perverse results"* (p. 2120). As the Advocate General proposed that the Court should review and alter the previous case law, in particular in cases since *Kermaschek*[8] which was the basis of the distinction, he proposed that the temporal effects of the judgement in *Cabannis-Issarte*[9] should be limited. The Court concluded that this was an equal treatment case and as *"the distinction drawn between rights in person and derived rights renders the fundamental rule of equal treatment inapplicable to the surviving spouse of a migrant worker, the rule in Kermaschek should be limited to certain circumstances."* The Court also limited the temporal effects of the judgement to claims made before the judgement was given.

This case is notable because the initial judgement in *Kermaschek* had been acted on in five other judgements of the Court, and had been accepted for twenty years. But the distinction previously drawn undermined *"the fundamental Community law requirement that its rules should be applied uniformly, by making their applicability to individuals depend on whether the national law relating to the benefits in question treats the rights concerned as rights in person or as derived rights."* In other words, the fact that the national law rules had not been harmonised had led to discrimination between family members and those individuals who had acquired rights of their own, and this was incompatible with free movement of workers, because it meant that family mem-

---

7 Case C-308/93 *Cabannis-Issarte* [1996] ECR I-2097. See also Case C-394/96 *Brown v. Rentokil* [1998] ECR I-4185 para. 27, where the Court expressly overruled Case C-400/95 *Larsson v. Fotex supermarked* [1997] ECR I-2557.
8 Case 40/76 *Kermaschek* [1974] ECR I-1669.
9 Case C-308/93 *Cabannis-Issarte* [1996] ECR I-2097 para. 34.

bers could lose their rights if they moved to another Member State. The unsatisfactory consequences of the *Kermaschek* judgement had gradually become clear.[10]

B. Choosing between Two Lines of Case Law

From time to time an Advocate General has pointed out to the Court that there is or seems to be a conflict between two sets of judgements, and that this situation needs to be clarified. A recent and important example of this situation is the *Altmark* case.[11]

The question before the Court concerned compensation paid by a Member State to a transport company with certain public service obligations that necessarily involved some loss-making activities. Insofar as the compensation merely offset the cost of carrying out the public service obligations, was the compensation to be regarded as State aid? One chamber of the Court, in the *Ferring* judgement[12] had decided that it did not constitute State aid. The Court of First Instance had taken the contrary view. The question had been considered by three Advocates General, and they disagreed. After the first Opinion of the Advocate General in the *Altmark* case, the Court reopened the oral hearing, and the Advocate General gave a second Opinion, in which he again disagreed with the *Ferring* judgement.

The Court in *Altmark* ruled that insofar as the compensation was to offset the cost of clearly defined public service obligations, and provided that four conditions were fulfilled to ensure that this is so, the compensation could not confer an advantage on the company concerned, and so was not a State aid.

Several points should be made:

- Four Member States supported the conclusion reached by the Court.

- The Court found it necessary to lay down four detailed requirements that must be fulfilled for the compensation to avoid being considered as State aid. These requirements largely resolved the differences of opinion that had arisen in the previous cases.

- Unlike the *HAG II* case, the Court did not follow the advice of the Advocate General in the case in question, but the opinion of another Advocate General in another case.

---

10 In Case C-127/08 *Metock* [2008] ECR I-6241 the Court (at para. 58) referred to a statement in its judgement in Case C-109/01 *Akrich* [2003] ECR I-9607 and said *"However, that conclusion must be reconsidered. The benefit of such rights cannot depend on the prior lawful residence of such a spouse in another Member State"* and then quoted two other judgements, implying that they should be followed rather than *Akrich*.
11 Case C-280/00 *Altmark* [2003] ECR I-7747. See Gulmann, State Aid and Compensation for Public Services, in: Baudenbacher and others (eds.), Liber Amicorum in honour of Bo Vesterdorf (2007), pp. 655–672.
12 Case C-53/00 *Ferring* [2001] ECR I-9067.

- For the second hearing, the Court had specifically asked for the views of the parties on the central legal issue (unlike *Keck*, where the Court asked about the economic position, in spite of the fact that the Court in cases referred by national courts is not supposed to concern itself with the facts).

- The question was important, since many public service obligations are compensated for out of state funds.

C. Revising the Reasons Given for Earlier Judgements

In at least one important series of cases, the Court has revised the reasons given for its conclusions in an earlier judgement.

In *Van Duyn*[13], the Court held that a private party, in litigation against a Member State, can rely on the terms of a directive binding the state, even if the directive has not been implemented by the state in question. The "useful effect" of the directive would otherwise be weakened. National courts can refer questions of EU law to the Court under what is now Article 267 TFEU, and questions about directives are not excluded. The question, therefore, was whether the provisions of the directive were capable of having direct effects.

At first this judgement was strongly criticised, by the Conseil d'Etat in France, and the Bundesfinanzhof in Germany. The Court subsequently in the *Ratti*[14] and *Marshall*[15] judgements put forward a reason that had not been given in *Van Duyn*. The Court said that since a directive imposes on Member States a duty to adopt certain measures by a given date, the state should not be allowed to take advantage of its own failure to carry out its obligations, in litigation in its own courts.

Some years later, when there was still scepticism about the principle stated in *Van Duyn*, the Court was asked in *Moorman*[16] to say what the legal basis of the principle was. The Court referred to Article 10 (the duty of Member States to cooperate with the Community institutions, now Article 4 TEU), although it had not mentioned Article 10 in this context since the *Van Duyn* judgement fourteen years before.

---

13   Case C-41/74 *Van Duyn* [1974] ECR 1337.
14   Case C-148/78 *Ratti* [1979] ECR 1629.
15   Case C-271/91 *Marshall* [1993] ECR I-4367.
16   Case C-190/87 *Moorman* [1988] ECR 4689.

D. Clarifying or Developing a Line of Reasoning

From time to time, the Court clarifies or develops a line of reasoning in an earlier judgement.

In *Bristol-Myers Squibb*[17], the European Court of Justice recognised that the established principles of law set out in *Hoffmann-La Roche*[18] (a leading case of 1978) on re-packaging of trademarked pharmaceutical products should be "clarified further" in light of recent related developments in the Court's case law.

The original decision in *Hoffmann-La Roche* concerned the parallel trading of Valium in Germany and the UK. Hoffmann-La Roche manufactured and marketed different types of packs in the two countries. In Germany, the firm sold 20 or 50 tablet packs for individuals, and packs of 100 or 250 tablets for hospitals. In the UK, the same product was marketed in packs of 100 or 500 tablets and at much lower prices. A parallel trader, Centrafarm, bought packs of valium in the UK, re-boxed them with the Hoffmann-La Roche trademark, and sold packs of 1000 tablets in Germany. Hoffmann-La Roche sued Centrafarm for infringing its trademark. The Court decided that the firm could prevent smaller firms from buying their products and re-boxing them as parallel imports unless four conditions were met:

> i) it is established that the use of the trademark right by the proprietor, having regard to the marketing system which he has adopted, will contribute to the artificial partitioning of the markets between Member States;

> ii) it is shown that the repackaging cannot adversely affect the original condition of the product;

> iii) it is stated on the new packaging by whom the product has been repackaged; and

> iv) the proprietor of the mark receives prior notice of the marketing of the repackaged product.[19]

The same point of law was again before the Court in the *Bristol-Myers Squibb* case, but there were also related points of law raised by other appeals that the Court heard with that case, which were appeals by large pharmaceutical firms as to different kinds of trademark infringements. The result of this interaction between the cases was that extensive passages in the *Bristol-Myers Squibb* judgement had been revised and elaborated on the four conditions in *Hoffmann-La Roche*, in particular against the *"artificial partitioning of the markets between the Member States"*, the importance of maintaining the integrity of the product in question, and other requirements.

---

17 Joined Cases C-427/93, C-429/93 and C-436/93 *Bristol-Myers Squibb* [1996] ECR I-3457.
18 Case C-102/77 [1978] ECR 1139.
19 Joined Cases C-427/93, C-429/93 and C-436/93 *Bristol-Myers Squibb* [1996] ECR I-3457 at para. 49. See also Case C-348/04 *Boehringer Ingelheim* [2007] ECR I-3391.

150   PRECEDENTS IN EU LAW

E. Reconciling Two Diverging Lines of Case Law

The Court cannot fairly be criticised for failing to clarify issues that it does not need to resolve. Each decision turns on its own facts, and, any judicial tribunal would avoid clarifying or elaborating the law through comments which were unrelated to the case before it. However, there have been occasions when the Court was dealing with cases on which there were two lines of case law, and the Court did not clearly choose between them.

In *Sydhavens Sten & Grus*[20], the Advocate General called attention to two approaches in the case law of the Court of Justice concerning state measures restricting competition. On one view, *"the mere finding that exclusive rights were conferred automatically made it possible to establish the existence of abuse""*. On the other, narrower view, EU law is infringed only if the enterprise in question *"merely by exercising the exclusive rights granted to it, is led to abuse its dominant position "*.

The two approaches, as they had developed, can be explained and contrasted more clearly as follows. In GB INNO[21] the Court had said that *"where the extension of the dominant position of a public undertaking or undertaking to which the state has granted special or exclusive rights results from a state measure, such a measure constitutes an infringement of Article 90 [now Article 106 TFEU] in conjunction with Article 86 [now Article 102 TFEU] "*. There was no reason to limit this principle to cases of (unjustified) extension of a dominant position and not to apply it to the unjustified creation of a dominant position, and in *Vlaamse Televisie*[22], the Court of First Instance ruled that legislation creating dominance without sufficient reasons in the public interest is contrary to European law.

However, the Court of Justice also made statements in *Crespelle* and other judgements[23] that a state measure creating a dominant position is illegal *only* if it is sufficiently likely to lead to an abuse, contrary to Article 102, by the enterprise concerned. That is clearly a different principle from that stated in GB INNO.

It now appears, although it is not entirely clear, that the Court has adopted the GB INNO principle.[24] Even if that is so, it does not imply that the judgements in the *Crespelle* line of cases were wrong, or no longer applicable, because they can be understood as dealing with cases from national courts in which the *only* objection made to the state measure was that it would lead to abuse contrary to Article 102. The word "only" crept into the case law in those cases, without its significance being explained. But if the GB INNO principle has now been accepted, it can be said in retrospect that the law would have been clearer if this had been explained in the *Cre-*

---

20 Case C-209/98 *Sydhavens Sten & Grus* [2000] ECR I-3743.
21 Case C-18/88 [1991] ECR I-5941 at pages 5980–5981.
22 Case T-266/97 [1999] ECR II-2329.
23 Case C-323/93 *Crespelle* [1994] ECR I-5077, in *Sydhavens Sten & Grus* itself, in Case C-67/96 *Albany* [1999] ECR I-5751 and in Joined Cases C-115/97 and others *Brentjens* [1999] ECR I-6025.
24 This is shown by the judgements in Case C-203/96 *Dusseldorp* [1998] ECR I-4075, Case C-475/99 *Glöckner* [2001] ECR I-8089 and Case C-462/99 *Connect Austria* [2003] ECR I-5197. Presumably there may be cases in which setting up a dominant position is justified, but the measure is contrary to EU law because it fails to deal with the likelihood of abuse, due e.g. to conflicts of interests; Case C-163/96 *Silvano Raso* [1998] ECR I-533.

spelle line of cases. Indeed, in *Klöckner*, two consecutive paragraphs of the judgement (paras. 39 and 40) state the two principles without suggesting that they are inconsistent. It is difficult to avoid the conclusion that there was a genuine difference of opinion within the Court that led to the two lines of cases, and that this was why the Court did not expressly make the choice that Advocate General Leger in *Sydhavens Sten & Gros* suggested should be made.

It may be relevant that (except for *Vlaamse Televisie*) all these cases were references from national courts, and in such cases the Court is usually careful to answer only the questions asked, even when it seems likely that other questions might have more clearly raised the questions of principle. It is certainly relevant that the area of state measures restricting competition is a difficult and sensitive one, and the Court was understandably cautious.

It is not possible to tell whether the lawyers in the *Crespelle* line of cases chose to challenge the conduct but not the dominant positions of the enterprises concerned because it was only the conduct that their clients wished to prevent, or because the lawyers were not sufficiently confident that the *GB INNO* principle would be maintained by the Court.

F. Emmot – Limiting a Precedent

In the *Emmot* judgement, the Court[25] said that until a directive is properly transposed, the state may not rely on an individual's delay in claiming under the directive against the state, and the limitation period cannot begin. The Court has since said the limitation periods may run, provided that they are reasonable,[26] and has said specifically that *Emmot* should be limited to its special facts.

In other cases, one has the impression that the Court is no longer satisfied with one of its previous judgements, but the Court does not comment on it.

G. Precedents and the Commission's Decisions

The Commission has now adopted many decisions imposing fines for price-fixing under Article 101 TFEU. The Commission is not always convincing when it argues that these decisions are completely consistent with one another on specific issues about the calculation of fines. The Commission has sometimes even argued that it is not bound by its own Notices, which

---

25   Case C-208/90 *Emmot* [1991] ECR I-4292 para. 33.
26   Case C-90/94 *Haahr Petroleum* [1997] ECR I-4142 para. 52. Case C-188/95 *Fantask* [1997] ECR I-6783. See Timmermans, Community Directives, in: XVIII Congress of FIDE, Fédération Internationale pour le Droit Européen Vol. I, (1998 Stockholm), pp. 35–36 and Barav, General Report, pp. 435–438.

is plainly inconsistent with the principle of legitimate expectations.[27] The General Court is, rightly, strict and careful to ensure that each decision treats the companies in the same case in a non-discriminatory way. But even in cases in which it is exercising full jurisdiction to reconsider the amount of fines, the Court is less strict to ensure that Commission decisions in different cases are consistent with one another, and the Commission often argues that it has a „discretion" that allows it to decide the same issue differently in different cases. Lawyers pleading before the General Court are not often successful when they argue that a given decision is inconsistent with the Commission's decisions in previous cases. No doubt the Court is reluctant to encourage lengthy comparisons between separate decisions.[28] However, the Court is careful to ensure that its own judgements are consistent, and the overall effect is gradually to oblige the Commission to be more consistent, too.

A situation in which the Commission appears to want to alter both its own practice and the case law of the Court in competition cases is discussed in part II below.

H. Creating an Exception – the Standing of the European Parliament to Sue

In what is known as the *Comitology* judgement[29], the Court rejected an argument by the Parliament that, although it was not named in the Treaty Article on challenges to the validity of EC measures (since modified, now Article 263 TFEU), the Parliament should have the same automatic standing to challenge measures as the Council, the Commission, and the Member States. The Court based its view on the words of the Treaty, and refused to extend them by analogy or otherwise. The Court considered that Parliament's prerogatives in the legislative process could be protected in other ways.

The Court partially reconsidered its position in the *Chernobyl* judgement.[30] The Parliament challenged a regulation fixing a maximum level of radioactive contamination in food. This regulation was based on the Euratom Treaty, but the Parliament argued that it should have been based on an Article in the EC Treaty that gave the Parliament a greater right to be involved, under the consultation procedure. The Court decided that the Parliament could sue in order to defend its prerogatives, because otherwise there would be a procedural gap in the legal protection provided by the Treaty. The Court said that it must be able *"to review the observance of the Parliament's prerogatives when called on to do so by the Parliament, by means of a legal remedy which is suited to the purpose which the Parliament seeks to achieve"*. (The Treaty was later modified to give the Parliament the same broad standing to sue as the other Institutions.) The Court, in

---

27 In the field of State aid, Case C-409/00 *Spain v. Commission* [2003] ECR I-1487 para. 95, Case C-91/01 *Italy v. Commission* [2004] ECR I- 4355 para. 45; under Articles 101–102: Case C-184/02P *Dansk Rorindustri* [2005] ECR I-5425 paras. 211–213, Case T-220/00 *Cheil Jedang* [2003] ECR II-2473 paras. 77 and 191. Fejo, How does the ECJ cite its previous judgements in competition law cases? in: Johansson, Wahl and Bernitz (eds.), Liber Amicorum in Honour of Sven Norberg (2006), pp. 195–217 says that the Court does not cite its own judgements consistently.
28 See however Case T-446/05 *Amann & Söhne* [2010] para. 145.
29 Case C-302/87 [1988] ECR I-5615.
30 Case C-70/88 [1990] ECR I-2041.

short, used the basic principle that the law must be observed (and, therefore, that there must always be a procedural remedy if the law is not observed), to fill the gap, though without reversing its judgement in the *Comitology* case.

I. Widening Precedents

The Court of Justice from time to time needs to decide questions that have not previously been considered. When it does so, it is naturally concerned to adopt a judgement that is consistent with, and based on, other principles in the European Union's legal order. It may also be anxious to adopt a judgement that is no broader than it is necessary to decide the case before the Court. The judges may consider that the arguments that have been made do not sufficiently discuss all the possible implications of the principles that have been suggested to the Court. Even if the Advocate General has discussed the implications as thoroughly as Advocates General usually do, the Court may think it is wise to decide one case at a time. That may well be right, and I certainly do not want to suggest any criticism of it. The Court has no control over the cases that come before it, and it would be natural if the Court sometimes considered that a case was not a suitable opportunity to state an important principle.

However, it sometimes happens that the Court decides a case on what appears at first sight to be a relatively narrow ground, or in rather special circumstances, and in later judgements cites the first judgement as an example of a broader principle. This might mean that in the first case, some of the judges had argued for a broader principle, and others had persuaded them to confine the judgement more narrowly. Alternatively, it may mean that since the first judgement, the judges have become more confident that they can see the implications of the broader principle, and that they are satisfied that the implications are satisfactory. The possibility that this may happen is something that the lawyer appearing before the Court needs to be aware of. The earlier precedent that he or she has read may prove to be broader or more important than the judgement itself seemed to imply. An apparently narrow precedent may prove to be regarded subsequently by the Court as an example of a broader principle.

A clear example was *Von Colson*[31] in which the Court said that *"in applying the national law and in particular the provisions of national law specifically introduced in order to implement Directive 76/207, national courts are required to interpret their national law in the light of the wording and purpose of the Directive"*. That sounded like a rule based on the directive in question, although the Court did refer to what is now Article 4 TEU.

But in *Marleasing*[32], the Court said *"... as the Court pointed out in its judgement in Von Colson ... the Member States' obligation arising from a Directive to achieve the result envisaged by the Directive and their duty under Article [5 EC, now Article 4 TEU] to take all appropriate measures, whether general or particular, to ensure the fulfilment of that obligation, is binding on all the authorities of Member*

---

31 Case C-14/83 *Von Colson* [1984] ECR 1891.
32 Case C-106/89 *Marleasing* [1990] ECR I-4135.

States including, for matters within their jurisdiction, the courts. It follows that, in applying national law, **whether the provisions in question were adopted before or after the Directive**, the national court called upon to interpret it is required to do so, as far as possible, in the light of the wording and purpose of the Directive in order to achieve the result pursued by the latter and thereby comply with the third paragraph of [Article 288 TFEU]" (emphasis supplied).

Later the Court went further, and it became clear that this principle applies to *all* directives, and even to national laws not specifically introduced to implement the directive in question, unless the interpretation consistent with the directive is clearly contrary to the words of the national legislation.[33]

However, this principle does not allow interpretations that would make national criminal law stricter.[34]

Broadening progressively the scope of an initially narrow judgement is the opposite of what the Court has done with the Emmot judgement, referred to above.

J. Distinguishing between Broad and Narrow Precedents

The lawyers in later cases should carefully study the Opinions of the Advocate Generals in the earlier cases, as well as the judgements. The Advocate Generals may have considered broader principles than the Court relied on. In these circumstances, the lawyer has to consider whether the Court was unconvinced by the Advocate General's broader arguments, or whether the Court merely chose to decide the broader issues another day. Before the Court decides the later cases, it may not be possible to see with confidence whether the Court will ultimately adopt the broader principle.

This may happen less often now than it used to in the past. But I call attention to this kind of situation for several reasons. The first is that in European Union law questions that have never previously arisen do sometimes need to be decided, and if the Court can with confidence decide them on broad grounds, that may reduce uncertainty and avoid unnecessary litigation subsequently. The second reason is that lawyers with a common law background tend to assume, probably more quickly than a civil law lawyer would assume, that a precedent is not much broader than the facts that gave rise to it. Common lawyers are not always quick enough to see judgements as examples of broader principles that have not always been stated in the judgements themselves.

The third reason is that it might be helpful if the Court, as well as the Advocate General, would sometimes say *"this case raises the important question whether and in what circumstances ... But in this case the Court does not need to answer that question"*. Without committing the Court in any

---

[33] Case C-268/06 *Impact* [2008] ECR I-2483 paras. 100 and 103.
[34] Case C-168/95 *Arcaro* [1996] ECR I-4705 para. 42.

way, that would help to alert lawyers reading the case later to the possibility that there may be a broad principle in substantially the terms tentatively visualised by the Court. The potential principle would then be brought to the attention of writers commenting on the judgement, and referred to in textbooks that now often tend merely to repeat or summarize what the Court said, rather than discussing its underlying assumptions or possible implications. It would also be helpful to judges, and their referendaires, in later cases, if their attention was called to an earlier judgement in which important issues had been raised and argued, even if they had not been decided. This might be particularly important if the later case was one that needed to be decided urgently, and if neither the judges nor the Advocate General had enough time to consider all the implications. I am thinking, of course, of urgent custody cases, of personal or family cases, and of other cases involving police and judicial cooperation in which new, undecided, and important questions are certain to arise.

If the Court were willing to refer to the possible existence of a principle without deciding it, the Court might be able to go some way to solve the problem of cases referred by national courts under Article 267 (ex-Article 234) in which the national court may not have asked the question that would have been most useful, at least for future cases, to ask. This may happen if the lawyers did not raise the most important question before the national court, and the result may be that the question was not argued, or was not sufficiently argued, before the Court itself. But even if that has happened, it might be very valuable if the Court was willing to point out that there might be a principle that would be relevant in similar cases in future. Sometimes the Court appears to do this by pointing out that the national court has *not* raised certain issues, and one has the impression that the Court is indicating that those issues would have been important if they had been raised.

One of the problems that the Court has with references is that the national court does not always ask the right question. Anything that the Court could do to call the attention of national courts to important questions that may arise would be useful. It would also help to ensure that lawyers would raise such questions before the national courts.

K. A Limitation on Precedents from Community Law in the Sphere of Police and Judicial Cooperation

The words of the *Arcaro* judgement[35], limiting the application of the *Marleasing* principle in the area of police and judicial cooperation, are so important that they should be quoted in full:

"*[the] obligation of the national court to refer to the content of the Directive when interpreting the relevant rules of its own national law reaches a limit where such an interpretation leads to the imposition on an individual of an obligation laid down by a Directive which has not been transposed or, more especially, where it has the effect of determining or aggravating, on the basis of the Directive and in the*

---

35 Case C-168/95 Arcaro [1996] ECR I-4705.

absence of a law enacted for its implementation, the liability in criminal law of persons who act in contravention of that Directive's provisions" (para. 42).

This is an extremely important principle. Presumably it also means that a national court may not impose or increase a criminal penalty, even when that would be appropriate or necessary to make EU law "effective", unless it is empowered to do so by national legislation. Principles and precedents that are well-established in Community law, such as that applied in *Pupino* (2005), may not lead to new or increased or retroactive criminal penalties.

"Effective access to justice" is one of the purposes for which EU legislation is envisaged by Article 81 TFEU.

This raises several other questions:

– May a criminal penalty be imposed or increased on the basis of a judgement, given after the offence was committed, by which the Court reversed one of its earlier judgements under which no penalty, or only a lower penalty, could have been imposed?

– May a penalty be imposed or increased on the basis of one or more judgements if there are other judgements of the Court under which the penalty could not have been imposed or increased?

– May a penalty be imposed on the basis of a directly applicable rule of EU law, if it could not have been imposed under a national law that is inconsistent with EU law?

L. The Jurisdiction of the Court of Justice under the Charter of Fundamental Rights

It will be seen that when the Court of Justice has decided to revise or modify its previous judgements, it has always been on technical legal grounds. This is primarily due to the relatively narrow scope of EU law, compared with the broad scope of the United States Constitution, and only secondarily because the Court has been in existence for only one quarter of the two centuries in which the US Supreme Court has been in operation. It is only recently that the Court has been actively applying fundamental rights principles. EU law is now broader in scope as a result of the new TEU and TFEU Treaties. Because the Charter of Fundamental Rights is now clearly part of EU law, the Court will be obliged to deal with many more, and more controversial issues, comparable to these with which the European Court of Human Rights has been dealing. It seems reasonable to expect that the Court may have to adapt or revise its case law more often in the future, in particular to ensure that the Charter is interpreted in the same way as the European Convention on Human Rights.

II. So when should the Court Correct or Clarify its Case Law?

On the basis of the cases summarised or referred to above, it seems that in practice the Court is likely to consider correcting or clarifying its previous case law (without necessarily having a duty to do so) if one of the following conditions are fulfilled:

1. If it has been asked to do so by the Advocate General, by one or more Member States, by a national court, by a Chamber of the Court itself, or by the General Court.

2. Presumably, if it has been asked to do so by the Commission. However, the Commission does not always have an interest in asking for the law to be clarified. In addition, if the Commission has itself contributed to or caused the lack of clarity, the Commission would presumably find it difficult to point out the issues that need to be resolved. In practice, the Commission is usually not the source of a change in the case law.

3. If there has been widespread and persistent criticism of the case law on the issue, in particular if it has come from national courts, or from objective and well-informed organisations with no direct or selfish interest in the practical results of the previous judgements.

4. If the legal uncertainty has given rise to a lot of litigation at national level or at the level of the EU Courts themselves, that could be ended if the law was clarified.

A. Other European Courts

A fifth, very important, situation in which the Court believes that it has a duty to consider changing its case law, is when it is inconsistent with a judgement of another European Court. There are several other types of situations in which one would expect that the Court would be willing to reconsider its case law, but in which it has not yet needed to consider whether it would do so.

One would expect that the Court would be ready to reconsider a previous judgement if it was giving rise to divergent interpretations by national courts of Member States, or if a national court asked the Court to reconsider. There are a number of former judges of the Court now in national Supreme Courts, and their views must have great weight. References to the Court under Article 267 TFEU should give the Court the opportunity to do that. Article 267 provides an on-going dialogue between the Court and the national courts, so there is much mutual influence. National courts, by references under Article 267, can make sure that the case law of the Court is, when necessary, clarified and corrected.

It would clearly also be appropriate for the Court to reconsider any judgement that appeared to be inconsistent with a judgement of the EFTA Court. In *Commission v. Denmark* [36], the Court followed the judgement of the EFTA Court in *EFTA Surveillance Authority v. Norway*,[37] and substantially clarified the previous Community case law. Generally one would expect the Court of Justice to participate in the widespread trend to cite the judgements of other Courts[38], especially when the judgements in question are concise and clear, as those of the EFTA Court are.

In fact, one of the most important reasons for the Court to reconsider its judgements in the future may prove to be that similar issues have been thoroughly considered by *other* courts, whether European or national.

This is so in particular because the General Court apparently considers that it is not part of its task to consider whether new principles should be developed. This would mean that the only opportunity to consider even a profoundly important development would be the case in the Court of Justice, and that Court would have to get the answer at the right first time. Since this cannot always be guaranteed, the role of the other European Courts is important.

B. Human Rights Issues

The Court is certainly willing to reconsider its previous judgements in the light of developments in the case law of the European Court of Human Rights.[39] Article 52 (3) of the Charter of Fundamental Rights provides:

---

36 Case C-192/01 [2003] ECR I-9693.
37 Case E-3/00 *EFTA Surveillance Authority v. Norway* [2000-01] EFTA Court Report 73. In Case T-308/00 *Salzgitter* [2004] ECR II-1933 para. 38, the General Court cited with approval the judgement of the EFTA Court in Case E-6/98 *Norway v. EFTA Surveillance Authority* [1999] EFTA Court Report 74. See Fredriksen, The EFTA Court 15 years on, 59 International and Comparative Law Quarterly (2010), pp. 731–760. See Baudenbacher, The EFTA Court in Action (2010), pp. 70–95; Rosas, Methods of interpretation – judicial dialogue, in: Baudenbacher & Busek (eds.), The Role of International Courts (2008), p. 185.
38 See Zeno-Zencovich, The Bingham Court, and Andenas and Fairgrieve – There is a world elsewhere, Lord Bingham and Comparative Law, in: Andenas & Fairgrieve, Tom Bingham and the Transformation of Law (2009, Oxford), pp. 823–830 and 831–866. Bronckers, The Relationship of the EC Courts with other International Tribunals, in: Monti and others (eds.), Economic Law and Justice in Times of Globalisation: Festschrift for Carl Baudenbacher (2007), pp. 51–74.
39 The Court already refers to the case law of the European Court of Human Rights when appropriate, to reconsider the Court's own judgements. See e.g. Case C-94/00 *Roquette Frères* [2003] ECR I-9011 para. 29, where the Court referred to the judgement of the Strasbourg Court of 16 April 2002 in *Colas Est and others v. France* No. 37971/97 in the Reports of Judgements and Decisions, and to *Niemietz v. Germany*, judgement of 16 December 1992 Series A No. 251-B, noting that it was given *after* the judgement in *Hoechst*, Joined Cases 46/87 and 227/88 [1989] ECR 2859. See also Cases C-238/99P and others *Limburgse Vinyl* [2002] ECR I-8375 para. 274 (*"The parties agree that, since Orkem, there have been further developments in the case law of the European Court of Human Rights which the Community judicature must take account when interpreting the fundamental right ..."*); Case C-84/95 *Bosphorus Hava Yollari Turizm* [1996] ECR I-3953; Case C-224/01 *Köbler* [2003] ECR I-10239 para. 49; Case C-117/01 *K.B. v. National Health Service Pension Agency* [2004] ECR I-541 para. 33. See also the opinion of Advocate General Jacob in Case C-168/910 *Konstantinides* [1993] ECR I-1191. See however Tridimas, The General Principles of EU Law (2nd ed., 2006), pp. 374–378.

"In so far as this Charter contains rights which correspond to rights guaranteed by the Convention for the Protection of Human Rights and Fundamental Freedoms, the meaning and scope of those rights shall be the same as those laid down by the said Convention. This provision shall not prevent Union law providing more extensive protection".

This means that if the case law under the Convention (whether of the Court of Human Rights or of a national court) appears to give greater protection than is given by a judgement of the Court of Justice, that court should reconsider the judgement when the occasion arises, to bring Union law into line with the case law under the Convention. No difficulty arises, however, if EU law goes further than the Convention.

As Tridimas has written

"…through respective developments in their jurisprudence and skilful judicial diplomacy, the ECJ and the ECHR are reaching a new state of symbiosis characterised by mutual respect and deference. The two courts do not compete but cooperate." [40]

The same thing can be said about the relationship between the Court of Justice and the EFTA Court.[41] It is often considered that the difference is that the Court of Justice is now obliged to follow the case law of the Court of Human Rights on the interpretation of the European Convention, but the Court follows the case law of the EFTA Court because of its clarity and soundness, without necessarily being obliged to do so. However, when the EFTA Court has decided a question of EEA law before the Court of Justice has had an opportunity to do so, the Court should follow the EFTA Court, because if it did not do so it would interfere with the homogeneity that the EEA Agreement is intended to ensure.[42] "*Ignoring EFTA Court precedents would simply be incompatible with the overriding objective of the EEA agreement which is homogeneity … The ECJ has contributed to the fulfilment of that objective by taking under consideration the EFTA Court case law although, in most cases, it has not done so expressly*".[43]

It is worth pointing out that the Court's original case law on fundamental rights was prompted by the comments of national courts in Germany, which were concerned because there were no express provisions in the original EC Treaties about fundamental rights.

---

40   Tridimas, The General Principles of EU Law (2nd ed., 2006), p. 299; see also pp. 347–348 and 556.
41   See Baudenbacher, The EFTA Court in Action (2010), pp. 70–95; Case C-13/95 *Süzen* [1997] ECR II-1259 (following the EFTA Court's judgement in E-2/96 *Ulstein*); Case C-192/01 *Commission v. Denmark* [2009] ECR I-9693 (following the EFTA Court's judgement in E-3/00 *EFTA Surveillance Authority v. Norway* [2001]; Temple Lang, The Importance of the EFTA Court, European Current Law (March 2006) xi.
42   Skouris, The ECJ and the EFTA Court under the EEA Agreement: A Paradigm for International Cooperation between Judicial Institutions, in: Baudenbacher and others (eds.), The EFTA Court: Ten Years on (2005), pp. 123–129; Busche, the Free Movement of Capital in the EEA – A Lehrstück in Homogeneity, in: Monti and others (eds.), Economic Law and Justice in Times of Globalisation: Festschrift for Carl Baudenbacher (2007), pp. 75–98.
43   Skouris, op.cit. at p. 125; See Case C-452/01 *Ospelt* [2003] ECR I-9743 para. 29 and in Case C-286/02 *Bellio F.lli* [2004] ECR I-3465 para. 34 "*both the Court and the EFTA Court have recognised the need to ensure that the rules of the EEA Agreement which are identical is substance with those of the Treaty are interpreted uniformly.*" See the Opinion of Advocate General Geelhoed in *Ospelt* at paras. 67–71.

Obviously, a judgement on a human rights issue that had been given before the Charter came into force may need to be reconsidered in the light of the Charter, which certainly altered the law in many important ways.

It seems likely that in the sphere of EU law, national courts will use the possibility of making references to the Court of Justice to obtain rulings on questions under the Charter since they cannot refer questions under the Convention to the Court of Human Rights. If, as it seems likely, national courts have a duty under Article 4 (3) TEU to raise questions of fundamental rights on their own initiative, such references may become frequent. National courts will be aware that when they refer a specific question to the Court they will get a single answer, and get it more quickly than a judgement would be obtained from the Court of Human Rights. This will make the Court of Justice, in the EU Member States, a more frequent source of rulings on fundamental rights then the Court of Human Rights.

The ability of individuals to bring cases to courts is a key ingredient in the success of the courts in question,[44] and it greatly increases the influence of the lawyers who represent them.

The German Constitutional Court has accepted that Union law, even before the coming into force of the new EU Treaties, provided protection for fundamental rights substantially similar to that provided under German constitutional law. However, if it were to appear that on any particular issue that was clearly not correct, one would expect the Court of Justice would be ready to reconsider whichever judgement was relevant. This, at least in theory, would be necessary to prevent it being argued in Germany that German courts should exercise judicial control over EU institutions.

C. Judgements Adopted Quickly

One important kind of situation in which the Court should be willing to reconsider its previous judgements concerns cases in which the Court has been obliged to adopt judgements quickly, because the cases involved questions of personal liberty or physical well-being of individuals.[45] In such cases it is natural to suppose that not enough consideration might have been given to the issues. Questions of fundamental rights might well be involved, and it would be desirable to make the applicable legal rules as clear as possible to all national authorities whose responsibilities might be affected. One difficulty in such cases is that it is not necessarily obvious who would be both willing and able to submit comprehensive and well-researched arguments on the issues involved. Lawyers representing families or accused persons would not be likely to have the time and the resources to do the work needed. In the General Court, it is unusual for a member of the Court to be asked to act as an Advocate General. Member States are not necessarily anxious to clarify rules that may have the effect of limiting their police powers. The

---

44   Slaughter & Helfer, Why States create International tribunals: a response to Profession Posner and Yoo, 93 California Law Review 899 (2005).
45   Article 62a, Protocol on the Statute of the Court of Justice, TFEU (accelerated procedure).

Court of Justice has a special responsibility in cases of this kind. It would be undesirable to allow a situation to develop in which the important issues were ultimately decided, perhaps years later, by the European Court of Human Rights.

D. Where the Commission is Reluctant to Reconsider

A second important kind of situation involves cases in which the Commission's policy is open to criticism, and the Commission has no interest in helping the Court to reconsider it. This is particularly likely to be a problem in technical areas. One example is official authorisation for genetically modified organisms, where the Court is likely to defer to the Commission's supposed expertise and presumed objectivity. Another area is the Commission's reliance on economic analysis in applying EU competition law. In cases under what is now Article 102 TFEU (abuse of dominant positions), the Commission has been allowed by the EU Courts to make economic arguments that are regarded by economists as superficial, legalistic and wrong. The Commission, plainly, has no interest in criticising its own practices, in particular because they enable it to use much simpler approaches than a serious economic analysis would allow. The Court, for its part, seems understandably reluctant to involve itself in issues of economic assessment, even when the Commission's practices have been subjected to criticism. Individual enterprises may not have an interest in arguing anything except the principal issues in their cases, and anyway cannot claim to be objective. Member States, even if they are well aware that the Commission's practices are unsatisfactory, may not have a sufficient interest in undertaking the necessary work. Even if the Court thought it necessary or desirable to reconsider its own case law and to look more critically at the Commission's economic theories, the Court would need a well-informed ally to help it to carry out the task.

For cases in these quickly-adopted or technical categories, it would be open to the Court to encourage interventions by well-informed organisations, and the Court could also ask the Commission to obtain reports on the situations in the industries in question, and to submit them to the Court. The Court would need to be sure that the Commission did not merely get reports written by those who were already involved in, or favourable to, its policies. The Court might need to consider giving legal aid to intervener organisations that might not be able to pay the expense of a substantial intervention, or the expense of gathering a substantial body of evidence. The Court may need to be more willing to accept interventions from organisations with expertise and experience to give, even when they have no direct interest in the practical result of the particular case. However, the Court would need to be careful to avoid being influenced by ostensibly "impartial" organisations that are in fact financed by interested multinational companies.[46]

Cases in these technical categories seem to be those in which it may be most difficult in practice to get the Court to reconsider its case law, even in circumstances in which the Commis-

---

46 See Case T-201/04 *Microsoft* [2007] ECR II-3601.

sion itself accepts that it needs to be reconsidered (as the Commission admitted to the Court in *British Airways*[47]).

The Court should also be more willing to reconsider its judgements in cases in which it has allowed the Commission to say that there was no evidence that confidential information had been released from the Commission (when there was no other source from which it could have come).[48] The Commission does not hesitate to defend its own convenience, and there is no reason why the Court should always allow it to do so.

E. Precedents and The Case Law on The Duty of National Authorities of "Loyal" Cooperation with the European Union

There have been many judgements based on what is now Article 4 TEU (previously Article 10 EC, the duty of national authorities and courts to cooperate with the Community and the EU).[49] This case law is now very diverse, and when a case arises in which some previous judgements are relevant, the Court naturally cites only the judgements that are most obviously applicable. However, when the Court does this, it usually refers only to the judgements, and not to the Article in the Treaty on which those judgements were based. This practice has two unfortunate consequences. First, it exposes the Court unnecessarily to criticisms that it is engaged in "judicial legislation". Second, it minimises the importance of the Treaty Article, because it fails to show how important its consequences are, and how broad its application is.

This occurs in cases where the Court is merely repeating a finding based on Article 10 made in an earlier judgement, without explaining it, and, therefore, without mentioning the reasons for the earlier finding. It is an example of the Court needing to clarify, though not to correct, an earlier judgement. It would probably be wise for the Court to refer to Article 4 (3) TEU as well as to its own previous judgements, unless the legal basis in Article 4 is very clear and well known, which is not the position in the case law. More frequent explicit references to Article 4 would help national courts to see the many implications of Article 4 more clearly and to fulfil their obligations without having to ask the Court for guidance unnecessarily.

---

47 Case C-95/04 P *British Airways* [2007] ECR I-2331.
48 See e.g. Case T-15/02 *BASF v. Commission* [2006] ECR II-497 pp. 698–701.
49 General Report, The duties of co-operation of national authorities and courts and the Community institutions under Article 10 EC, XIX FIDE Congress, Federation International pour le Droit Européen (2000, Helsinki), pp. 373–426; Skouris, The Principle of Procedural Autonomy and the Duty of Loyal Cooperation of National Judges under Article 10 EC, in: Andenas and Fairgrieve (eds.), Tom Bingham and the Transformation of Law (2009, Oxford U.P.), pp. 493–507; Temple Lang, The development by the Court of Justice of the duties of cooperation of national authorities and Community Institutions under Article 10 EC, 31 Fordham International Law Journal (2008), pp. 1483–1532.

F. What should National Courts do?

If a case comes before a national court in which the issue is one that has already been decided by the Court of Justice, the court should normally follow the judgement of the Court.[50] If the national court believes that the Court should or is likely to alter or revise its previous judgement, the court may refer the question again to the Court, giving its reasons.

If the issue before the national court is one which the Court of Justice has *not* decided, the court may decide the issue itself, or refer the question to the Court. If it is the court of final appeal in the national legal system, it may be required by Article 267 TFEU to refer the question. If it chooses to decide the question itself, it should decide whatever it believes is correct, but bearing in mind that the question may be brought to the Court of Justice. It would, therefore, be inappropriate to decide in a way which the Court was clearly unlikely ultimately to accept. This means that the national court may decide to take the risk of anticipating a future change in the case law of the Court, if it considers that there are sufficient reasons, of the kinds discussed here, for doing so. A national court that is faced with an issue not decided by the Court of Justice, but decided by other national courts, may decide to follow the other national courts, if they have all agreed, even though it is not bound to do so. If, however, national courts have disagreed with one another, it may be desirable or even legally necessary for the court that is faced with this disagreement to refer the question to the Court of Justice, in order to establish a uniform interpretation of EU law on the question. This would be appropriate if the question was likely to arise again, or if uniform interpretation was particularly important (e.g., in customs classification cases), or if it were important for some other reason to get it finally resolved. Article 4 (3) TEU (ex-Article 10) imposes a duty on national courts to refer a question under Article 267 TFEU if a significant difference of view has developed between national courts, whether in the same or in different Member States.[51]

G. A National Court's Duty to Correct a Previous Judgement

Another situation in which a national court may have a duty to resolve the issues arising is where it seems that one of its own previous judgements, which it would usually follow, is contrary to EU law.[52] National courts have a duty to raise points of EU law on their own initiative. A national court, therefore, should not follow a previous national judgement if it seemed to be incorrect or contrary to the case law of the Court, unless it decided to ask the Court to reconsider its previous judgement.

A national court may be asked by e.g. the national competition authority or by some other public authority, or by the government of its Member State, to refer a question to the Court of Justice. In theory the Commission might intervene in the national court, either to express a

---

50   Bingham J. (as he then was), *Customs and Excise Commissioners v. Aps Samex* [1983] All E.R. 1042 explained why the Court was in general better placed than a national court to decide EU law questions.
51   Case C-283/81 *Cilfit* [1982] ECR 3415.
52   See in particular Case C-224/01 *Köbler* [2003] ECR I-10239.

view on the question, or to suggest that the question should be referred to the Court of Justice. However, the Commission intervenes in national courts surprisingly rarely, although it is expressly authorised to do so in competition cases by Regulation 1/2003. It seems reasonable to say that the Commission may intervene in a national court in any case in which a significant issue of EU law arises, even without being authorised by a regulation. In *Hasselblad v. Orbison*[53] the Commission intervened in a national court, without having a specific legal basis for doing so, other than what is now Article 4 TEU. A national court presumably would have a duty under Article 4 to allow the Commission to intervene if it had a reason to do so. The Commission does not consider that it should normally intervene in a national court, except at the request of the court, because that might appear to interfere with the jurisdiction of the Court of Justice to decide questions which the national court feels unable to decide without judicial advice.

H. The Role of the Advocate General in Persuading the Court to Revise its Case Law

In many of the cases described here, it has been the Advocate General, not the Commission, who has advised the Court to change its case law.[54]

The role of the Advocate General may be crucial when the Court is asked to reconsider and revise a previous judgement. If the Advocate General advises the Court to do this, the Court can be expected to reconsider its case law carefully, whether or not it ultimately decides to change it. If the Advocate General reconsiders the case law and advises against change, the Court would presumably be likely to follow that advice, perhaps without very profound analysis. If the Advocate General does not raise the question, the Court would be less likely to do so on its own initiative. If reconsideration is needed, the normal responsibility of the Advocate General to summarise and balance the arguments on both sides of each question becomes particularly important.

This has implications for other European Courts. The General Court, in cases in which it would be appropriate for the Court of Justice to reconsider its case law, should consider nominating an Advocate General for the purpose of setting out the arguments for and against change, and discussing these arguments in a way which it might be difficult for the General Court itself to

---

53   *Hasselblad (UK) v. Orbison* [1984] 3 Common Market Law Report 540, 679 at p. 692. See now Case C-429/07 X BV [2009] ECR I-4833 (an intervention in accordance with Regulation 1/2003). In *Conex Banninger v. Commission*, High Court, England, HC09C04594, Judgement dated 29 July 2010, the Commission was defendant, not intervener.

54   The Commission argues now more often cases in the EU Courts as a litigant, defending its own interests and its own convenience, and less often than in the past acts as an impartial adviser to the Court, proposing clarification of the law even when it would increase the obligations of the Commission. Examples of this change are the Commission's efforts to say that it was not bound by its own Notices on competition law questions, and that Article 265 TFEU (on failure to act) does not apply to "comitology" procedures, and the Commission's efforts to restrict its obligations to disclose documents under Regulation 1049/2001 (e.g. Cases T-121/05 and T-166/05 *Borax Europe* [2009] ECR II-28; Case T-36/04 *Association de la presse internationale* [2007] ECR II-3201).

do.⁵⁵ The General Court could then either follow the Court of Justice case law, perhaps indicating that it should be reconsidered, or adopt a new position, if it considered that to be justified e.g. as an exception to a principle that had previously been considered to be a general one.

The situation is more difficult for the EFTA Court, which does not appoint an Advocate General. Neither does the European Court of Human Rights, but in that Court one would expect that if its case law on a given issue needed to be reconsidered, there would normally be a dissenting or concurring judgement that would form the basis for the views to be analysed.

The importance of the Advocate General's role in this context means, of course, that the Advocate General may need more time than is usually available to reconsider the fundamental principles or assumptions of the case law. This may be especially difficult to ensure in urgent cases, even in situations in which previous judgements have also been adopted hurriedly and without as much consideration as it might be desirable. Where precedents need to be reconsidered, the Advocate General should discuss all the arguments for and against change.

An Advocate General may feel more free than the Court itself to refer to and discuss the judgements of other courts, whether European or national, and this trend can be expected to develop in the future. An Advocate General may well consider that it is now part of his or her responsibilities to call the attention of the Court to the judgements of *other* courts, in particular the EFTA Court and the European Court of Human Rights.

I. "Soft law" as a Reason for Reconsideration of the Court's Case Law

Occasionally statements made by the Commission or the European Parliament might be sufficient reasons for the Court of Justice to reconsider its case law. Neither of the other institutions, of course, has power to change the law by its own actions. But either institution might legitimately call attention to uncertainty or some other feature of the case law that is considered to be unsatisfactory, and this might in practice be enough to lead the Court to reconsider.⁵⁶

J. "Soft Law" – the Question of the Commission's Guidance Document on Exclusionary Abuses

Among the statements that might have this result are the Commission's "Notices" or "Guidelines", for example in competition law. These bind the Commission itself, in accordance with

---

55   In Case T-177/01 *Jégo-Quéré* [2002] ECR II-2365 the Court did not nominate an Advocate General, presumably because it was following the Opinion of Advocate General Jacobs in Case C-50/00P *Unión de Pequeños* [2002] I-6677.
56   In Case C-280/00 *Altmark* [2003] ECR I-7747 the Advocate General referred to the implications of the *Ferring* judgement for the Commission's investigation of subsidies: Opinion paras. 94–98.

the principle of legitimate expectations, as the Court has repeatedly determined.[57] However, these statements are not always consistent with the Court's existing case law. When they go further than the case law, that may cause no difficulty. But when, as in the case of the Commission's "Guidance" on the enforcement of what is now Article 102 TFEU, on exclusionary abuses of dominant positions[58], the Commission's statements are inconsistent with the Court's case law, other issues arise. It is curious that the Guidance document does not mention the fact that it is inconsistent with the Court's case law, and does not discuss the legal and other issues that are likely to arise as a result. If the Guidance document was intended to encourage or invite the Court to reconsider its case law, it might have been more frank and more helpful to say so. It would certainly have been useful to suggest legal reasons, as distinct from economic reasons. This was not done. Merely describing the Guidance as the Commission's own enforcement priorities does not avoid this difficulty, because it is obviously untrue (several of the suggestions made are so unusual or extreme that they cannot be priorities), and because some of the Commission's suggestions would be accepted by the Court only if the Court was willing to change its case law. When, as in the case of Article 102, the Commission has apparently adopted "soft law" in order to encourage the Court to change its case law, the Court should presumably consider doing so, even if the Commission has not made its wishes clear, and even if the Commission's specific proposals are not satisfactory.[59]

Because of these difficulties, the General Court might be wise to appoint an Advocate General in some future case under Article 102,[60] so that the whole problem caused by the Commission's apparent wish to change the case law on exclusionary abuses (to which it has itself contributed) can be fully discussed. If this were not done, there is a risk that the case law under Article 102 will develop primarily through references from national courts under Article 267 on spe-

---

57 E.g. Case C-184/02P *Dansk Rørindustri* [2005] ECR I-5425 paras. 211–213. Case C-409/00 *Spain v. Commission* [2003] ECR I-1487 para. 95.
58 Guidance on the Commission's enforcement priorities in applying Article 82 of the EC Treaty to abusive exclusionary conduct by dominant undertakings, OJ No. C-45/7, 24 February 2009. See Azizi, Prospective Conduct Announcements by the Community Administration: some personal reflections, in: Johansson, Wahl & Bernitz (eds.), Liber Amicorum in Honour of Sven Norberg (2006), pp. 11–23. The complexity of the situation should not be underestimated. There are three lines of thought involved: (i) the better known line of judgements of the EU Courts, including Case T-203/01 *Michelin II* [2003] ECR II-4071, Case C-95/04P *British Airways* [2007] ECR I-2331; (ii) the less well known line of judgements of the Courts, based expressly on the words of Article 102 (b), including Joined Cases C-40/73 and others *Sugar Cartel-SZV*, [1975] ECR 1663 paras. 399, 482–483 and 523–527, Case C-41/83 *Italy v. Commission (British Telecommunications)* [1985] ECR 873, Case C-311/84 *Telemarketing CBEM* [1985] ECR 3261, Joined Cases C-241/91P *RTE and ITP ("magill")* [1995] ECR I-743 para. 54, Case C-41/90 *Höfner and Elsner* [1991] ECR I-1979 pp. 2017–2018, Case C-258/98 *Carra* [2000] ECR I-4217, Case T-201/04 *Microsoft* [2007] ECR II-3601 paras. 643–648; (iii) the Commission's Guidance document, which is primarily economic statements, containing features which are inconsistent with both lines of judgements, and for which there is no legal authority.
59 Centre for European Policy Studies, Treatment of Exclusionary Abuses under Article 82 of the EC Treaty (2009): Temple Lang, Anticompetitive Non-pricing abuses under European and national antitrust law, in; Hawk (ed.), 2003 Fordham Corporate Law Institute (2004), pp. 235–340; Temple Lang, The Requirements for a Commission Notice on the Concept of Abuse under Article 82 EC, in: Mentula (ed.), 2007 Competition Law Yearbook (Helsinki), pp. 271–305.
60 See Greaves, Judge Edward Acting as Advocate General, in Hoskins & Robinson, A True European: Essays for Judge David Edward (2003), pp. 91–98.

cific issues, and a suitable opportunity for a much-needed reconsideration of the whole case law on exclusionary abuses will not arise.

K. Numerous Interventions as a Reason for Reconsideration

The Courts of the EU have gradually allowed an increasing number of interventions by representative organisations in direct actions. In references from national courts it is the national court that decides whether an intervention is admissible, not the Court of Justice. In at least one of these cases, the *Akzo* case on legal privilege for in-house lawyers[61], the large number of interventions by lawyers' organisations was due to the fact that the Court's previous case law was widely considered to be too restrictive.

It should be recognised that there is a weakness in the system of references under Article 267 TFEU. When a national court asks a very important question, on which the views of representative organisations might be very useful, they are unable to make submissions to the Court of Justice, except when they have intervened already in the national court. This has the effect of depriving the Court of what might be valuable arguments that would be admissible if the question had not arisen under Article 267. If interventions were allowed at the stage when the case is before the Court, that would delay the case, in particular if the importance of the question did not become clear until after written arguments had been filed, as has sometimes happened. This means that the national court needs to understand fully the importance of the question, before the reference is made, and the potential value of interventions. It would also mean that the Court should allow interveners to give evidence of facts, even though the Court in Article 267 does not make findings of facts.

Under the "Community method" of legislating, the Commission has the exclusive right to propose new measures for consideration by the Parliament and the Council. There are good reasons for this,[62] but it has one undesirable result. It means that when the Commission believes that it would be inconvenienced by a certain reform, it may not make a proposal at all. The result is that the Parliament and Council are not given an opportunity to consider whether any reform is needed. Of course, a reform that would need new legislation cannot be achieved by a judgement of the Court of Justice. But when there is a considerable body of well-informed opinion in favour of a reform, but the Commission is unwilling to propose it or to allow it to be discussed, the Court might be willing to allow interventions from representative organisations, so that any legal questions that are within the Court's competence can be considered by the judges. Whatever the merits of the controversy over legal privilege may be, it was certainly desirable that the Court should reconsider a question on which there was a widely-held view that change is necessary, but on which the Commission was unwilling to make any proposal, apparently because it believes that its own interests or convenience would be affected.

61　Case C-550/07P *Akzo Nobel* [2010] – judgement dated 14 September 2010; see Case T-201/04 *Microsoft* [2007] ECR II-3601 (a total of fourteen interveners).
62　Temple Lang and Gallagher, The Role of the Commission and Qualified Majority Voting, Occasional paper No. 7 (Institute of European Affairs, Dublin).

Rather similar situations seem to be arising in two other cases. As already mentioned, on the concept of exclusionary abuse under Article 102 TFEU, the Commission's Guidance document is very different from the Court's case law, and the Commission has so far made no proposals to reconcile them or to clarify the legal position. Unless the Commission explains the problem frankly to the Court, it seems likely that the many difficulties can be explained only by objective and well-reasoned interventions. The second of these problems concerns the Commission's procedure in competition cases, on which the Commission is reluctant to consider a radical reform. The Court would be helped to consider detailed improvements that could be brought about by case law by more objective assessments than are likely be made by a company that has been fined for infringement of Articles 101 or 102 TFEU.[63]

One would expect the Union Courts to allow lawyers' organisations to intervene concerning the Commission's procedure in competition cases and anti-dumping cases.

L. Changed Circumstances

In *Commission v. Denmark*[64] Advocate General Mischo pointed out that the Commission had argued that *"the judgement of the [EFTA] Court*[65] *must be viewed as an element in the development of the law. Since the judgement in Sandoz, practically 20 years ago, the methods used to determine health risks had undergone considerable changes ... The judgement of the [EFTA] Court reflects this development"*. He went on *"I will take as my starting point the EFTA Court's judgement."*[66] The Court in its judgement[67] relied repeatedly on the judgement of the EFTA Court, but without referring to changed circumstances, and rejecting the interpretation of *Sandoz* proposed by Denmark.[68] In general, the mere fact that circumstances have changed is not a sufficient reason for reconsidering a judgement, but there may be situations in which it would be enough. A more likely situation is when new evidence becomes available that alters the Court's previous assessment of facts.

---

63 Temple Lang, Three possibilities for Reform of the Procedure of the European Commission in Competition Cases under Regulation 1/2003, in: Baudenbacher, (ed.) 17th St Gallen International Competition Law Forum (2010) Temple Lang, Do we need a European Union competition court? in: Baudenbacher and others (eds.), Liber Amicorum honour of Bo Vesterdorf (2007), pp. 343–361.
64 Case C-192/01 *Commission v. Denmark* [2003] ECR I-9693 p. 9711; Case C-238/99P *Limburgse Vinyl* [2002] ECR I-8375 (duty to revise the Court's case law in the light of developments in the Court of Human Rights).
65 Case E-3/00 *EFTA Surveillance Authority v. Norway* EFTA Court Report 2000/01, p. 73.
66 Case C-192/01 *Commission v. Denmark* [2003] ECR I-9693 p. 9712. See also p. 9720.
67 Case C-192/01 *Commission v. Denmark* [2003] ECR I-9693 pp. 9739–9740.
68 In Joined Cases T-74/00 and others *Artegodan* [2002] ECR I-4945 para. 178 the Court referred to the need for re-evaluation of the balance of benefit and risk of medicinal products in the light of new data, by the competent authorities (not by the Court itself). See Demetriou and Higgins, Free Movement and Environment: seeing the wood for the trees, in: Hoskins & Robinson (eds.), A True European: Essays for David Edward (2003), pp. 193–201; Temple Lang, Article 82 and EU Rules on National Measures Restricting Competition During a Recession, 2009 Jura Falconis, pp. 253–289. In Case C-89/08P *Commission v. Ireland* [2009] ECR I-11245 paras. 70 et seq., the Court held that a State aid is considered an existing aid if it was not an aid when it was put into effect, but became an aid due to evolution of the common market without having been altered by the Member State.

In her opinion on legal professional privileges for employed layers[69], Advocate General Kokott explained that the right to be protected against discrimination on the basis of age resulted from developments in national laws, and the right of access to the Commission's files in competition cases was developed because the Commission both investigates and decides. In the *Akzo* case it was argued that the ending of notifications of agreements in competition cases, making companies rely on self-assessment, was a change of legal circumstances that made it appropriate to recognise privileges for employed lawyers.

M. The Fédération Internationale Pour Le Droit Européen (FIDE)

Since the Commission does not always propose that the Court should reconsider its previous judgements even when that seems desirable, there may be other bodies whose views, if they called for reconsideration of the Court's case law, should be listened to. One of these is FIDE, which is one of the few bodies which would be in a position to call attention to the need for reconsideration of any aspect of the Court's case law, if the question arose from the subject of a FIDE conference. The role of FIDE has altered greatly since it was launched in the 1960s, and its *raison d'être* is now not as clear as it once was. If there was a need for reconsideration of the Court's case law on some issue that FIDE had discussed, one would expect the Court to listen carefully to any consensus that might emerge. FIDE congress subjects have not always been chosen with this in mind, but there is no reason why they should not be.

N. The Role of the Grande Chamber in Reconsidering Case Law

It seems that in cases in which the Court is considering whether some of its previous case law should be reconsidered, clarified, or revised, the Court arranges for the cases to be decided by the Grande Chamber. This is to ensure that all the issues are fully analysed, and to add weight to whatever is finally decided.

I hope that it would not be thought presumptuous or disrespectful to the Court if a lawyer who wanted to argue for reconsideration of previous case law were to suggest that the case was suitable for the Grande Chamber, giving the reasons for a possible change in the Court's view of the law. If a lawyer believes that the case law should be reconsidered, the sooner that suggestion is made the better, in particular to avoid the need to re-open the oral hearing and to have, perhaps, two hearings and two Advocate General's Opinions. This might be particularly useful in cases referred from national courts under Article 267 TFEU, in which there is only one set of written arguments.

---

69   Case C-550/074P *Akzo Nobel*, opinion dated 29 April 2010, paras. 93–96. In the judgement, given on 14 September 2010, the Court considered that changed circumstances did not necessitate a change in the case law: para. 69–76 and 83–87. In considering whether Regulation 1/2003 had changed EU law in some respect relevant to legal privilege, the Court looked only at the words of the Regulation, and did not consider the implications of the regime of voluntary compliance with EU competition law that the Regulation established.

O. The Scope of Arbitrators for Innovation

The position of an arbitrator deciding a case to which EU law applies is not the same as that of a national judge in a EU or EEA Member State. The traditional view has been that an arbitrator, unless acting on the basis of public law, has no power to refer a question to the Court of Justice.[70] An arbitrator would be wise to comply with all the duties imposed on national courts by Article 4 (3) TEU (ex-Article 10 E), but strictly speaking they may not apply. An arbitrator is not expressly required by Regulation 1/2003 to follow a decision of the European Commission in the same competition case, and the Commission is not required by Article 15 of that Regulation to provide information to arbitrators, although the Commission has done so in some cases. Clearly an arbitrator should not make an award that would be contrary to any rule of EU law, because it would be unenforceable in the EU and the EEA States.

The terms of the agreement under which the arbitrator is acting may give more scope for an innovative award than a national court would usually consider that it could have, even in the light of the duties of national courts to innovate if necessary to provide "effective" remedies for infringements of EU law (not, of course, only EU competition law).[71] Most arbitrators do not consider that they are as bound to follow precedents as national courts, and they often feel free to adopt procedural innovations if that is necessary. This relative freedom, if the arbitrator considers that it is available, may be useful in devising interim measures (successive Presidents of the Court of First Instance and the General Court have often been practical, pragmatic, and innovative in interim measures cases) and in devising remedies.

The Court of Appeal in England has pointed out the advantages of arbitration in competition cases involving essential facilities, excessive prices and discrimination.[72] Since the Commission is extremely reluctant to investigate excessive pricing cases, in spite of the clear words of the Treaty, and because of the difficulties of complainants to get evidence in discrimination cases, arbitration should be encouraged in such cases. In essential facility cases, the difficulties of deciding the terms on which access should be granted are well known, and the Commission has consistently avoided deciding them. (Whether the Commission will be able to continue to avoid carrying out its responsibilities in these respects is not discussed here. The point being made is that since the Commission is reluctant to decide such cases, arbitrators should be encouraged to do so.)

The Commission, which for some time in the past suspected that arbitral awards might have anticompetitive effects, has now approved arbitration arrangements in the context of merger cases and of cases involving legally binding commitments under Article 9 of Regulation 1/2003. The Commission has referred to the possibility of arbitration, in its Merger Remedies Notice, in the Regulation 823/2000 on liner shipping companies and in Regulation 1400/2002 on motor vehicles. The Commission is, therefore, much more favourable to arbitration than it was.

---

70 Case 102/81 *Nordsee v. Reederei Mond* [1982] ECR 1095.
71 Case C-432/05 *Unibet* [2007] ECR I-2271.
72 *Attheraces v. British Horseracing Board* [2007] EWCA Civ 38, [2007] UKCLR 309, para. 7, per Mummery L.J.

Insofar as arbitral awards are publicly available, and in the absence of judgements of national or European courts, the General Court and the Court of Justice could look for inspiration to arbitral awards. In addition, an award might be made in terms that were not fully consistent with the existing case law of the Courts, if the arbitrator considered that appropriate because there were grounds of the kinds described in this paper for believing that the case law was incomplete or unsatisfactory or inapplicable to the case in question. Arbitrators, in other words, are free to be more innovative than national judges, and there is no objection in principle under EU law if they innovate when they consider it appropriate or necessary to do so.

P. The Case Law on References by Arbitrators to the Court of Justice and the EFTA Court

An arbitrator might try to refer a question of EU law to the Court of Justice, to give the Court an opportunity to reconsider the judgement in *Nordsee v. Reederei Mond*, in which it held that private arbitrators have no power to refer questions. In a case in which a question of EU law clearly needed to be decided, it would be expensive, inconvenient, and slow to bring the question before a national court exercising a supervisory jurisdiction over the arbitrator, merely so that the court could refer the question under Article 267 TFEU. Admittedly, the Court of Justice would be reluctant to increase its case-load by accepting what might prove to be a large number of references from arbitrators, and the need to go through the supervising national court would provide a screening mechanism that would keep down the numbers of such cases. The Court unfortunately has not got a power corresponding to the power of the US Supreme Court to refuse to hear a case (the power to "refuse certiorari" in US terminology). The Court therefore cannot choose what references it will accept from national courts, and therefore could hardly find a way of exercising a discretion in choosing what references it would accept from arbitrators. But the following criteria, which would not involve discretion, can be suggested.

One possibility would be for the Court to accept, at least in the case of an arbitrator acting on the basis of a decision of the European Commission, that the arbitration has the public law features that have been thought necessary under Article 267 TFEU.[73] An arbitrator who is appointed or approved by the Commission, if he was not allowed to refer a question to the Court, might have to refer the issue back to the Commission, which would then have to adopt a decision and, if necessary, defend it in the General Court. That would be an unnecessarily complicated, inconvenient and expensive procedure. Another possibility is for the Court to accept references from arbitrators in cases in which the European Commission has intervened or given the arbitrators information to enable them to carry out their duties. An arbitration on the basis of an international treaty, bilateral or multilateral, to which a Member State was a party should also be treated differently from a purely private arbitration. Also, it seems unreasonable to treat e.g. the International Chamber of Commerce International Court of Arbitration

---

73 See generally Blanke, The Use and Utility of International Arbitration in EC Commission Merger Remedies (2006, Groningen), in: Brealey & Green (eds.), Competition Litigation (2010, Oxford U.P.), pp. 604–620.

as something less than a small local court in a Member State, when the lowest courts in Member States have the power to refer questions to the Court of Justice.

It is also suggested that the Court should accept a reference from an arbitrator who is *not* subject to the supervision of a national court of an EU Member State, and who, therefore, is not able to have a question of EU law brought indirectly before the Court under Article 267. The Commission ought to be willing to inform or advise an arbitrator in this situation, if the arbitrator asks for information. In such a situation it would be more convenient to allow the arbitrator to refer a question to the Court directly, instead of obliging the parties to ask a national court in the EU to refer the question to the Court later at the stage when the award was being enforced in the EU, which is, of course, possible.[74] This is so in particular because it is not clear how far a national court should reconsider an arbitral award at the enforcement stage, and a direct reference to the Court by the arbitrator would avoid delay and expense. If there was no award in favour of the claimant, there would be nothing to enforce, and, therefore, no opportunity to bring the question of EU law before the Court. It certainly also would seem unreasonable, and indeed undesirable, for the Court to refuse to accept a reference from an arbitrator who had raised a question of EU law on his or her own initiative, since the fact that the parties had not raised it might suggest that they were not likely to do so subsequently. An arbitral tribunal has a duty to give an enforceable award, and should be helped if it tries to fulfil that duty.

These are all situations that are different from the *Nordsee* case, and the Court could accept references in these cases without overruling the *Nordsee* case, and without the risk of allowing too many references. It seems that the Court should do so, and certainly that the Commission should indicate that it would advise the Court to consider exceptions to the general rule stated in the *Nordsee* case. The Commission has no reason to discourage arbitrators from obtaining authoritative guidance on issues of EU or EEA law.

III. Conclusions – and the Future

The Court has been cautious in reconsidering its own previous case law, and has changed it only when there were clear reasons for doing so.

This is natural and wise, in a newly established legal system. It would have weakened the authority of the Court and of its case law if the Court had been thought too ready to change its previous judgements. If this caution has sometimes led to judgements being delayed while the judges satisfied themselves that the implications had been foreseen as far as possible, that was a small price to pay. It has been suggested, above in this paper, that the Court would be wise to refer expressly to Article 4 (3) TEU (ex-Article 10) EL when referring to its own previous judgements that are in fact based on that principle.[75] It is respectfully suggested also that when

---

74   Case C-126/97 *Eco Swiss China Time v. Benetton* [1999] ECR I-3055.
75   Temple Lang, The Development by the Court of Justice of the Duties of Cooperation of National Authorities and Community Institutions under Article 10 EC, 31 Fordham International Law Journal (2008), pp. 1483–1532, at p. 1488.

the Court takes judgements of the EFTA Court and the European Court of Human Rights into consideration, it should always do so expressly. It is apparently now not the practice to do this in all cases.[76] It would be helpful if the Court would expressly call the attention of lawyers appearing before it to all of the authorities on which it may base its judgements.[77] It is very helpful that Advocates General increasingly refer to judgements of the other European Courts.

The increased workload may now mean that the judges have less time than formerly for the research and reflection that is needed to ensure that judgements do not need to be reconsidered because of questions that might have been foreseen if there had been more time to foresee them. This risk is partly off-set by the fact that many of the fundamental principles of the EU legal system have now been established, and changes in the case law on technical issues, if and when they are necessary, are less likely to reduce confidence in the authority of the Court. If there are problems in the future, they are likely to arise in the area of freedom, security and justice, where there has not yet been time to establish all the fundamental principles. The questions will not all be purely technical, cases may be urgent, and some of the Court's judgements may be controversial. The case law of the European Court of Human Rights, although helpful, will certainly not resolve all the questions that may come before the Court in this area. No doubt the Court will continue to be cautious in this sphere, too.

We are at the start of a new era. Because the Charter of Fundamental Rights is to be interpreted in the same way as the European Convention on Human Rights, the Court of Justice will make greater use of the case law of the European Court of Human Rights than it has done in the past. Both Courts, no doubt, will make greater use of the increasing number of national judgements on fundamental rights, as the Court of Human Rights already does. The "precedents" used by all these courts will be more numerous, and richer, than they have ever been. This means more work for lawyers appearing before the courts, but the results will be better law, and more dialogue between the courts.[78] Dialogue between courts in Europe is uniquely extensive, and is important for public acceptance of European law. Nowhere else in the world is judicial dialogue so frequent and so explicit.

A dialogue between courts of high standing may be valuable, not only to provide different perspectives, but on occasion to correct defects. The US Supreme Court, which has no such dialogue except with lower courts (and has the advantage of continuity due to life tenure), has sometimes been so widely regarded as wrong that respect for its authority has declined. In Eu-

---

76   Skouris, The ECJ and the EFTA Court under the EEA Agreement: A Paradigm for International Cooperation between Judicial Institutions, in: Baudenbacher and others, (eds.), The EFTA Court Ten Years on (2005), p. 125.
77   Lord Bingham, The Business of Judging (Oxford 2000) wrote *"It is, surely, an abnegation of the judicial role if a judge allows himself to be influenced in his decision by considerations to which he does not allude"*.
78   The Court of Justice might think it appropriate, on occasion, when giving directions to counsel about the question to be discussed at a hearing, to ask specifically for comments on specified relevant judgements of *other* courts. It is unsatisfactory for a lawyer whose case is decided against him on the basis of a judgement of another court which he did not know that he should have cited. Advice to counsel always to consult the case law of the European Court of Human Rights and the EFTA Court would be appropriate, but it might be useful to call attention specifically to judgements of national courts, unless the lawyers come from the Member State in question and can be expected to know them.

rope, which depends more heavily on its legal order because it has as yet no political unity to sustain it, it is even more important that nothing similar should happen. The dialogue between courts provides a more open discussion than collegiate decisions can create. The difficulties of developing a comprehensive body of case law under the Charter of Fundamental Rights should not be underestimated, and it is valuable that there are three European Courts that may be in a position to contribute to it. The legal order of Europe is a wholly new invention, and the more courts that can contribute to it, the better.

All this is important, and not only for lawyers. The principal set of values available to the European Union involves human rights and the role of law. They are in the hands of the three European Courts. They need to work carefully together to maintain these values. The European Community was astonishingly successful in ending enmities in Western Europe. Creating good governance and consolidating human rights, particularly in Central Europe, is more difficult. It will depend, among other things, on the European Courts. The promise of economic development, even if it is fulfilled, is not enough. The principle of effective judicial protection of fundamental rights, set out in Article 47 of the Charter of Fundamental Rights and in Article 6 and 13 of the Convention on Human Rights, and clearly a part of EEA law, will be one of the most important foundation stones for these values.

The jurisdiction of the European Court of Justice overlaps with that of the EFTA Court on EEA matters, and with the jurisdiction of the European Court of Human Rights on fundamental rights issues. The Court of Justice already has a close and mutually valuable dialogue with national courts in EU Member States. (Most of the fundamental principles of the Court's case law on the duties of national authorities under Article 4 (3) TEU have come from references from national courts).[79] The Court of Justice is in the centre of this complex. If the Court allowed some references from arbitrators, it would establish a dialogue with the only remaining important group of legal decision-makers in Europe who are not already linked to it. The relationships between these three European Courts (and between the Court of Justice and the EFTA Court and national courts) are rightly described as a *"symbiosis"*. No doubt it will become the most interesting kind of *"symbiosis"*, which is co-evolution.

---

79 Temple Lang, The development by the Court of Justice of the duties of cooperation of national authorities and Community Institutions under Article 10 EC, 31 Fordham International Law Journal (2008), pp. 1483–1532.

Discussion

PAUL MAHONEY
I will now open the discussion. Please do not hesitate to ask any questions that you may have.

VICTOR COMELLA FERRERES
When reading decisions by the ECJ and the European Court of Human Rights one gets the impression that in general the ECJ tends to be a little bit more categorical in its rulings, whereas the European Court of Human Rights is more sensitive to the circumstances of the case. I wonder whether there might be an institutional explanation for that, namely, that we can see the ECJ as sort of the Supreme Court of a quasi federal politic. For that Supreme Court it is very important to fix the meaning of the law that is generated by that politic. The European Court of Human Rights is a sort of a more external, sort of international court that adds a layer of protection to human rights but the main reasons for the existence of that court is not to guarantee a certain level of uniformity. So, interestingly when the ECJ deals with human rights, it tends to be a little bit less categorical. Is there something to this?

JOHN TEMPLE LANG
I agree that the tone is different. I have much greater difficulty in giving you a convincing explanation. Some of it is certainly a difference of style in writing the judgements, but nothing more than a difference in style. Also, you have to bear in mind that the case law of the Court of Justice on human rights issues is 31 years old. In fact, it has not developed as much as the case law of the Court of Human Rights, obviously. The other factor which I think is important is, of course, that in the Court of Human Rights you have the possibility, which is also frequently used, of having concurring and dissenting opinions. So, what you described as the categorical ipsidictis of the Court of Justice is simply the result of a certain number of judges having agreed on a certain text. That is what they have agreed on. They do not discuss alternatives. They do not, generally speaking, give more than the minimum reasons. I do not think I have any further comment, but I agree that there is a difference in tone.

CARL BAUDENBACHER
Mr Mahoney, I would have a further comment right on this question. There is another huge difference and I became fully aware of that a couple of weeks ago when I participated in a workshop of the Advocates General of the ECJ: The fact that there is an Advocate General gives the ECJ the feeling that they can be particularly brief because there is always this broadly formulated opinion by the Advocate General. Whether the opinion of the Advocate General can replace the lack of elaborated reasoning in many cases may be doubted, but at least that is obviously the approach.

LUCIUS CAFLISCH

I find it difficult to answer your question because I know one side better than the other. But if what you say is true, there is a general explanation, namely, that the European Union, as the Community is called now, is a far more integrated and also smaller community than that formed by the 47 Member States of the Council of Europe which are all parties to the European Convention on Human Rights as well.

Yes, there is, as it has been suggested, a possibility for judges to express their dissenting or separate opinions which, of course, erodes the authority behind this or that judgement. There are judgements that were adopted in the Grand Chamber by 9 to 8 votes, such as Al-Adsani v. the United Kingdom.

The absence of an Advocate General has also been mentioned, particularly in Professor Lang's paper. Indeed, the European Court of Human Rights has no Advocate General. It does, however, have somebody similar: the Commissioner on Human Rights who, under Protocol No. 14, can now intervene in chamber and Grand Chamber cases. But he does not tell the Court what to do. He informs it of the human rights situation in a given country; he is an informant rather than an Advocate General. The idea of having Advocates General is still being discussed, however. It came up again in Interlaken but frankly, I do not think that having Advocates General is very suitable for a human rights court.

PAUL MAHONEY

The significant difference between the nature of the two systems explains in part the difference in the style of and in the purpose served by the judgements. EU law is much more directly integrated into the national legal orders of the Member States than is the ECHR; and the mechanism whereby national courts can seek preliminary rulings from the Luxembourg Court has the consequence that not only that the ruling is binding on the particular court that has sought the ruling in that particular case in the national proceedings, but that the whole body of interpretive jurisprudence emanating from the ECJ is binding on the national courts throughout the EU, given the exclusive mission that is conferred on the ECJ by the Treaties of ensuring the unity of interpretation of EU law. On the other hand, the Strasbourg Court is much more obliged to convince and to explain, in order to secure the adhesion of the national courts. Consequently, the judges in Strasbourg are aware that the judgements have a pedagogical function as well as a purely declaratory, interpretive function. They have to convince. Also, the role of the Luxembourg Court is more limited in the sense that it is mostly concerned with the interpretation of black-letter law, EU law, whereas the Court in Strasbourg has a phenomenal jurisdiction covering the whole range of human activity where the exercise of one of the guaranteed rights or freedoms may be at stake. The Strasbourg Court, therefore, digs much deeper into national law and national prerogatives. The international judicial control exercised in Strasbourg is based on the principle of subsidiarity and on the notion of democracy whereby, normally speaking, it is for each society to decide at the local level how they want to organise the lives of their people. The Strasbourg Court is essentially there to make sure that the national authorities have not gone outside their margin of democratic discretion. This explains the softer touch, if you like; it explains why the exercise of judicial restraint is more necessary in Strasbourg and why it is more visible. In sum, I suspect that the difference in style is linked to the difference in function that Luxembourg and Strasbourg judgements serve.

SIMON PLANZER

Thank you very much for four fine and rich presentations. When I reflect the description of the jurisprudence of the Swiss Supreme Court in Professor Kaddous' presentation, I cannot help to note a certain irony of the Court's practice. Prior to the referendum on the Agreement on the European Economic Area in 1992, one of the central arguments against its ratification was the fear of foreign judges. According to your description of the jurisprudence, the Swiss Supreme Court has voluntarily followed the case law of the ECJ, even if the case law changed direction. It may thus be legitimate to ask whether there is still de facto a difference between this judicial situation and the judicial situation of Switzerland as an EEA member. We should also consider in this context that the Swiss Supreme Court notes, as you say, that there cannot be two different systems of free movement of person. Could you possibly comment on that?

CHRISTINE KADDOUS

I fully agree with this statement. I just tried to show how the Federal Court follows the case law rendered by the European Court of Justice, without always mentioning the reasons why it takes into consideration specific judgments. Clearly, our Supreme Court is very open to consider European case law in relation to the Bilateral Agreements. However, there are two different positions defended in Switzerland: the one which results from the practice of the Federal Tribunal as discussed above and the other, more political, held by the Swiss Government as to the sensitive issue related to sovereignty and to the question of the submission to a "foreign judge". There is of course a lack of transparency in the political field in Switzerland. However transparency is not total either in the practice of the Federal Court, as all the decisions are not always motivated in an appropriate manner. The Federal Court has a duty to take into account the case law of the European Court of Justice, prior to the date of the signature of the FMP Agreement, but it took the point of view of following, in certain circumstances, the case law rendered after the date of signature, because it appeared to it quite logical to adopt such an approach as the text of the agreement is based on the European Union *acquis*. So, if the source of inspiration of the bilateral agreement is European Union law, it is difficult for a judge to convincingly try to defend a different interpretation than the one given in relation to that *acquis*. However, it is worth noting the courageous approach adopted by the Swiss Federal Court in the case rendered in September 2009. Even if it did not clarify its position as to the existence or to the no existence of a duty to take into consideration the Metock judgment of the European Court of Justice, it pleaded in favour of a parallel interpretation, because the FMP agreement aims at creating parallel legal situations in Switzerland and in the European Union. And I think this approach is the correct one to be adopted in order to maintain the equivalence of legislation in the field of the free movement of persons; otherwise the agreement would not function properly and its *effet utile* will be jeopardised.

SIMON PLANZER

Hence, is it correct that you have not found evidence in the jurisprudence that the Swiss Supreme Court did not follow case law passed by the ECJ posterior to the signing of the bilateral agreements?

CHRISTINE KADDOUS

No, there is the case law rendered in relation the reimbursement of health care.

CARL BAUDENBACHER

There is one famous case in Switzerland concerning the obligation of the country to pay so-called helplessness allowance to non-residents, which concerns mainly commuters who have spent their whole working life in this country but always the night in France, Italy or Germany or Austria. Had the Swiss Supreme Court decided that this new case law applies, it would have had consequences of probably half a billion Swiss Francs a year. And so, quite understandably by a professor, the court said this is new case law. The court was supported by an opinion written and paid by the government. It was a controversial issue, so they passed it on to the negotiators. And I am quite sure that one day the Commission will come with that and say, now we adjust the agreement exactly on this point. But in my view this is the only case.

I would like to make two more remarks. If we now think of the subject of the conference, the role of precedent, it seems to me that the case law of the European Court of Human Rights is more elaborate on this issue than the case law of the Court in Luxembourg. It has been mentioned that the fact that concurring and dissenting opinions are possible may shed more light on the precedential strength of a judgement. On the other hand in the ECJ, as I mentioned briefly yesterday morning, sometimes you do not even know whether there has been overruling or not. I mentioned briefly the case law on the famous transfer of undertakings directive. That is a directive which states that if an acquirer takes over a business or part of a business, he does not only take over the assets, material and immaterial assets, but also the employment relationships. The case law of the ECJ has been more and more expansive, in particular in the 1990s. In a famous case, *Christel Schmidt*, the European Court of Justice held that the transfer of a sheer activity of one single worker qualifies as a transfer of undertaking. That was the famous cleaning lady *Christel Schmidt* who had cleaned the surfaces of a small savings and loans bank in Northern Germany every night. Then the management fired her and they hired a cleaning firm to do that same work. So, *Christel Schmidt* was employed by this cleaning firm and was assigned the same job again and she was paid the same salary but she had to clean a larger surface so that her working conditions had deteriorated. She went to the local union and the local union advised her on bringing a case. A low labour court in Germany referred this question to the ECJ and the ECJ finally said that this qualifies as a transfer. That is a case which had huge consequences for the restructuring of big corporations. The ECJ was criticised for that. In a later case, a test case supported by the unions, they wanted to go even one step further. They said, not only should this directive apply if a sheer activity is transferred or outsourced, but also if an activity has been outsourced in the past to service provider number one and this contract with service provider number one is terminated and the contract is given to a second service provider after a tendered procedure. We had the first cases on this issue. The factual situation was on an oil drilling platform in Western Norway, where cleaning services and catering services had been outsourced. A contract had been concluded for three years. After three years the contract was put out for tender again and another company got the contract. So, these people claimed that this amounted to a transfer of undertaking. The Court said in Süzen that this is not a transfer. But it did not make clear whether with *Sodexho* it had overruled *Christel Schmidt*. So, there was a lot of discussion in academic literature and in particular practicing lawyers wrote about the judgement that they did not know at all where they stood. In the meantime there have been additional rulings on this subject in which the ECJ even seemed to take back part of the *Sodexho* judgement. Now, there is a situation with the utmost legal insecurity.

My second point concerns something the chairman said right now. I think it is a very important statement. Function matters. The Court of Human Rights has a different function than the Court in Luxembourg, but I may add from my own perspective, also size matters. The EFTA Court is a small court consisting of three judges. We have noticed that on a number of politically sensitive issues, where we had to give judgement first – for instance concerning the compatibility of state alcohol monopolies, the free movement of goods or tobacco or state gambling monopolies, but also on certain with taxation issues – we gave a ruling which was according to the law as it stood at the time, whereas the ECJ later on gave a ruling which probably took more policy considerations into account. I would say, if you are only three judges, you have to stick to the law. If you are larger, then you can more easily enter into a broader approach which would also take into account considerations that may be outside of strictly legalistic ones.

JOHN TEMPLE LANG
There is another consideration that occurs to me. I do not know whether I am right, but it seems to me that one of the problems of the Court of Justice is that there is a fairly high turnover of judges. One of the aspects of this is that judges come up for reappointment and they become inevitably, humanly sensitive to the possibility that their government may want to know and want to be assured that they will not support judgements that are contrary to the interests of the convenience of the government. What I conclude from this is that the Court of Justice, I suspect, is probably reluctant to expressly overrule its own judgements because that would encourage governments of Member States to say openly more often to the court that they never liked that previous judgement in Case X and that they are asking the Court to reverse it. The more often the Court indicates its willingness to reverse its own judgements, the more it would be exposed to pressure from national governments. I am not sure how important this is, but I would be surprised if it was not from time to time a factor in the failure of the Court to explicitly overrule its own judgements where fairly clearly, notably in the Emmett case, they really need to be overruled.

LUCIUS CAFLISCH
I wish to comment on the proposition that Human Rights Court practice may be more elaborate when it comes to precedent. That is probably necessary considering the caseload of the Court. And the law applicable to the Court is quite specific on this point. I have cited two provisions, Article 30 and 43 of the Convention, which specifically pertain to the question of precedent. In Protocol No. 14, which is now fully applicable, there is a further provision which al-

lows three-member panels to judge cases both on admissibility and on the substance in areas where there is already well-established case law. I think that this perfectly illustrates that case law and the acceptance of case law or departure from such law loom very large in the thoughts of the Court.

CHRISTINE KADDOUS

I just want to add a comment about the case law of the European Court of Justice. In my point of view, its case law is very transparent as to the issue of reconsideration of previous decisions. This transparency was notably obvious in the cases I mentioned, in the Akrich and the Metock cases but also in Keck and Mithouard. The Court of Justice does not hesitate to indicate clearly in its case that it is reconsidering a previous decision, whereas other jurisdictions don't like to state it expressly or even try to hide it. So, I would rather support that transparency is at the advantage of the European Court of Justice. However, I must admit that the Court does not always give the necessary explanations on the reasons why it reconsiders its previous judgments. One can easily imagine that the reversal is often the result of intense deliberations, with the consequence that the judges composing the chamber did not agree or did not fully agree on the detailed motivation which should be given and which led to the reconsideration of the previous decisions. This is a rather unsatisfactory situation from a legal point of view that should be avoided as much as possible.

PAUL MAHONEY

If the Strasbourg Court overrules previous case law, it is to raise the level of human rights protection available for the individual applicant. "Overruling" judgements thus go against the respondent government, which represents the general interest. I am not aware that there have been any cases of reversal of case law in favour of the respondent government, lowering a previously existing level of human rights requirements incumbent on it. And indeed, some judges in separate opinions have argued that, as a matter of principle, that it is not possible: It is not possible for the Court to go back on case law so as to reduce the level of protection available. It is a bit like a lobster pot: once the government has got into it, it cannot get out; there is only one way forward. This issue may come to the fore in the future, with the recent wave of anti-terrorist and security legislation in various countries, which does appear to represent a step backwards in terms of human rights protection. It will be interesting to see how the Strasbourg Court reacts if it is confronted with arguments to that effect.

In Luxembourg three weeks ago we had a meeting between the British judges of the ECJ and judges from the higher British courts. The latter judges said that, although they do not like the style of the Luxembourg judgements, they prefer them. They are told: Do this or do that. And at least they know that the cases are binding; whereas with the Strasbourg judgements, which are more diffuse, they quite often do not know whether the judgement is binding, how it is binding and what it is exactly that they must or must not do. The fact that EU law has primacy over national law, and the fact that the Treaty clearly gives a monopoly of interpretation of EU law to the ECJ, make life much easier for the national judges. They can accept that, and they find it relatively easy to operate with the more categorical judgements. They prefer them.

On another point, life will become interesting in the future with the accession of the EU to the European Convention on Human Rights. This will integrate the precedents on human rights matters between the two Courts, but fears have been expressed in some quarters that this accession may mean that the Strasbourg Court will start intruding into the monopoly of interpretation that the ECJ has over EU law; in particular in relation to those guarantees in the European Convention on Human Rights where there is a reference back to national law, domestic law. Was a contested measure "lawful", "prescribed by law" or "in accordance with the law", for example? In an EU context that will be a reference back to EU law. In such cases, the Strasbourg Court will be obliged to look at the EU law and what it requires in the circumstances. There are some judges in Luxembourg who are a little worried that accession of the EU to the Human Rights Convention will not simply mean unification of case law on human rights issues between the two Courts, but may mean even some sort of inroads being made into their monopoly of interpretation of EU law as it is.

SIMON PLANZER

I would like to briefly come back to Professor Caflisch's remark that in a judicial system, which does not recognise a stare decisis doctrine, a lower court runs the risk that its judgement is reversed by higher courts if it does not follow accepted case law. But this does also offer the chance to lower courts to suggest new approaches. And occasionally, the higher courts may choose to follow those suggestions. At the ECJ, such attempts have also occurred as we know, for instance in Jégo Quéré.

JOHN TEMPLE LANG

It seems to me that the fear of the court in Strasbourg that the Chairman has referred to, is an exaggeration primarily because of two things. First, the court in Strasbourg has said in the *Bosphorus* judgement that the protection of human rights by the Court of Justice is equivalent to the protection in Strasbourg and, therefore, that there is normally no need for the Strasbourg Court to review judgements of the Court of Justice on human rights issues. I am paraphrasing what the court in Strasbourg said but I think that this is a fair way of paraphrasing it. The other reason why I think it is unlikely that the court in Strasbourg will criticise the Court of Justice too frequently is because the Court of Justice may well, quite properly in applying the charter, go further than the Strasbourg Court would be entitled to go applying the Convention. So, the fear, if a fear is to be expressed, is that the Court of Justice will go further than expected rather than the Strasbourg Court would go further than expected.

PAUL MAHONEY

The *Bosphorus* judgement concerned an action brought against a State as regards measures it had taken in order to fulfil its obligations under an EU text. The argument of the respondent Irish Government was that it had no discretion as to how it implemented the EU text. The Court in Strasbourg accepted that an international obligation of that nature would normally constitute a sufficient justification for the national measures in question, so that there would not be a violation of the Human Rights Convention, given that the EU system provided an "equivalent protection" of human rights already. There was a presumption of compliance with the European Convention standards within the EU system. The need for that interpretive construction of State responsibility for actions of international organisations so as to allow people to bring a case in Strasbourg against a state and so indirectly challenge an action by an EU institution will disappear as soon as the EU accedes to the Human Rights Convention. It is, therefore, an open question whether the Strasbourg Court will continue to maintain the same degree of judicial restraint in relation to cases brought, not against a State, but directly against the EU, in other words one of the EU institutions. The Strasbourg Court may say that it recognises the EU institutions as enjoying a margin of appreciation comparable to the notion of "equivalent protection" that it applied in the *Bosphorus* case. But that is by no means sure. We will have to wait and see. The degree of judicial control that the Strasbourg Court will exercise in relation to EU acts is an issue here. How deeply will it go into the question of compliance with human rights standards in EU cases? A "light-touch" control as in *Bosphorus* or stricter control as in cases against States?

The fear that I was referring to and which I do not share – I agree with John Temple Lang there – is a different fear, namely that the Strasbourg Court may be prompted to say things about the interpretation of EU law or even the basic features of the EU law in its judgements. To give one example: By virtue of the right of access to a court under the Human Rights Convention, if persons feel that there has been an unlawful interference with one of their rights and obligations as protected under national law, they are guaranteed that it will be a judge, a court, that decides that dispute and not an administrative authority and there must be a reasonable degree of access to court. Individuals do not have unlimited or free access directly to the ECJ. So, it may well be that there will be challenges brought against EU law on that ground. To give another example: potential complainants are obliged under the European Convention to exhaust domestic remedies before applying to Strasbourg. Under EU law, EU acts implemented within the national legal system may be challenged before the national courts; these courts, but not the parties, are empowered and sometimes obliged to refer the case to Luxembourg for an authoritative preliminary ruling on the issue of EU law raised in the case. What if a national court unreasonably refuses to refer a case to the Luxembourg Court? Could that be considered to be an interference with the free access to a court? In which event, would the Strasbourg Court have to look at whether under EU law there should have been a reference to the Luxembourg Court? It may, therefore, be that indirectly the Strasbourg Court will be called on to interpret pure matters of EU law; and that is what is raising some fears in EU circles. I do not share those fears, but it is easy to say that there is a whole range of interesting issues concerning the relationship between the European High Courts that will explode once the EU accedes to the Human Rights Convention.

CHRISTINE KADDOUS
It is rather a question what is going on in the negotiations for the accession for the European Union to the open Convention of Human Rights. These kinds of issues may be discussed with provisions on this point.

PAUL MAHONEY
I do not know at what stage exactly the procedure is at the moment, but the Council of the European Union, that is the EU institution that represents the governments, was recently in the

process of drafting a mandate to give to the European Commission. On the basis of that mandate the European Commission will then have to negotiate with the Council of Europe the terms of an accession agreement. There will be an international treaty between the EU and the Council of Europe covering the terms of the EU accession. The Lisbon Treaty, in Protocol No. 8, lists conditions which must be fulfilled within the framework of accession. In particular, the specificity of the EU and of EU law and the prerogatives of the institutions of the EU must be duly taken into account in the arrangements figuring in the accession agreement. It may be that the agreement will say something about the relationship between the two Courts, but I do not know. The terms of the mandate and what is going on between the government representatives and the European Commission are confidential. The accession agreement will have to be ratified by all the 27 EU States according to their national procedures and by all the 47 Council of Europe States according to their national procedures. Among the 47 Council of Europe States, there is the Russian Federation, Armenia, Azerbaijan etc. who may have their own interests as to how the relationship between the EU and the Council of Europe should develop.

CARL BAUDENBACHER
And this country probably also has its own interests, the country which is hosting this conference.

4th Panel
Precedent in WTO Law

Introduction

MICHAEL WAIBEL

I am honoured to chair the last panel of this conference on the subject of precedent in the World Trade Organization (WTO).

In February 2008, the Appellate Body (AB) decision in US – *Stainless Steel* triggered a debate on precedent in the WTO. It held that WTO panels had to advance cogent reasons in order to depart from a previous decision of the AB, but also highlighted that *"it was well settled that AB reports are not binding, except with respect to resolving the particular dispute between the parties"*.

The AB expressed a deep concern about the panel's decision to depart from well-established AB jurisprudence clarifying the interpretation of the same legal issues. It was essential for the security of predictability of the world trading system that *"absent cogent reasons, an adjudicatory body will resolve the same legal question in the same way in subsequent cases"*.

The EC had requested that the AB confirms that there is not only an expectation that panels follow AB findings, but an obligation by virtue of the hierarchically superior position of the AB with respect to panels. The United States took the view that binding precedent would undermine the legitimacy of the WTO and would go against the grain of what the drafters of the WTO covered agreements intended.

The implications of this ruling by the Appellate Body and the continuing debate about the role of precedent in the WTO is the subject of this panel. On account of their strong persuasive power, Appellate Body decisions are often regarded as a form of non-binding precedent. Panels routinely incorporate reasoning from Appellate Body decisions into their decisions.

We have three distinguished panellists to enlighten us about this subject. Let me introduce them briefly.

The first speaker is Professor Rachel Brewster, who is on the faculty of the Harvard Law School, where her research and teaching concentrate on international trade and international relations. She has a background both in law and political science and has published widely in international law journals. She will engage us in a thought experiment, showing us what a rigorous application of a doctrine of precedent would mean for the WTO and express some scepticism about whether the current WTO legal order does conform to such a system.

Our second speaker is Professor Akio Shimizu from Waseda Law School. His research concentrates on international trade law. He is currently a visiting fellow at the Lauterpacht Centre for International Law at the University of Cambridge where his main research project is examining the WTO's jurisprudence since its inception. He is an extremely well qualified speaker to enlighten us about this subject. He has an LL.M. degree from Yale Law School and is routinely teaching at US law schools in a visiting capacity. He's going to give us a sense of how some of the Appellate Body decisions have developed by looking further at the *US – Stainless Steel* decision in particular.

The last speaker is Mrs Juhi Sud, who is a senior associate in the law firm Vermulst Verhaeghe Graafsma & Bronckers which specialises in WTO dispute settlements. She is admitted to the Brussels and Delhi bars and is a graduate of the Free University of Brussels and Delhi University. Previously, she has worked as an assistant to the Belgian ambassador to India. She will be looking at the focal point of the discussion at precedent in the WTO legal order and the zeroing case law by the panels and the Appellate Body.

Before turning the discussion over to Professor Brewster, let me offer a few general thoughts on precedent in the WTO legal order. Let me do that by comparing the situation of WTO law with general international law. The well known Article 59 of the Statute of the International Court of Justice states: *"The decision of the court has no binding force except as between the parties and in respect of that particular case"*. In the German Interests in Upper Silesia case, the Permanent Court of International Justice (PCIJ) summarized the rationale for the equivalent provision in the statute of the PCIJ: the object of *"Article 59 is simply to prevent legal principles accepted by the Court in a particular case from being binding on other states or in other disputes."*

The rule that we have in Article 59 is really about protecting states against rules being binding on them without their consent, which is one of the foundational principles of international law. States for that very reason are traditionally very adverse to the suggestion that engagements other than those which they have expressly undertaken may be invoked against them. And, therefore, they oppose the development of international law by the way of a doctrine of precedent. And that continues to be very much the default position in international law.

There is in international law a permanent tension between a desire for consistency between decisions in different cases, in similar but different cases and the desire of states to be safeguarded in their ability to consent to every rule of international law before it becomes binding on them. And this is particularly important in areas of international law that do not contain a set of uniform obligations. Let me explain. What amounts to a breach of international law in general depends on the actual content of international legal obligations and especially, insofar as treaties are concerned, these vary considerably from one state to the next. Even customary international law is not uniform in its application to states. In many areas of international law there is, therefore, no uniform set of international legal obligations. This may be contrasted with the position in WTO law, where, because of the single undertaking approach, on the whole the set of legal obligations that bind WTO members are the same.

And this leads me to my first question to the panel. Holding all else equal, would we, therefore, expect less resistance to a system of precedent in the WTO? There are other structural reasons for a difference in terms of acceptance of precedent between general international law and WTO and these include the hierarchy between the panels and the Appellate Body and in general the much higher degree of specificity of WTO legal rules as compared to general international law.

My second question to the panel is: What precisely do we mean by the term precedent? It appears that when we talk about precedent in relation to WTO law, that term is often used in a very loose sense. So, precedent can mean a variety of things. Do we mean, as we use the term in ordinary language, that because something was done in the past on account of reason we would like to do the same thing in the future? Is it a reason for deciding a similar case in the future in the same way because a series of related cases might crystallise a precedent? Do we mean by precedent a decision rule that has persuasive force but is not binding? Do we mean a rule that has been solidified in a long line of decisions, thatthereby enhances the authority and legitimacy of that rule? Do we view precedent as a contribution to the stock of legal knowledge that builds on the wisdom of various WTO panellists, responding to arguments presented to them by lawyers?

In this context, Sir Hersch Lauterpacht has remarked in "The Function of Law in the International Community in 1933":

"The imperceptible process in which the judicial decision ceases to be an application of existing law and becomes a source of law for the future is almost a religious mystery into which it is unseemly to pry ... It is of little import whether the pronouncements of the Court are in the nature of evidence or of a source of international law they are largely identical with it."

So, Hersch Lauterpacht suggests in that quotation that international courts, even in 1933, and we have since then advanced beyond that position, play a critical role in the development of international law because the distinction between interpreting and creating law as far as international law is concerned is a fiction.

There is interpretive power on behalf of international courts and tribunals because courts and tribunals are required, routinely, to interpret broad provisions, fill gaps and clarify ambiguities. These judicial interpretations are then routinely looked at by states, courts, other courts and academics as evidence of the content of international law. So, seen in this light, is it really useful to distinguish in the context of WTO law whether judicial decisions are evidence of international law or are a source of law? Is it useful to distinguish a notion of non-binding precedent and binding precedent? Is it useful to distinguish between de facto precedent and de jure precedent? Is it a misnomer or is it even a hypocritical distinction? As a practical matter, do interpretations of provisions adopted by the Appellate Body of the WTO not radiate far outside the confines of a particular dispute?

My third question is: why would a system of precedent emerge in the WTO law in the first place? If we look at the precedent in common law systems, the development of precedent, as we have heard already during this conference, has been intimately linked to the wide availability of judicial decisions. And if we look again at the interval period, back then it was noted that international law lacked precedential effect largely because the decisions of international courts and tribunals were not widely available. Now, with respect to the WTO, that position has fundamentally changed. Panel reports and Appellate Body reports are available. Does that simple fact almost automatically account for a gradual development of a system of precedent over time?

Fourthly, what are the incentives for the actors in the WTO to establish a system of precedent? What are the costs and benefits? The adjudicators, on the one hand, in WTO disputes may be inclined to try and impose their policy preferences on the international trading system. And this might explain why they are ready to expend time and effort to develop reasoning that will stand the test of time and will be accepted by peers in this system. They generally will want future generations of WTO panellists and future generations of WTO Appellate Body members to defer to their decisions. This factor might explain why such a system of precedent could develop. Adjudicators are generally reluctant to admit that they or their peers were wrong in the past. This consideration could give rise to a system of precedent. From the perspective of litigants in WTO disputes, it may depend quite considerably on whether they expect to be repeat players in similar cases in the future. Do they expect to derive benefits from the development of a precedent with respect to a particular legal question or not? We can see that quite clearly in the zeroing case law.

The next question is, whether the debate over the role of precedent in the WTO is in reality a proxy battle over who has interpretive power and the power to develop international trade law in the WTO more broadly; about how interpretative authority ought to be shared. It is linked to the broader debate whether the WTO dispute settlement system is a proper judicial system. Should it be rule-bound or should it rather be a system of diplomacy with judicial elements of dispute settlement? Turning to concrete decisions, the decision in US – *Stainless Steel*: Is that decision a radical departure from previous cases decided by the Appellate Body or is it a gradual evolution in the development of the WTO Dispute Settlement Body into a fully fledged judicial body? The Appellate Body does not use the word precedent in that decision. Why? Did it anticipate that using the term precedent would lead to strong reactions by Member States? Why has the issue of precedent come up almost exclusively in the context of zeroing cases? Are these cases special? Is it perhaps because of Article 17 Paragraph 6 of the Anti-Dumping Agreement?

Finally, a very broad, general question: Does the WTO regime with the Dispute Settlement Understanding at its core, often called the jewel in the crown of the WTO, provide a glimpse into the future for the role of precedent in dispute settlement in international law more generally?

The System of Precedent
(or the Lack Thereof) at the WTO

RACHEL BREWSTER[1]

The United States government consistently denies the existence of a system of jurisprudence at the World Trade Organization (WTO), insisting rather that there is simply a series of case reports. This may appear to be a minor semantic point, but it is a telling statement. Whether the WTO is ambitiously engaged in an experiment of law development through its dispute resolution system or is more modestly settling disputes on a case-by-case basis is an issue of significance to governments. Questions regarding the existence of a system of precedent (or the lack thereof) at the WTO engage similar issues – in particular, who has the institutional competence to issue binding interpretations of the WTO agreements?

Formally, the WTO's Dispute Settlement Understanding (DSU) does not have a system of precedent. Nonetheless, there are questions regarding whether the WTO is developing an informal system of precedent and whether such developments are beneficial for the international trading system. It is these questions that my presentation will address. My discussion will cover three topics. I will begin with a review of the dispute settlement process. While some participants here are intimately familiar with the WTO dispute resolution process, I would like to highlight some institutional design features of the system that would become important if the WTO adopted a rigorous system of precedent. I will then define what I mean by precedent and distinguish between horizontal and vertical systems of precedent. Finally, I will discuss what implications a system of precedent would have for the WTO dispute resolution.

I. WTO Dispute Resolution

Let me begin my discussion with some background on the WTO system of dispute resolution. All Member States of the WTO have standing to bring legal claims through the Dispute Settlement Understanding (DSU). The complaining state and the respondent state engage in consultations to resolve the dispute for at least 60 days. If the parties have not reached a mutually-acceptable solution by the end of that time, the complaining state can request the formation of a panel to adjudicate the dispute. The Dispute Settlement Body (DSB) will then vote on whether to establish a panel. The voting rule is that of reverse consensus – the request to establish a panel is accepted unless there is a consensus of states against establishing a panel. Ef-

---

[1] Thank you to the University of St.Gallen and Professor Carl Baudenbacher for hosting this conference. Additional thanks are due to Simon Planzer for organizing the conference and to Michael Waibel for moderating this panel. Andrew Breidenbach provided valuable assistance in preparing this presentation.

fectively, the member state that requested the panel would have to vote against it for the vote to fail. No request for a panel has ever been refused (although parties can and do delay the request for a DSB meeting).

The panel consists of three ad hoc arbitrators. I use the term ad hoc because there is no standing body of lower court judges. Unlike a lower court, the panelists are selected by the disputing Member States for that specific case. There is not a vetting process for panelists, like there is for Appellate Body members. Although the WTO Secretariat keeps a list of persons who could serve as arbitrators, there is no requirement that the panelist is to be selected from that list. The WTO Secretariat is formally involved with the selection of arbitrators only if the parties cannot agree. The panelists do not unlike a standing body of lower court judges, expect to regularly hear cases in the future. Most panelists serve only once and few panelists will serve more than two or three times. Consequently, there are few opportunities for panelists to develop group norms regarding interpretation or precedent. In addition, since there is no expectation that a panelist who performs well will be promoted to the Appellate Body, there is little incentive for panelists to adopt norms that are deferential to the Appellate Body's decisions.

The panel hears issues of fact and law and issues a report detailing its factual findings and its application of WTO rules to those facts. If the parties do not appeal the case, then the DSB adopts the panel's report by reverse consensus. If either party announces its decision to appeal, then the case is assigned to the Appellate Body.

The Appellate Body is a standing body of seven judges. The judges are designed to be geographically representative, but they are also representative of the largest economies. From the inception of the WTO, the United States, the European Communities and Japan have always had a representative on the Appellate Body, and a Chinese judge recently assumed a seat on it as well. Although it is not explicit in WTO rules, it seems unlikely that any of these four states will be without a member of the Appellate Body in the foreseeable future.

Although, there are seven members of the Appellate Body, only three judges are assigned to hear each appeal. There is no procedure for an en banc appeal, where all of the members of the Appellate Body would rehear the case. The Appellate Body's review is limited to issues of law; the Appellate Body hearing is not designed to hear factual evidence and the Appellate Body panel is supposed to accept the panel's finding of fact. The DSB adopts the Appellate Body report by reverse consensus.

The WTO litigation process often continues on to a second "compliance" stage (Article 21.5 hearings) of adjudication and then a third "remedy" stage (Article 22.6 arbitrations) if the respondent state fails to come into compliance with the decision of DSB. These stages are less relevant to the system of precedent so I do not discuss them here.

In addition to establishing the dispute resolution process, the text of the DSU sets out the overarching goals of the institution. First, the process is designed to provide multilateral means of resolving disputes and thereby end unilateral state actions (most notably US unilateral sanctioning through Section 301). Second, the process is designed to provide security and predictability to the multilateral trading system by clarifying the existing provisions of the WTO texts. Third, the DSU makes explicit that the dispute resolution process is not designed to create new rules: The DSU states that the DSB, the Appellate Body and the panels may neither add to nor diminish the rights and obligations provided in the WTO agreements. Finally, it is notable that the DSU text does not include the words "precedent" or "stare decisis." This silence is not dispositive but is suggestive that the Member States could not reach an agreement on whether a system of precedent would be beneficial. The DSU text goes into great detail on how the system should function, including panel procedures and applicable rules. The absence of any mention of stare decisis or precedent would be surprising if there were a consensus among the Member States that such a system was intended.

II. Systems of Precedent

Against this background, then, it is interesting to consider how a system of precedent would function at the WTO. I want to be explicit in what I mean by precedent as to avoid confusion.

The idea of precedent implies more than a judgement that the prior decision is persuasive and remains a good reason for justifying the outcome of a case. Rather, the idea of precedent is that the established rule has a special status independent of its persuasiveness. Precedent is content independent.[2] The hallmark of precedent is a sense of obligation, not simply persuasiveness: A judge must abide by a rule even if she is not persuaded by the logic or the wisdom of the rule. The judge is constrained from adopting the rule that she believes to be superior. In this way, precedent can change the meaning of a text. For instance, if there are two equally reasonable interpretations of the text, a system of precedent can make only one of these interpretations valid in future cases.

Precedent has two aspects: horizontal and vertical. Horizontal precedent – what American lawyers call stare decisis – is the idea that a court must follow its own previous decisions unless there is some articulated "special justification" for deviating from that rule. Vertical precedent refers to the obligation of a lower court or arbitrator to follow the rulings of a higher court. Vertical precedent alters the judge's or arbitrator's reading of the legal text. Even if the judge or arbitrator believes that the legal rules established by the higher court are in error, he is under an obligation to follow the higher court's ruling.

How would these concepts play out in the WTO system? First, I will discuss horizontal precedent and then turn to a discussion of vertical precedent.

---

2   See Frederick Schauer, Precedent, 39 Stan. L. Rev. 571 (1987).

A. Horizontal Precedent

Does it exist at the WTO now?

I am hard-pressed to think so. There is certainly a practice of citing past decisions, but this practice does not indicate that there is system of precedent at the WTO. A court or an arbitration panel may cite a decision because it finds the reasoning persuasive, not because it believes itself to be bound by that decision. Furthermore, there is not much in the language of WTO opinions that indicates that it is actually bound by past decisions. The Appellate Body has never said that it would have decided a case differently but for the existence of precedent.

If we believed that a system of horizontal precedent at the WTO would be a positive development, what conditions would we want for the creation of precedent?

There is no obvious answer here, but there are a few immediate concerns that we should consider. While every WTO Appellate Body decision could be given precedential effect, each such decision represents the view of only a minority of the Appellate Body. As such, any one opinion is not representative of the entire Body. We could have an odd situation where a minority opinion could bind the majority into the future. Here, the lack of an en banc rehearing procedure is important. Because the full Appellate Body cannot hear a case, the potential problem of 'minority precedent' will be a recurring one. An alternative may be to adopt a system similar to that of the Mexican Supreme Court, which permits a ruling to become precedent only if a particular issue has been decided the same way in five consecutive cases. This mitigates (although does not completely avoid) the concerns with a minority opinion binding the majority.

In addition, it is far from clear that a system of horizontal precedent is consistent with the overarching goals of the WTO DSU. As discussed above, the WTO dispute resolution system aims to clarify the text and to provide predictability and stability to the international trading system. Yet, it also closely guards the rights and obligations of states as set out in the text of WTO agreements. Remember, these agreements are detailed political deals, based as much on what is politically feasible as on broad principles. The concern with horizontal precedent within the WTO system is that it can alter the rights and obligations of Member States.

Consider a situation where there are two equally reasonable interpretations of a WTO text. If the Appellate Body adopts a system of precedent and selects interpretation A as the operative interpretation, then this interpretation now has a superior status to interpretation B. A government that legitimately relied on interpretation B to justify its policy can now no longer do so. This seems to diminish the rights of that state – the state may find its policies declared out of compliance with WTO law because of the precedential effect of decisions, even if a later Appellate Body panel of judges deems the state's interpretation of the text a reasonable interpretation.

There is also a subtle issue here of equal access to WTO rule making. Most dispute settlement engages developed states. Developed states are a small minority of the WTO membership but are involved as parties in a majority of the WTO disputes. As a result, developed states would have a greater ability to shape precedent. Developing countries, who use the system less frequently, may find that many issues of great importance are already resolved by the time these states bring a complaint.

How does this balance against the need for stability and predictability in the world trading system?

It is not obvious that a system of precedent is necessary to achieve stability and predictability in the world trading system.[3] As the conference's panel on international arbitration discussed, international businesses frequently send their disputes to arbitration (where there is not a robust system of precedent) without undermining the stability and predictability of the international economic system. Similarly, the WTO system also does not appear to be in a state of crisis without a system of precedent. The current system of relying on the persuasive power of past opinion appears to be serving the Appellate Body well. Its case law is relatively consistent even without a system of precedent and it retains the flexibility to adapt its rules to new developments, such as the treatment of measures aimed at environmental or health and safety goals.

B. Vertical Precedent

Does it exist at the WTO now?

There is some evidence that the Appellate Body is attempting to develop a system of vertical precedent. As other members of this panel have discussed, decisions of the Appellate Body in recent zeroing cases appear to be arguing that panelists have an obligation to follow Appellate Body interpretations of the WTO Agreements. Most notably, in US – Stainless Steel, the Appellate Body stated that, *"[w]e are deeply concerned about the Panel's decision to depart from well-established Appellate Body jurisprudence clarifying the interpretation of the same legal issues. The Panel's approach has serious implications for the proper functioning of the WTO dispute settlement system, as explained above."*[4] Here, the Appellate Body seems to be saying that the ad hoc panelists should accept Appellate Body decisions on interpretative issues even if the panelists believe that the Appellate Body's interpretation is in error. Indeed, the panelists in the US – Stainless Steel dispute had decided that the Appellate Body's previous interpretations were in error, noting that:

> *"We are troubled by the fact that the principal basis of the Appellate Body's reasoning in the zeroing cases seems to be premised on an interpretation that does not have a solid textual basis in the relevant treaty provisions. We recall the rules on treaty interpretation (supra, paras 7.3– 7.5) which we have to follow in these proceedings. We are of the view that a good faith inter-*

---

3 Arguably, the greatest service that the DSU has done in terms of providing predictably and stability to the international trade system has nothing to do with issues of interpretation. The major benefit of the DSU has been ending the pre-Uruguay Round practice of some states (mostly the United States) of making independent judgements on the legality of other state's practices and unilaterally imposing sanctions.

4 *United States – Final Anti-Dumping Measures on Stainless Steel from Mexico* – Report of the Appellate Body, WT/DS344/AB/R, 30 April 2008, at p. 162.

pretation of the ordinary meaning of the texts of Articles VI:1 and VI:2 of the GATT 1994 and Article 2.1 of the Anti-Dumping Agreement, read in their context and in light of the object and purpose of the mentioned agreements, does not exclude an interpretation that allows the concept of dumping to exist on a transaction-specific basis. We recall that according to the standard of review that we have to follow in these proceedings (supra, paras 7.1–7.2), we are precluded from excluding an interpretation which we find permissible, even if there may be other permissible interpretations."[5]

How would a system of vertical precedent function?

A system of vertical precedent is much less concerning than a system of horizontal precedent. The DSU text implicitly establishes the Appellate Body as a higher legal authority than the panels. Although the DSU text never explicitly states that the Appellate Body's determination should be given greater legal authority than the panels' analysis, the Appellate Body can reverse the panel's legal analysis.[6] The institutional design of the DSU thus indicates that the Appellate Body was intended to have greater authority than ad hoc panels in interpreting the WTO Agreements. Having a system of vertical precedent may also be functionally desirable. The Appellate Body does not have the authority to remand cases, an institutional design feature that is problematic if the panel follows its own legal theory and thereby fails to make findings of fact on issues that are legally relevant under the Appellate Body's preferred legal analysis. An explicit system of vertical precedent may mitigate (although not eliminate) this problem.

While the idea of vertical precedent is straightforward, it is less clear how a system of vertical precedent would practically function within the DSU system. As I highlighted earlier, ad hoc panelists are quite different from lower court judges. In a domestic court system, the higher court has some control over the lower courts. The control can be direct (the power to remand a case for reconsideration) or indirect (control over the lower judge's likelihood of promotion). The Appellate Body lacks both of these mechanisms to control. It cannot remand cases back to the panel for reconsideration if the panel fails to follow the Appellate Body's ruling. Failing to follow the Appellate Body's rulings might decrease the panelist's probability of being selected for another WTO panel, but then again might not. The Member States select the panelists, not the Appellate Body, so the panelist could be selected again if the Member States approve of the panel's reasoning.

Naturally, many panelists may accept the Appellate Body's ruling as binding on them as a legal matter, so the matter of control would be moot. Not all panelists have believed this to be the case, however. As the US – Stainless Steel panel demonstrates, panelists have been known to reject prior Appellate Body rulings. In these cases, the Appellate Body's limited control over the panelists will limit the extent to which that body can implement a system of vertical precedent.

---

5 *United States – Final Anti-Dumping Measures on Stainless Steel from Mexico* – Report of the Panel, WT/DS344/R, 20 December 2007, at p. 7.119.
6 Article 17 (13) of the Dispute Settlement Understanding.

As a final note, I want to point out that all of the discussion of precedent at the WTO has been on the liability side of WTO litigation and not the remedy side. That is, all of the Appellate Body's rulings are on questions of what qualifies as a violation of the WTO Agreement. On the remedy side of WTO litigation – where the question is what actions the complaining state is permitted to undertake in face of continuing non-compliance by the respondent state – there are only arbitration panel rulings. Under the DSU system, an arbitration panel reviews (and almost always modifies) the complaining state's request for a remedy, but this decision is not subject to appeal.[7] This feature of the DSU's institutional design is notable because it means that the system of precedent would apply only to issues of liability, and not to the (equally important) issue of remedies. This is particularly odd given the divergent approaches arbitration panels have taken towards calculating retaliation awards.[8] If there is an area in need of greater predictability, the remedy regime is a far more obvious candidate for governmental and scholarly attention.

---

7   Article 22 (6) of the Dispute Settlement Understanding.
8   See Holger Spamann, The Myth of 'Rebalancing' Retaliation in the WTO Dispute Settlement Practice, 9 J. Int'l Econ. L. 31, 75–77 (2006) (critiquing the methodology of calculating retaliation on several grounds and noting that the panel frequently appears to be splitting the difference between the figures offered by the two parties).

Introduction to Treaty Interpretation by the WTO Panels and Appellate Body

AKIO SHIMIZU

Before I start, I would like to thank Professor Baudenbacher and all the other organisers for inviting me to this conference and for giving me an opportunity to speak.

As our Chair, Dr. Michael Waibel, very expertly summarized in the beginning, there is no doctrine of precedent for adjudication between states in international law. Does that mean we can just say, that with the WTO law being part of public international law, that there is no doctrine of precedent in the WTO dispute settlement procedures at all? If the answer is yes, there is not much to add. The answer, of course, cannot be just simply "yes" or "no". Binding adjudicatory decisions ascertain the rights and obligations of disputants at a particular moment and the parties to an adjudicated dispute must comply with the decision. The WTO Appellate Body and the panels issue reports that are always adopted by the Dispute Settlement Body as they are. The disputing WTO members addressed in the recommendations and rulings in the reports must comply with them.

The existence of the compliance can be scrutinized in the DSU Article 21.5 proceedings. By definition, the Article 21.5 panel, and the Appellate Body if it is appealed, are bound by the legal interpretations included in the reports by the original panel and the Appellate Body.

The more important question is what is meant by saying previous Appellate Body and panel reports are not binding in subsequent cases in the regular dispute settlement proceedings. Are the interpretations provided by the panels and the Appellate Body entirely case specific? The panel in US – Stainless Steel (Mexico) made a famous decision in 2007 "to respectfully disagree" with the previous interpretation developed by the Appellate Body regarding the consistency of simple zeroing with the Anti-Dumping Agreement.[1] The panel must have considered previous interpretations as being not case specific but that they had some meaning for subsequent cases. Otherwise the panel did not have to "respectfully disagree" with the previous interpretation of the Appellate Body and could have made their decision entirely on their own.

The Appellate Body stated in the same case that *"subsequent panels were not free to disregard the legal interpretation and the ratio decidendi contained in previous Appellate Body reports"*[2] and reversed the panel's finding that simple zeroing in reviews was not inconsistent with the GATT

---

1 Panel Report, *United States – Final Anti-Dumping Measures on Stainless Steel from Mexico*, WT/DS344/R, adopted 20 May 2008, as modified by Appellate Body Report WT/DS344/AB/R, DSR 2008:II, 599, para. 7.106.
2 Appellate Body Report, *United States – Final Anti-Dumping Measures on Stainless Steel from Mexico*, WT/DS344/AB/R, adopted 20 May 2008, DSR 2008:II, 513, para. 158.

1994 and the Anti-Dumping Agreement. Mr Vermulst, who was supposed to be here, was focusing his presentation on the treatment of zeroing in the anti-dumping proceedings by the related panels and the Appellate Body. I'm sure Ms Sud will tell us on his behalf all about zeroing itself as well as about the findings made by the panel and Appellate Body on zeroing. I will not say anything more about zeroing itself but would like to briefly point out a few other things that I noticed in this Appellate Body report.

The Appellate Body in US – Stainless Steel (Mexico) based its idea that subsequent panels were not free to disregard the legal interpretation and the *ratio decidendi* contained in previous Appellate Body reports on ensuring security and predictability in the WTO dispute settlement system. The Appellate Body referred to Article 3.2 of the Dispute Settlement Understanding, which contained the words, security and predictability. Security and predictability are pursued not uniquely in the WTO dispute settlement procedures but in any system of adjudication. The Appellate Body made a general statement: "*[A]n adjudicatory body will resolve the same legal question in the same way in a subsequent case.*"[3] It sought reinforcement of its argument in a footnote[4] by referring to an article by Sir Hersh Lauterpacht published in 1931, which was introduced by our Chair at the beginning of this session, and a decision of the ICTY (International Criminal Tribunal for the Former Yugoslavia) made in March 2002 as well as a decision of the ICSID (International Centre for Settlement of Investment Disputes) Arbitration Tribunal made in March 2007.

The ICTY decision was especially pertinent for the Appellate Body. The ICTY found that *"each Trial Chamber was not free to disagree with decisions of law made by the Appeals Chamber"* because of the right of appeal, the fair trial requirement and the right of the accused to have like cases treated alike.[5] The hierarchical structure of the WTO dispute settlement system necessarily requires panels to follow previous Appellate Body reports that addressed the same legal issues.[6]

One thing I would like to add is that the Appellate Body decision in US – Stainless Steel (Mexico) had an important qualification. It stated that an adjudicatory body would resolve the same legal question in the same way in a subsequent case "absent cogent reasons".[7] Future panels are not asked to blindly follow previous Appellate Body decisions. If there are cogent reasons, panels do not have to accept previous Appellate Body interpretations and the Appellate Body do not have to follow its own previous reports, either. The Appellate Body did not elaborate on the qualification of cogent reasons. It only cited an ICSID Arbitration Tribunal decision in 2007, which stated, "*subject to compelling contrary grounds, it has a duty to adopt solutions established in a series of consistent cases*".[8] It shows that "cogent reasons" can be replaced with "compelling contrary grounds". What "cogent reasons" and "compelling contrary grounds" could mean more specifically remains to be answered in the future.

---

3   Ibid., para. 160.
4   Ibid., footnote 313 to para. 160.
5   Ibid.
6   Ibid., para. 161.
7   Ibid., para. 160.
8   Ibid., footnote 313 to para. 160.

It is sure at this moment that the Appellate Body did not consider the Panel in *US – Stainless Steel (Mexico)* to have cogent reasons to justify its deviation from the interpretation on zeroing in the previous Appellate Body reports.

Notwithstanding what the Appellate Body said in its report for *US – Stainless Steel (Mexico)*, subsequent panels and, for that matter, the Appellate Body chambers have not been disregarding previous panel and Appellate Body reports. On the contrary, they have closely scrutinized previous findings. This is obvious if you just look at the footnotes in any panel or Appellate Body report, as Professor Brewster pointed out. You will find extensive citations to previous panel and Appellate Body reports. Citations to GATT 1947 panel reports were frequently made in the earlier WTO cases and they included both adapted and unadapted GATT 1947 panel reports. Recent panel reports refer to so many previous reports that they usually include a very long list of cited reports. It seems, panels cite previous panel and Appellate Body reports when they agree with the interpretations that were shown in them. Even when panels do not agree with some previous panels, they still cite them just to say that they don't agree with them. The cases of disagreement are fewer in number than those of agreement. The Appellate Body also extensively cites previous panel and Appellate Body reports. When the Appellate Body does not agree with previous panels, they says so of course. When it does not agree with the interpretations provided by previous Appellate Body reports, it does not appear to say anything about that.

Why do the panels and the Appellate Body cite so many previous reports? Obviously because there are all these panel and Appellate Body reports that can be referred to. The reports go in detail with a number of pages; hundreds of pages or more than a thousand pages in some cases. They often contain a number of issues on interpretations. The fact that the same or similar issues, both substantive and procedural, keep appearing in different cases, promote more citations to previous decisions.

Unlike international arbitration, it is relatively easy to look for previous cases in the WTO. They are all in an online database. The parties in a dispute before a panel or the Appellate Body always refer to the old reports. Valuable technical assistance is given to the panels and the Appellate Body by the WTO Secretariat and the Appellate Body Secretariat respectively. They have been dutifully archiving and analysing the past reports as their publications suggest.

The WTO dispute settlement procedures are said to be treaty text oriented. To begin with, the claims made by the challenging parties have to be based on some provisions in the WTO agreements. The panels and the Appellate Body interpret relevant provisions in the agreements and apply them. As it is now well known, they do so in accordance with the customary rules of the interpretation of public international law, which are considered mainly to be expressed in Articles 31 and 32 of the Vienna Convention of the Law of Treaties.

The more previous reports the panels and the Appellate Body cite, the more authoritative and convincing they look. Who do they have to convince? Most of all, they obviously have to convince the disputing parties and in case of the panels, they also have to convince the Appellate

Body. The Appellate Body often states in their reports that the original panels erred in various legal issues. The Appellate Body is supposed to do that. It is their job to do so. The panels, however, may try to avoid being reversed by the Appellate Body. One way for the panels to be more convincing and to avoid being reversed is to carefully observe the previous decisions made by the Appellate Body regarding similar legal questions.

Even though there is no formal doctrine of binding precedent in the WTO dispute settlement procedures, past cases may have had *de facto* precedential effect even before the Appellate Body expressed its opinion on this issue in *US – Stainless Steel (Mexico)*.

Here is one final question I would like to raise. What if there is a country which persistently argues against the idea of precedential effect in general or against a particular interpretation given by the Appellate Body? Does it or should it have anything to do with the idea of *de facto* precedent? Such a WTO member country may choose to violate the WTO rules despite the dispute settlement procedures and the possibility of retaliation. We need to be very careful about pursuing the doctrine or *de facto* doctrine of precedent in the WTO dispute settlement procedures.

Thank you very much for your kind attention and I am looking forward to hearing more about zeroing from the next speaker.

Precedent in WTO – Zeroing Cases

EDWIN VERMULST AND JUHI SUD[1]

I. Introduction

On behalf of Edwin Vermulst and myself, I would like to thank you all for being here today and I would also like to thank the organisers for giving us this opportunity to speak on the subject of precedent in the WTO.

Much has already been said on the topic by my co-panelists and a mention of certain important zeroing cases has been made. Therefore, it would perhaps be a good idea to just take a step back and consider the interesting question – what is anti-dumping and what is zeroing – and then review the various panel and Appellate Body rulings concerning zeroing, from the point of view of precedent. Through this presentation the endeavor is to make the topic a little bit more lively as zeroing is universally considered to be a very technical issue.

Before starting with the zeroing cases let us first review what the Understanding on Dispute Settlement ("DSU") and the WTO Agreement basically say:

- The WTO Agreement Article XVI:1 states as follows: *"Except as otherwise provided under this Agreement or the Multilateral Trade Agreements,* **the WTO shall be guided by the decisions, procedures and customary practices followed by the CONTRACTING PARTIES** *to GATT 1947 and the bodies established in the framework of GATT 1947."* (Emphasis added)

- DSU Article 3.2 provides that: *"The dispute settlement system of the WTO is a central element in providing* **security and predictability to the multilateral trading system***. The Members recognize that it serves to preserve the rights and obligations of Members under the covered agreements,* **and to clarify the existing provisions of those agreements in accordance with customary rules of interpretation of public international law***. Recommendations and rulings of the DSB cannot add to or diminish the rights and obligations provided in the covered agreements."* (Emphasis added)

- Finally, DSU Article 19.2 provides that: *"In accordance with paragraph 2 of Article 3, in their findings and recommendations, panel and* **Appellate Body cannot add to or diminish the rights and obligations provided in the covered agreements***."* (Emphasis added)

---

1 Vermulst Verhaeghe Graafsma & Bronckers Advocaten, Brussels. E-mail: edwin.vermulst@vvgb-law.com; juhi.sud@vvgb-law.com.

As it can be observed, the central principles regarding dispute settlement are enshrined in the aforementioned articles. Article 3.2 of the DSU establishes the three pillars of the system. First, that the dispute settlement system is central to providing security and predictability to the multilateral trading system. Second, that the existing provisions of the covered agreements need to be clarified in accordance with customary rules of interpretation of public international law. Last, that the recommendations and rulings of the DSB cannot add or diminish the rights and obligations provided in the covered agreements. This latter point is also reiterated in Article 19.2 of the DSU.

It may be useful to consider the actual practice in WTO disputes. As it was also brought to our attention by Professor Shimizu, in every dispute there are routinely cross-references to other panel and Appellate Body reports. Indeed, parties to the dispute and third parties refer to previous panel and Appellate Body rulings to support their arguments and to develop interpretations. Panels and the Appellate Body note and review previous findings in response to the references made by parties to the dispute and third parties. The focus is on the reasoning and approach of the previous panels and the Appellate Body and, if necessary, support for reaching their decisions is found in those reports. Eventually, there seems to be an inherent unsaid approach of the existence of a hierarchy in the system whereby a panel ruling overruled by the Appellate Body is considered determinant of the issue. Needless to say, exceptions exist and the issue of zeroing seemed to be one. In the cases that will be discussed below, the above-mentioned points will be repeatedly observed.

II. The Zeroing Cases

Moving on to the concept of "zeroing", we will take a quick look at the concept itself and the various zeroing cases, which are significant with regard to today's discussion topic.

It is important to note that 84 of the 414 disputes notified to the DSB until 15 September 2010 have involved anti-dumping issues. The dumping margin calculation technique known as "zeroing" has been an issue in 13 of those 84 disputes. A list of these cases is provided below.

7 cases in which the Appellate Body ruled on zeroing issues:

1. EC – Bed Linen (India) [March 2001];

2. US – Corrosion Resistant Steel Sunset Reviews [August 2004];

3. US – Softwood Lumber V (Canada) [August 2004]; US – Softwood Lumber V (compliance) [August 2006];

4. US – Zeroing (EC) [April 2006]; US – Zeroing (EC) (compliance) [May 2009];

5. US – Zeroing (Japan) [January 2007]; US – Zeroing (Japan) (compliance) [August 2009];

6. US – Stainless Steel (Mexico) [April 2008];

7. US – Continued Zeroing [February 2009].

4 additional cases in which panels discussed zeroing:

1. EC – Malleable Cast Iron Tube or Pipe Fittings (Brazil) [March 2003];

2. US – Shrimp (Ecuador) [January 2007];

3. US – Shrimp (Thailand) [February 2008];

4. US – Carrier Bags (Thailand) [February 2010].

2 on-going cases where panels are established:

1. US – Zeroing (Korea) [May 2010];

2. US – Shrimp (Vietnam) [May 2010].

A. What is Zeroing?

What is actually "zeroing"? "Zeroing" refers to the practice, conducted in some jurisdictions, of replacing the actual amount of dumping calculated, for model or sales comparisons that yield negative dumping margins, with a value of zero prior to the final calculation of a weighted-average margin of dumping for the product under investigation. Zeroing has the effect of overstating dumping margins by denying the full impact of non-dumped or negatively-dumped models/export sales on the dumping margin for the product as a whole.

The practical application of this concept is a bit complicated but very interesting. First, per Article 2.1 Anti-Dumping Agreement ("ADA"), 'dumping' is said to occur when *"the export price of the product exported from one country to another is less than the comparable price, in the ordinary course of trade, for the like product when destined for consumption in the exporting country."* In simple words, if an exporter sells the same product at a cheaper price to a customer in the European Union than he sells it to a customer in his own home market, he is said to be dumping. A dumping margin calculation basically entails a comparison between the export price and the domestic sales price called the normal value of the product in question. The various provisions of Article 2 establish the manner in which a dumping margin calculation consistent with the ADA is to be made.

In specific, Article 2.4 ADA lays down that *"a fair comparison shall be made between the export price and the normal value."* Article 2.4.2 ADA provides comparison methods for establishing the existence of dumping. There are two preferred comparison methods:

(i) the method whereby the weighted average normal value is compared with the weighted average of prices of all comparable export transactions; or

(ii) the method whereby the normal value and export prices are compared on a transaction-to-transaction basis.[2]

The exceptional comparison method entails the comparison of the weighted average normal value with the prices of individual export transactions, and may be resorted to if a pattern of export prices which differ significantly among different purchasers, regions or time periods is found.

---

2 Article 2.4.2 ADA: *"Subject to the provisions governing fair comparison in paragraph 4, the existence of margins of dumping during the investigation phase shall normally be established on the basis of a comparison of a weighted average normal value with a weighted average of prices of all comparable export transactions or by a comparison of normal value and export prices on a transaction-to-transaction basis. A normal value established on a weighted average basis may be compared to prices of individual export transactions if the authorities find a pattern of export prices which differ significantly among different purchasers, regions or time periods, and if an explanation is provided as to why such differences cannot be taken into account appropriately by the use of a weighted average-to-weighted average or transaction-to-transaction comparison."*

The table below provides an example of how zeroing is applied when export price and normal value comparisons are made and how it results in inflating the dumping margin.

Simple Zeroing						Without Zeroing		With Zeroing	
Sales Date	Export Trans.	Do-mestic Trans.	Export Avg.	Do-mestic Avg.	Avg.-to-Avg.	Trans.-to-Trans.	Avg.-to-Trans.	Trans.-to-Trans.	Avg.-to-Trans.
02-Sep	5	20	30	30	0	15	25	15	25
04-Sep	5	25	30	30	0	20	25	20	25
08-Sep	25	25	30	30	0	0	5	0	5
10-Sep	30	25	30	30	0	-5	0	0	0
12-Sep	35	25	30	30	0	-10	-5	0	0
16-Sep	35	35	30	30	0	0	-5	0	0
18-Sep	40	35	30	30	0	-5	-10	0	0
20-Sep	45	40	30	30	0	-5	-15	0	0
24-Sep	50	40	30	30	0	-10	-20	0	0
		Amount Dumping			0	0	0	35	55
		Dumping %			0.0%	0.0%	0.0%	13.0%	20.4%

As explained in the example above, the specific sales transactions which resulted in negative dumping margins were replaced by a zero and this resulted in an increase in the dumping margin.

In addition to simple zeroing just discussed, there is also model zeroing. When comparing export price and normal value, investigating authorities generally make the comparison on model-by-model basis or product control number basis, before the results of these model-based/product control number-based calculations are weighted to come to a dumping margin for the exporter concerned. The example below shows a comparison of model sales transactions. Because the non-dumped transaction was replaced by zero, from a zero dumping margin there is a 10% dumping margin. So the effective result of zeroing in this case was the finding of a positive dumping margin when in reality there was no dumping. As a result of model zeroing, dumping will be found as soon as one model is dumped even if all other models are not dumped.

Model Zeroing				
Model	Export Trans.	Domestic Trans.	Unit Dumping	Model Zeroing
A	100	50	-50	0
B	100	100	0	0
C	100	100	0	0
D	100	100	0	0
E	100	150	50	50
TOTAL	500			
	Amount Dumping		0	50
	Dumping %		0.00%	10.00%

Having understood the basic concepts, let us move on to review the various zeroing cases and then evaluate the conclusion regarding the concept of precedent in the WTO through the eyeglass of the "zeroing" cases.

B. The Zeroing Cases

EC – Bed Linen

This was the first case concerning zeroing. In this case, India challenged the European Union for applying model zeroing in an original investigation and alleged a violation of Article 2.4.2 ADA by the European Union.

The Panel agreed with India that model zeroing was not allowed under Article 2.4.2 first sentence and held that:

> "Margin of dumping ... can only be established for the product at issue, and not for individual transactions concerning that product, or discrete models of that product."[3]

The Panel also noted that:

> "Article 2.4.2 specifies that the weighted average normal value shall be compared with 'a weighted average of prices of all comparable export transactions'. In this case, the European Communities' calculation of the final weighted average dumping margin for the product did not, in fact, rest on a comparison with the prices of all comparable export transactions. By counting as zero the results of comparisons showing a 'negative' margin, the European Communities, in effect, changed the prices of the export transactions in those comparisons. It is, in our view, impermissible to 'zero' such 'negative' margins in establishing the existence of dumping for the product under investigation, since this has the effect of changing the results of an otherwise proper comparison."[4]

The Appellate Body upheld the Panel finding and stated that:

> "Whatever the method used to calculate the margins of dumping, in our view, these margins must be, and can only be, established for the product under investigation as a whole."[5]

Additionally, the Appellate Body also noted that:

> "By 'zeroing' the 'negative dumping margins', the European Communities ... did not take fully into account the entirety of the prices of some export transactions, namely, those export

---

3   Panel Report, *EC – Anti-Dumping Duties on Imports of Cotton-type Bed Linen from India*, WT/DS/141/R, para. 6.114.
4   Ibid., para. 6.115.
5   AB Report, *EC – Anti-Dumping Duties on Imports of Cotton-type Bed Linen from India*, WT/DS/141/AB/R, para. 53.

transactions involving models of cotton-type bed linen where 'negative dumping margins' were found. Instead, the European Communities treated those export prices as if they were less than what they were. This, in turn, inflated the result from the calculation of the margin of dumping ... Furthermore, we are also of the view that a comparison between export price and normal value that does not take fully into account the prices of all comparable export transactions – such as the practice of 'zeroing' at issue in this dispute – is not a 'fair comparison' between export price and normal value, as required by Article 2.4 and by Article 2.4.2."[6]

EC – Malleable Cast Iron Tube or Pipe Fittings

The next dispute, where the issue of zeroing was challenged, was brought by Brazil. It challenged the European Union for using model zeroing and claimed that the European Union acted inconsistently with Articles 2.4 and 2.4.2 ADA.

The Panel considered the European Union's assertion that zeroing had limited impact on the dumping margin, i.e., 2.72%, to be irrelevant and held that:

> "... the European Communities violated Article 2.4.2 of the Anti-Dumping Agreement by failing to consider the weighted average of 'all comparable export transactions'. **We find support for this finding in the EC – Bed Linen dispute, where the Appellate Body upheld the panel's finding** in that case that the practice of 'zeroing' does not fully take into account the prices of 'all comparable transactions' as required by Article 2.4.2."[7] (Emphasis added)

The Panel in this case thus explicitly referred to and found support in the Appellate Body ruling in EC – Bed Linen. This practice, as we will observe in the following cases, developed further.

US – Softwood Lumber V (Canada)

In this case, Canada challenged the use of model zeroing by the US in the underlying investigation and alleged an inconsistency with Articles 2.4 and 2.4.2 ADA.

Relying on the interpretation of the requirement of Article 2.4.2 by the Appellate Body in EC – Bed Linen, the Panel held that the US acted inconsistently with Article 2.4.2 ADA by not taking into account all comparable export transactions when calculating the overall margin of dumping in the investigation at issue.[8]

On appeal, amongst other issues, the US argued with respect to the relevance of the Appellate Body Report in EC – Bed Linen, by referring to the Appellate Body's statement in Japan – Alcoholic Beverages II, that dispute settlement reports "are not binding, except with respect to resolving the particular dispute between the parties to that dispute". The US therefore claimed that the Ap-

---

6   Ibid., para. 55.
7   Panel Report, EC – Anti-Dumping Duties on Malleable Cast Iron Tube or Pipe Fittings from Brazil, WT/DS219/R, paras. 7.216–7.217.
8   One panelist had a dissenting opinion.

pellate Body report in EC – Bed Linen did not govern the US' appeal and among others, that it was not a party to the dispute in EC – Bed Linen, that the arguments raised in that case were different and that its practice of zeroing was not at issue in that appeal.

The Appellate Body upheld the Panel ruling in that case and confirmed its findings in EC Bed Linen. With regard to the relevance of the EC – Bed Linen Appellate Body report, it did not give any further clarification than available previously on the issue of precedent. The Appellate Body in that case quoted the Appellate Body ruling in Japan – Alcoholic Beverages II that:

> "[a]dopted panel reports are an important part of the GATT acquis. They are often considered by subsequent panels. They create legitimate expectations among WTO Members, and, therefore, should be taken into account where they are relevant to any dispute. However, they are not binding, except with respect to resolving the particular dispute between the parties to that dispute."

Additionally, it also referred to the Appellate Body's clarification in US – Shrimp (Article 21.5 – Malaysia) that:

> "[t]his reasoning [from Japan – Alcoholic Beverages II] applies to adopted Appellate Body Reports as well. Thus, in taking into account the reasoning in an adopted Appellate Body Report – a Report, moreover, that was directly relevant to the Panel's disposition of the issues before it – the Panel did not err. The Panel was correct in using our findings as a tool for its own reasoning."[9]

It is interesting to note the Appellate Body's conclusion in that case which explicitly restricted itself to mentioning that the reasoning and findings of previous Appellate Body had been considered:

> "…bearing these previous findings in mind, and noting Article 3.2 of the Understanding on Rules and Procedures Governing the Settlement of Disputes (the 'DSU')… we have given full consideration to the particular facts of this case and to the arguments raised by the United States on appeal, as well as to those raised by Canada and the third participants. In **doing so, we have taken into account the reasoning and findings contained in the Appellate Body Report in EC – Bed Linen, as appropriate.**"[10] (Emphasis added)

US – Zeroing (EC)

The next case that one would look at is US – Zeroing (EC). This is an important case as regards zeroing and the issue of precedent. The European Union challenged the following in this case – (i) model zeroing as applied, (ii) model zeroing 'as such' (e.g. US practice or methodology of zeroing) and (iii) simple zeroing under the weighted average-to-transaction method in

---

9   AB Report, US – Final Dumping Determination on Softwood Lumber from Canada, WT/DS264/AB/R, para. 111.
10 Ibid., para. 112.

periodic reviews. We will discuss the relevant issues under each of the above-mentioned categories of challenges.

Model Zeroing as Applied in 15 Original Investigations

First, in the context of model zeroing, the Panel held model zeroing to be inconsistent with Article 2.4.2 and found the zeroing in question identical to that challenged in EC – Bed Linen and US – Softwood Lumber V. The Panel in this case decided not to depart from previous Appellate Body findings and noted as follows:

> "[i]n the anti-dumping investigations at issue in this dispute USDOC calculated aggregate margins of dumping in a manner that, with respect to the treatment of weighted-average export prices that were above normal value, was identical in relevant respects to the zeroing methodology considered by the panels and Appellate Body in EC – Bed Linen and US – Softwood Lumber V.
>
> In this respect, we are mindful of our obligations under Article 11 of the DSU. At the same time, we note that the issues raised by the United States regarding the meaning of the term 'margin of dumping' and the relevance of the historical background of Article 2.4.2 of the AD Agreement were addressed by the Appellate Body in US – Softwood Lumber V.
>
> Although previous Appellate Body decisions are not strictly speaking binding on panels, there clearly is an expectation that panels will follow such decisions in subsequent cases raising issues that the Appellate Body has expressly addressed. The Appellate Body has stated that adopted Appellate Body reports should be taken into account where they are relevant to any dispute. In US – Oil Country Tubular Goods Sunset Reviews, the Appellate Body specifically stated that: '… following the Appellate Body's conclusions in earlier disputes is not only appropriate, but is what would be expected from panels, especially where the issues are the same'. We also note that Article 3.2 of the DSU refers to the DSU as 'a central element in providing security and predictability to the multilateral trading system'. Therefore, we do not believe that it would be appropriate for us to depart from the Appellate Body's conclusion…"[11]

Model Zeroing 'as such'

With regard to the 'as such' claims concerning model zeroing, the Panel held that the US zeroing methodology, as it relates to original investigations, is a norm which, as such, is inconsistent with Article 2.4.2 ADA.

The US appealed that the Panel had erred in ruling that the zeroing methodology is a measure challengeable 'as such'. The Appellate Body upheld, albeit for different reasons, the Panel findings, that the use of zeroing while calculating the overall dumping margin using the weighted average-to-weighted average comparison method in original proceedings can be challenged 'as such'.

---

11   Panel Report, US – Laws, Regulations and Methodology for Calculating Dumping Margins (Zeroing), WT/DS294/R, paras. 7.28–7.31.

Simple Zeroing in 15 Periodic Reviews

In this context the Panel held that Article 2.4.2 ADA does not preclude simple zeroing in periodic reviews nor in other reviews. It relied on several Appellate Body reports to interpret the concept of 'investigation' and to conclude that:

> "First, the phrase 'the existence of margins of dumping during the investigation phase' in Article 2.4.2 read in its ordinary meaning in context of the AD Agreement as a whole means that **Article 2.4.2 applies to the phase of the 'original investigation'** i.e. the investigation within the meaning of Article 5 of the AD Agreement, **as opposed to subsequent phases of duty assessment and review. Second, our interpretation of the meaning of this phrase as limiting the applicability of Article 2.4.2 to investigations within the meaning of Article 5 is also consistent with the distinction made between investigations and subsequent proceedings in various Appellate Body decisions.**"[12](Emphasis added)

The Appellate Body in turn overruled the Panel findings on Article 9.3 and did not address the European Union's appeal of the Panel findings on Article 2.4.2, which was conditioned on the Appellate Body affirming the Panel's Article 9.3 findings. The Appellate Body reiterated the findings in EC – Bed Linen and US – Softwood Lumber V and resorted to its reasoning in the latter dispute that dumping is defined in relation to the product as a whole. Thus, multiple comparisons at an intermediate stage are permissible, but a dumping margin is to be established for the product as a whole. Applying this to Article 9.3, the Appellate Body ruled that the dumping margin for an exporter limits the maximum duty that can be levied on the entries of the subject product from that exporter. Thus, a comparison has to be made between the duties collected on all the entries of the subject product from an exporter with that exporter's dumping margin calculated for the product as a whole.

US – Softwood Lumber V (Compliance)

In order to implement the Appellate Body report in the original US – Softwood Lumber V case, the USDOC recalculated the dumping margins. In the new calculations, it used the transaction-to-transaction method and zeroed the non-dumped transactions. Canada challenged the consistency of this with Articles 2.4.2 and 2.4 ADA and relied on the Appellate Body report in the original case.

The Panel rejected Canada's claim; reviewed the scope of the Appellate Body ruling in US – Softwood Lumber V and gave its own reasoning as follows:

> "In the absence of any definition of the phrase 'margins of dumping' in Article 2.4.2, and in the absence of any obligation under the T-T methodology to ensure that 'all comparable export transactions' are represented in a weighted average export price, we see no reason why a Member may not, when applying the transaction-to-transaction comparison methodology, es-

---

12 Ibid., para. 7.220.

tablish the 'margin of dumping' on the basis of the total amount by which transaction-specific export prices are less than the transaction-specific normal values."[13]

"To conclude, neither the ordinary meaning of the first sentence of Article 2.4.2 as a whole, nor the ordinary meaning of the phrase 'margins of dumping' in particular, require that all transaction-specific comparisons under the T-T comparison methodology must be treated as 'intermediate values' and aggregated, without zeroing, in order to arrive at a single margin of dumping for the product as a whole. Nor is such an approach mandated – in the context of the T-T comparison methodology – by the Appellate Body's interpretation of the phrase 'margins of dumping' in US – Softwood Lumber V. Indeed, broader contextual considerations demonstrate that the application of the Appellate Body's interpretation beyond the confines of the W-W comparison methodology would lead to absurd results that could never have been intended by the Appellate Body, let alone the drafters of the AD Agreement."[14]

The Appellate Body reversed the Panel findings and held that the use of zeroing in the transaction-to-transaction method in original investigations violated Article 2.4.2 ADA and relied to a certain extent on the interpretation provided by the Appellate Body in US – Zeroing (EC):

"The text of Article 2.4.2 implies that the calculation of a margin of dumping using the transaction-to-transaction methodology is a multi-step exercise in which the results of transaction-specific comparisons are inputs that are aggregated in order to establish the margin of dumping of the product under investigation for each exporter or producer. Contrary to the United States' submission, the results of the transaction-specific comparisons are not, in themselves, 'margins of dumping'.

Furthermore, the reference to 'export prices' in the plural, without further qualification, suggests that all of the results of the transaction-specific comparisons should be included in the aggregation for purposes of calculating the margins of dumping. In addition, the 'export prices' and 'normal value' to which Article 2.4.2 refers are real values, unless conditions allowing an investigating authority to use other values are met. Thus, in our view, zeroing in the transaction-to-transaction methodology does not conform to the requirement of Article 2.4.2 in that it results in the real values of certain export transactions being altered or disregarded."[15]

"In sum, the results of the transaction-specific comparisons cannot be considered margins of dumping within the meaning of Article 2.4.2. The 'margins of dumping' established under the transaction-to-transaction comparison methodology provided in Article 2.4.2 result from the aggregation of the transaction-specific comparisons. Article 2.4.2 does not permit an investi-

---

13 Panel Report, *US – Final Dumping Determination on Softwood Lumber from Canada (Article 21.5)*, WT/DS264/RW, para. 5.28.
14 Ibid., para. 5.65.
15 AB Report, *US – Final Dumping Determination on Softwood Lumber from Canada (Article 21.5)*, WT/DS264/AB/RW, paras. 86–87.

gating authority, when aggregating the results of transaction-specific comparisons, to disregard transactions in which export price exceeds normal value."[16]

US – Zeroing (Japan)

In this case multiple zeroing types under different methodologies were challenged as can be observed from the table below.

AD Investigation	Zeroing Type	Zeroing Method	WTO Challenge	Panel Decision	Appellate Body Decision
Original Investigations	Zeroing Procedures	T-by-T & WA-to-T	As such	Challengeable Measure	Upheld
Original Investigations	Model & Simple	T-by-T & WA-WA	As such	Model zeroing inconsistent with Article 2.4.2; simple zeroing not inconsistent with Articles 2.4.2 & 2.4	Inconsistent with Articles 2.4.2 & 2.4
Original Investigations	Model	WA-WA	As applied	Inconsistent with Article 2.4.2	Inconsistent with Article 2.4.2
Periodic Reviews	Simple	WA-to-T	As such	Not inconsistent with Articles 2.4.2 & 9.3	Violates Articles 2.4 & 9.3
Periodic Reviews	Simple	WA-to-T	As applied	Not inconsistent with Articles 2.4.2 & 9.3	Violates Articles 2.4 & 9.3
New Shipper Reviews	Simple	WA-to-T	As such	Not inconsistent with Articles 2.4.2 & 9.5	Violates Articles 2.4 & 9.5
Sunset Reviews	Simple	WA-to-T	As applied	Not inconsistent with Articles 2 & 11.3 ADA	Inconsistent with Art 11.3

We will discuss the main issues under the relevant headings below.

Simple Zeroing as such in Original Investigations, Periodic and New Shipper Reviews
The Panel held that simple zeroing 'as such' is permissible in original investigations, periodic and new shipper reviews. This Panel, while finding simple zeroing 'as such' permissible in original investigations, explicitly noted that *"while we recognize the important systemic considerations in favour of following adopted panel and Appellate Body reports, we have decided not to adopt that approach"*, for the specific reasons noted in the report. Among others, the Panel clarified that Japan's extension of the Appellate Body's findings in US – Softwood Lumber V of "product as a whole" to the context of simple zeroing is not acceptable. Additionally, concurring with the Panel in US – Softwood Lumber V (Compliance), this Panel held that the use of the word 'product' in these provisions does not preclude the possibility of establishing a dumping margin on a transaction-specific basis.

---

16   Ibid., at para. 94.

The Panel concluded that the fact that *"the terms 'dumping' and 'margin of dumping' in Article 2.1 and Articles VI:1 and VI:2 are defined in relation to 'product' and 'products', does not warrant the conclusion that these terms, by definition, cannot apply to individual transactions and inherently require an examination of export transactions at an aggregate level in which the same weight is accorded to export prices that are above normal value as to export prices that are below normal value."* The Panel also noted that the text of Article 2.4.2 *"does not support"* the view that the ADA and GATT Article VI *"must be interpreted to mean that there exists a general prohibition of zeroing"* and if zeroing is generally prohibited under Article 2.4.2, the results of the average-to-average method would not differ from those of the average-to-transaction method, which would undermine the rationale of that latter method.

The Panel, furthermore, concurred with the analysis of the panel in US – Zeroing (EC) that the applicability of Article 2.4.2 is limited to investigations within the meaning of Article 5 of the ADA. It considered that the fair-comparison obligation in the first sentence of Article 2.4 ADA is an independent obligation and there is no Appellate Body report rendering zeroing inconsistent with Article 2.4 on its own. Moreover, concurring with the Panel in US – Zeroing (EC), it held that the fair-comparison requirement cannot be interpreted to generally prohibit zeroing.

Therefore, while complying with the obligation to make an objective assessment of the matter in question, the Panel referred to and concurred with the ruling of the previous panels, notably the Panel in US – Zeroing (EC).

Regarding simple zeroing 'as such' in periodic and new shipper reviews, in addition to the reasoning in the context of Articles 2.1 and 2.4.2 ADA, the Panel relied on the US – Zeroing (EC) panel's reasoning on several points. Notably with regard to Article 9.3 it held that this article requires the limiting of the duty amount to the dumping margin established under Article 2, and the obligation to pay the duty is on the importer on an import-specific basis. The latter obligation would be violated if the dumping margin is calculated by an aggregation of export prices during a review period without zeroing. According to the Panel, notably in a retrospective duty-assessment system, a member may be precluded from collecting duties in respect of the lower-than-normal-value export transactions of a particular importer at a particular point of time because the prices of export transactions to other importers exceed normal value at a different point in time. The Panel concluded that Article 9.3:

> *"Especially when interpreted in light of the express reference to a prospective normal value system in Article 9.4 (ii), lends further support to the view that it is permissible within the meaning of Article 17.6 (ii) of the AD Agreement to interpret Article VI of the GATT 1994 and the relevant provisions of the AD Agreement to mean that there is no general requirement to determine dumping and margins of dumping for the product as a whole, which, by itself or in*

conjunction with a requirement to establish margins of dumping for exporters or foreign producers, entails a general prohibition of zeroing."[17]

Per the Panel, even if it is assumed *arguendo* that Article 2.4.2 could be construed as prohibiting zeroing under any comparison method, it would still not uphold Japan's claim because Article 2.4.2 cannot be interpreted to be applicable to reviews under Articles 9.3 and 9.5. On this point as well, the Panel relied on the reasoning of the Panel in *US – Zeroing (EC)*. Accordingly, the Panel found no violation with regard to simple zeroing as applied in periodic and new shipper reviews.

The Appellate Body reversed all of the Panel's findings regarding the consistency of simple zeroing as such and as applied in original investigations, and regarding periodic and new shipper reviews. The Appellate Body found "*no reason to depart*" from its findings in *US – Softwood Lumber V (Compliance)* and relied on reasoning that "*the text of Article 2.4.2 indicates that the calculation of a margin of dumping using the T-T comparison methodology is a multi-step exercise in which the results of transaction-specific comparisons are inputs that are [to be] aggregated in order to establish the margin of dumping of the product under investigation for each exporter or producer and in aggregating the results of transaction-specific comparisons*".[18] The Appellate Body considered that an investigating authority may not disregard the results of comparisons in which export prices are above normal value and that the absence of the phrase "*all comparable export transactions*" in the context of the transaction-by-transaction comparison methodology does not suggest that zeroing should be permissible under that methodology.

The Appellate Body found inconsistency with Articles 9.3 and 9.5 ADA based on the *US – Zeroing (EC)* Appellate Body's reasoning that "dumping" and "dumping margins" can only exist at the level of a product, and the dumping margin acts as a ceiling for the total amount of anti-dumping duties that can be collected in both duty-assessment systems. It suggested a hybrid methodology and rejected the mathematical equivalence argument on the ground that an investigating authority is obliged to aggregate the results of all transaction-specific comparisons and the export transactions would be more limited in the Article 2.4.2 second sentence (as they would be limited to the ones falling within the particular pricing pattern).

The Appellate Body also held that zeroing in administrative and new-shipper reviews is inconsistent with Article 2.4 ADA based on the *US – Zeroing (EC)* Appellate Body's reasoning as it leads to the collection of anti-dumping duties in excess of the dumping margin and contravenes the fair-comparison obligation.

Simple Zeroing as Applied in Sunset Reviews

The Panel did not find zeroing as applied in the sunset review investigations in question to be inconsistent with Articles 2 and 11.3. The reason was that the margins of dumping relied upon by USDOC were margins calculated during periodic reviews and not those calculated in orig-

---

17 Panel Report, *US – Measures Relating to Zeroing and Sunset Reviews*, WT/DS322/R, para. 7.209.
18 AB Report, *US – Measures Relating to Zeroing and Sunset Reviews*, WT/DS322/AB/R, para. 120.

inal investigations. Given its earlier finding that the ADA *"does not proscribe simple zeroing in periodic reviews within the meaning of Article 9.3"*, it held that relying on dumping margins calculated in periodic reviews on the basis of simple zeroing did not violate the ADA.

The Appellate Body reversed the above Panel finding. It recalled its finding in the case *US – Corrosion-Resistant Steel Sunset Reviews* that when investigating authorities rely on past dumping margins in making their likelihood determination in a sunset review, these margins must be consistent with Article 2.4 and noted that the Panel had found that the USDOC relied on past margins that were calculated during periodic reviews on the basis of simple zeroing. Therefore, having previously concluded that zeroing in periodic reviews is inconsistent with Articles 2.4 and 9.3, the Appellate Body found the determinations in the sunset reviews at issue to be inconsistent with Article 11.3.

US – Stainless Steel (Mexico)

This case is very important from the point of view of the topic of today's discussion. In this case, Mexico challenged (i) model "Zeroing Procedures" as such and as applied in the original investigation; (ii) simple "Zeroing Procedures" (weighted average-to-transaction comparison methodology) as such and as applied in five periodic reviews.

Model "Zeroing Procedures" as such and as Applied
The Panel held model "Zeroing Procedures" to be inconsistent as such with Article 2.4.2 ADA and accordingly also upheld the as applied claim. While recalling the panel decisions in *EC – Bed Linen*, *EC – Tube or Pipe Fittings*, *US – Softwood Lumber V*, *US – Zeroing (Japan)*, *US – Shrimp (Ecuador)* and the Appellate Body decisions in *EC – Bed Linen* and *US – Softwood Lumber V*, and noting that the issue was the same as the one addressed by the Appellate Body in *US – Softwood Lumber V*, it "only partially" agreed with the Appellate Body's reasoning with respect to the consistency with Article 2.4.2 ADA, although it came to the same conclusion.

Simple "Zeroing Procedures" as such and as Applied in Periodic Reviews
In the context of simple "Zeroing Procedures" as such and as applied in periodic reviews, the Panel first discussed the "significance of WTO jurisprudence". It referred to the cases *US – Zeroing (EC)* and *US – Zeroing (Japan)*, where the WTO-consistency of simple zeroing in periodic reviews was questioned before the panels. In both cases, while panels found this practice not to be inconsistent, the Appellate Body reversed the decisions of both panels. The Panel made it clear that it is not bound by Appellate Body decisions:

> "We recall that we are not, strictly speaking, bound by previous Appellate Body or panel decisions that have addressed the same issue, i.e. simple zeroing in periodic reviews, which is before us in these proceedings. There is no provision in the DSU that requires WTO panels to follow the findings of previous panels or the Appellate Body on the same issues brought before them. In principle, a panel or Appellate Body decision only binds the parties to the relevant dispute. Certain provisions of the DSU, in our view, support this proposition."[19]

Referring to prior Appellate Body reports on the question of precedent including the Appellate Body's opinion in US – OCTG Sunset Reviews that *"following the Appellate Body's conclusions in earlier disputes is not only appropriate, but is what would be expected from panels, especially where the issues are the same"*, the Panel considered that:

> "This indicates that even though the DSU does not require WTO panels to follow adopted panel or Appellate Body reports, **the Appellate Body de facto expects them to do so to the extent that the legal issues addressed are similar.**"[20] (Emphasis added)

The Panel knowingly decided to follow the reasoning of the Panels in US – Zeroing (EC) and US – Zeroing (Japan), understanding that those Panel rulings were reversed by the Appellate Body. The Panel noted that it was compelled to disagree with the Appellate Body based on its analysis stemming from its own appreciation of the facts and the legal arguments presented by the parties in the case, in pursuance of its obligation under Article 11 DSU to carry out an objective examination of the matter. It thus concluded that simple zeroing is not inconsistent with GATT Articles VI:1 and VI:2 and ADA Articles 2.1 and 9.3.

The Panel disagreed with the Appellate Body's views that *"the margin of dumping has to be determined for the product under consideration as a whole"* and reasoned that Articles VI:1 and VI:2 of the GATT 1994 and Article 2.1 ADA do not *"compel a definition of 'dumping' based on an aggregation of all export transactions"* and that those provisions do not *"exclude an interpretation that allows the concept of dumping to exist on a transaction-specific basis"*. With regard to the Appellate Body's view that dumping has to be calculated for individual exporters or foreign producers subject to such proceeding, implying that the margin of dumping calculated for the product under consideration as a whole *"operates as the ceiling for the anti-dumping duties that may be collected from importers of that product"*, it reasoned that duties are paid by importers and the importer-or transaction-specific character of the payment of duties must be considered in interpreting Article 9.3. The Panel emphasized that *"an importer does not incur liability for the payment of anti-dumping duties on the basis of the totality of exports made by an exporter"* and that Articles 9.3.1 and 9.3.2 must be interpreted in this light. On the lines of the Panel in US – Zeroing (EC), this Panel also reasoned that an interpretation of the relevant treaty provisions that prohibits zeroing in all contexts would render the exceptional comparison method *"inutile"*.

---

19 Panel Report, *US – Final Anti-dumping Measures on Stainless Steel from Mexico*, WT/DS344/R, para. 7.102.
20 Ibid., para. 7.105.

The Appellate Body reversed the Panel's findings in line with the reasoning of the Appellate Body in *US – Zeroing (EC)* and *US – Zeroing (Japan)*. The Appellate Body held that – pursuant to Articles VI:1 and VI:2 GATT 1994, and various ADA provisions – (i) "dumping" and "margin of dumping" are exporter-specific concepts and "dumping" is product-related, (ii) "dumping" and "margin of dumping" have the same meaning throughout the ADA, (iii) an individual margin of dumping is to be established for each investigated exporter, and the amount of duty levied in respect of an exporter shall not exceed its margin of dumping and (iv) the purpose of an anti-dumping duty is to counteract "injurious dumping" and not "dumping" *per se*. The Appellate Body held that:

> "The notion that 'a product is introduced into the commerce of another country at less than its normal value' in Article VI:1 of the GATT 1994 suggests that the determination of dumping with respect to an exporter is properly made not at the level of individual export transactions, but on the basis of the totality of an exporter's transactions of the subject merchandise over the period of investigation and if it were permissible to determine a separate margin of dumping for each individual transaction, several margins of dumping would exist for each exporter and for the product under consideration."[21]

The Appellate Body saw "*no basis in Article VI:2 of the GATT 1994 or in Articles 2 and 9.3 of the Anti-Dumping Agreement for disregarding the results of comparisons where the export price exceeds the normal value when calculating the margin of dumping for an exporter.*"[22]

In response to Mexico's claim under Article 11 DSU concerning the Panel's failure to follow previous adopted Appellate Body reports addressing the same issues, the Appellate Body clearly outlined that it is well settled that Appellate Body reports are not binding, "*except with respect to resolving the particular dispute between the parties*" but this does not mean that subsequent panels are free to disregard the legal interpretations and the *ratio decidendi* contained in previous Appellate Body reports adopted by the DSB.[23] While criticizing the Panel's approach, the Appellate Body systematically delineated that:

- Previous panel reports (*Japan – Alcoholic Beverages II*), Appellate Body reports (*US – Shrimp (Article 21.5- Malaysia)*) are part of the GATT acquis, create legitimate expectations and should be taken into account where relevant to the dispute, and referred to the *US – OCTG Sunset Reviews* Appellate Body finding in this context.

- WTO Members attach significance to reasoning provided in previous panel and Appellate Body reports.

---

21 AB Report, *US – Final Anti-dumping Measures on Stainless Steel from Mexico*, WT/DS344/AB/R, para. 98.
22 Ibid., para. 103.
23 Ibid., para. 158.

- When enacting or modifying laws and national regulations pertaining to international trade matters, WTO Members take into account the legal interpretation of the covered agreements developed in adopted panel and Appellate Body reports.

- Legal interpretation embodied in adopted panel and Appellate Body reports becomes part and parcel of the *acquis* of the WTO dispute settlement system.

- Ensuring "security and predictability" in the dispute settlement system, as contemplated in Article 3.2 DSU, implies that, absent cogent reasons, an adjudicatory body will resolve the same legal question in the same way in a subsequent case.

- In the hierarchical structure contemplated in the DSU, panels and the Appellate Body have distinct roles to play and to strengthen the dispute settlement system in the multilateral trading system: The Appellate Body was established as a standing body.[24]

It is relevant to note that the Appellate Body also clarified the scope of its authority pursuant to Article 17.6 of the DSU, to review "*issues of law covered in the panel report and legal interpretations developed by the panel*" and accordingly, per Article 17.13 of the DSU, to "*uphold, modify or reverse*" the legal findings and conclusions of panels. It concluded that although it did not find a violation of Article 11 DSU by the Panel, it had deep concern about the Panel's decision to depart from well-established Appellate Body jurisprudence clarifying the interpretation of the same legal issues. The Appellate Body noted that the Panel's approach has serious implications for the proper functioning of the WTO dispute settlement system.

The Appellate Body in this case, therefore, clarified the effect of precedent to some extent in the following words:

> "The creation of the Appellate Body by WTO Members to review legal interpretations developed by panels shows that Members recognized the importance of consistency and stability in the interpretation of their rights and obligations under the covered agreements. This is essential to promote 'security and predictability' in the dispute settlement system, and to ensure the 'prompt settlement' of disputes. **The Panel's failure to follow previously adopted Appellate Body reports addressing the same issues undermines the development of a coherent and predictable body of jurisprudence clarifying Members' rights and obligations under the covered agreements as contemplated under the DSU.** Clarification, as envisaged in Article 3.2 of the DSU, elucidates the scope and meaning of the provisions of the covered agreements in accordance with customary rules of interpretation of public international law. **While the application of a provision may be regarded as confined to the context in which it takes place, the relevance of clarification contained in adopted Appellate Body reports is not limited to the application of a particular provision in a specific case.**"[25](*Emphasis added*)

---

24 Ibid., para. 161.
25 Ibid., para. 161.

US – Shrimp (Ecuador)

This case is relatively straightforward where the Panel followed the reasoning of the Appellate Body in the cases discussed above. In this case Ecuador challenged model zeroing by the US in an original investigation and relied upon the Appellate Body ruling in US – Softwood Lumber V.

The Panel noted that while it is not strictly speaking bound by the Appellate Body's reasoning in US – Softwood Lumber V, it is *"reminded that adopted Appellate Body Reports create legitimate expectations among WTO Members,"* and that *"following the Appellate Body's conclusions in earlier disputes is not only appropriate, but is what would be expected from panels, especially where the issues are the same"*. While holding that the US acted inconsistently with Article 2.4.2 ADA, the Panel considered that:

> *"Thus, in our view, **there is now a consistent line of Appellate Body Reports, from EC – Bed Linen** to US – Zeroing (EC) that holds that 'zeroing' in the context of the weighted average-to-weighted average methodology in original investigations (first methodology in the first sentence of Article 2.4.2) is inconsistent with Article 2.4.2 …*
>
> *We have, as is our duty, carefully considered the Appellate Body's reasoning in US – Softwood Lumber V and taken into consideration the consistent line of Appellate Body Reports as mentioned in the previous paragraph. **We find the Appellate Body's reasoning persuasive and adopt it as our own** …*
>
> *As a final point, we note that neither the Panel nor the Appellate Body report in US – Softwood Lumber V addressed explicitly the issue of the inconsistency of the 'all others' rate as calculated by the USDOC. In this regard, we consider that our finding that Ecuador has established that the calculation of the margins of dumping for Exporklore and Promarisco was inconsistent with Article 2.4.2 means that the calculation of the 'all others' rate as the weighted average of the individual rates necessarily incorporates this inconsistent methodology."*[26] (Emphasis added)

---

26 Panel Report, US – Anti-Dumping Measure on Shrimp from Ecuador, WT/DS335/R, paras. 7.40-7.42.

US – Continued Zeroing (EC)

In this case, once again different zeroing methods and types used by the US were subject of a challenge by the European Union. The table below provides an overview of the same as well as the Panel and Appellate Body decisions in this case.

AD Investigation	Zeroing Type	Zeroing Method	WTO Challenge	Panel Decision	Appellate Body Decision
Continued use of zeroing methodology in successive proceedings in which duties resulting from the 18 anti-dumping duty orders are maintained			Whether challengeable	Failed to identify specific measures at issue; "outside terms of reference"	Are 'measures' and challengeable
4 Original Investigations	Model	WA-WA	As applied	Inconsistent with Article 2.4.2 ADA	Not appealed
37 Periodic Reviews	Simple	WA-to-T	As applied	29 measures inconsistent with Articles 9.3 ADA and VI:2 GATT 1994	Upheld
				7 measures: EU did not established zeroing has been used	Reversed Panel, completed analysis and found inconsistent with Articles 9.3 ADA and VI:2 GATT 1994
				1 preliminary measure – "outside terms of reference"	Reversed Panel but not found inconsistent – EU challenged "premature"
11 Sunset Reviews	Model	WA-WA	As applied	Inconsistent with Article 11.3 ADA	Upheld
				3 preliminary measures excluded – "outside terms of reference"	Reversed Panel but not found inconsistent – EU challenged "premature"

Model Zeroing in Original Investigations and Sunset Reviews

As regards model zeroing, following the previous panel and Appellate Body findings, the Panel in this case held that model zeroing in original investigations is inconsistent with Article 2.4.2 ADA and agreed with the Appellate Body's reasoning in US – *Softwood Lumber V*. Likewise, the Panel found model zeroing in sunset reviews to be inconsistent with Article 11.3 and relied upon the Appellate Body's reasoning in US – *Zeroing (Japan)*.

Simple Zeroing in Periodic Reviews

The Panel found simple zeroing in periodic reviews to be inconsistent with Articles 9.3 ADA and VI:2 GATT 1994. The Panel's approach in this case was rather reluctant. The Panel made it clear that it was inclined to agree with the US – *Stainless Steel (Mexico)* panel's reasoning that dumping may be determined for individual export transactions. At the same time the Panel noted that the Appellate Body had reversed the US – Stainless Steel (Mexico) panel's findings in this context for the reason that if the above-mentioned reasoning were to be followed, several margins of dumping would exist for each exporter and for the product under consideration and this cannot be reconciled with the interpretation and application of several provisions of the ADA (injury under Article 3; price undertakings under Article 8).

The Panel also noted that it tended toward the view that 'dumping' is not necessarily and exclusively an exporter-specific concept, and found the reasoning of the US – Stainless Steel (Mexico) panel to be persuasive but the Appellate Body had reversed the panel's findings reiterating that dumping is necessarily an exporter-specific concept.

This Panel also shared the concerns of the US and the US – Stainless Steel (Mexico) panel that prohibiting simple zeroing in periodic reviews would favour importers with high margins but the Appellate Body had reversed that finding of the panel. The reasoning being that the prohibition of simple zeroing in periodic reviews does not preclude Members from carrying out an importer-specific inquiry in determining liability for the collection of duties, as long as the duty collected does not exceed the exporter-specific margin of dumping established for the product under consideration as a whole.

Finally, regarding the mathematical equivalence argument this Panel also shared the view of the US –Stainless Steel (Mexico) panel.

Simple Zeroing in Periodic Reviews
Regarding simple zeroing in periodic reviews, this Panel "*generally found the reasoning of earlier panels on these issues to be persuasive*"[27] but considered that it was faced with a situation where the adopted Appellate Body reports consistently reversed the panel findings that simple zeroing in periodic reviews is not WTO-inconsistent. Therefore, it evaluated the systemic question of the role of adopted Appellate Body reports. The Panel recalled the Appellate Body's considerations in *Japan – Alcoholic Beverages II, US – Shrimp (Article 21.5- Malaysia), US – OCTG Sunset Reviews, US – Stainless Steel (Mexico)* and the latter Appellate Body's concern about "*the security and predictability*" of the system. Then, reviewing its own obligations under Article 11 DSU in light of Article 3.2 DSU, it agreed with the Appellate Body that "*security and predictability in the multilateral trading system may also be furthered by the development of consistent jurisprudence and applying it to the same legal questions, **absent cogent reasons to do otherwise***". The Panel noted that:

> "*it is obviously incumbent upon any panel to consider prior adopted Appellate Body reports, as well as adopted panel reports, and adopted GATT panel reports, in undertaking the objective assessment required by Article 11. Prior adopted reports form part of the GATT/WTO acquis, and, as stated by the Appellate Body, create legitimate expectations among WTO Members, and, therefore, should be taken into account where they are relevant.*

---

27   Panel Report, *US – Continued Existence and Application of Zeroing Methodology*, WT/DS350/R, para. 7.169.

> *However, we do not consider that the development of binding jurisprudence is a contemplated element to enable the dispute settlement system to provide security and predictability to the multilateral trading system. Clearly, it is important for a panel to have cogent reasons for any decision it reaches, regardless of whether or not there are any relevant adopted reports, and whether or not the panel follows such reports. An essential part of a panel's task under Article 11 is to explain its objective assessment of the matter before it. ...*" (Emphasis added)

> "*In our view, however, a panel cannot simply follow the adopted report of another panel, or of the Appellate Body, without careful consideration of the facts and arguments made by the parties in the dispute before it. To do so would be to abdicate its responsibilities under Article 11. By the same token, however, neither should a panel make a finding different from that in an adopted earlier panel or Appellate Body report on similar facts and arguments without careful consideration and explanation of why a different result is warranted, and assuring itself that its finding does not undermine the goals of the system.*"[28]

The Panel ultimately concluded that:

> "*In addition to the goal of providing security and predictability to the multilateral trading system, we recall that Article 3.3 of the DSU provides that '[t]he prompt settlement of situations in which a Member considers that any benefits accruing to it directly or indirectly under the covered agreements are being impaired by measures taken by another Member is essential to the effective functioning of the WTO and the maintenance of a proper balance between the rights and obligations of Members'. Given the consistent adopted jurisprudence on the legal issues that are before us with respect to simple zeroing in periodic reviews, we consider that providing prompt resolution to this dispute in this manner will best serve the multiple goals of the DSU, and, on balance, is furthered by following the Appellate Body's adopted findings in this case.*"[29] (Emphasis added)

Therefore, the Panel broke the chain of the predecessor panel rulings on the issue but effectively said that it would be perfectly legitimate for it to deviate from the Appellate Body's jurisprudence, but since the Appellate Body would almost surely overrule it, the result would be a delay in final settlement of the dispute which would be at odds with the goal of promptly settling the dispute.

The Appellate Body started its analysis with an examination of Article 17.6 (ii) of the ADA and reiterated that on the basis of the first sentence of that article, panels adjudicating disputes under the ADA must apply Articles 31 and 32 of the Vienna Convention on the Law of Treaties. It also considered that the second sentence of that article envisages the possibility that application of Articles 31 and 32 may give rise to an "interpretative range." Subsequently, it con-

---

28   Ibid., paras. 7.179–7.181.
29   Ibid., para. 7.182.

secutively considered and rejected the US arguments with respect to the concept of "dumping" and "margins of dumping" in the ADA, implications for importer-specific duty assessment in periodic reviews, discrimination between prospective normal value systems and the US' retrospective duty assessment system, "mathematical equivalence" and the historical background of the dumping concept. It concluded that zeroing is inconsistent with Article 9.3 ADA on the basis of the application of Article 17.6 (ii) first sentence.

With regard to the relevance of prior Appellate Body reports and the European Union's claim of violation of Article 11 DSU by the Panel, it reiterated the reasoning and findings of the Appellate Body in US – Stainless Steel (Mexico). In one of its conditional appeals, the European Union had requested that, if the Panel report were to be construed as finding that a panel can invoke 'cogent reasons' for departing from previous Appellate Body rulings on the same issue of legal interpretation, the Appellate Body modify or reverse such a panel finding for the reason that only the Appellate Body itself should have the power to invoke such cogent reasons. The Appellate Body considered that it did not have to rule on the European Union's conditional appeal because although the Panel report was at places ambiguous, in the end the Panel followed the previous Appellate Body reports and, therefore, appeared "*to have acceded to the hierarchical structure contemplated in the DSU.*"

The Appellate Body's approach regarding the issue of precedent in US – Stainless Steel (Mexico) and in this case, when compared to the US – Softwood Lumber V case, demonstrates a significant shift.

US – Shrimp (Thailand), US – Carrier Bags (Thailand)

In both cases Thailand challenged model zeroing by the US in original investigations and claimed that zeroing in those cases was identical to that considered inconsistent by the Appellate Body in US – Softwood Lumber V.

The Panels in both these cases having established that Thailand had demonstrated that the methodology used by the USDOC was the same in all legally relevant respects as the methodology reviewed by the Appellate Body in US – Softwood Lumber V, adopted the same approach as the US – Shrimp (Ecuador) Panel and took into consideration:

(i) the US – Shrimp (Ecuador) Panel's understanding of US – Softwood Lumber V;

(ii) that there was a consistent line of Appellate Body reports condemning "zeroing" in the context of the weighted average-to-weighted average methodology in original investigations; and

(iii) the fact that following the Appellate Body's conclusions in earlier disputes is appropriate and would be expected from panels, especially where the issues are the same.

Both panels held that Thailand had established a *prima facie* case in both disputes and the US-DOC did not calculate the dumping margins in the investigations concerned on the basis of the "product as a whole" in that it failed to take into account all comparable export transactions in calculating the margins of dumping.

III. Conclusion

Having reviewed the various zeroing cases, the conclusion seems to be that through these cases, while very carefully making clear that there is no precedent in WTO law, for all intents and purposes, the Appellate Body's case law comes very close.

The desirability of this is self-evident. The lack of consistent panel and Appellate Body decision-making would affect the predictability and non-discrimination principles of the WTO and undermine the legitimacy of the prior Appellate Body decisions. For instance, the panel's suggestion in US – Continued Zeroing (EC) that the consistency of zeroing might vary from case to case would create a serious time consistency problem for WTO members. Under the panel's view, it is quite possible that the US could practice zeroing when computing margins for a pasta producer from Italy but be prohibited from using zeroing when computing margins for a pasta producer from Japan. As a result, two firms with identical home and export prices could have dramatically different dumping margins.

Discussion

PARTICIPANT
First, I would like to ask, whether you would say that zeroing is exclusively an importer oriented concept or can zeroing also be made in a purely domestic background? Because I see zeroing more as an entry strategy into markets and not as much a strategy of importing goods or exporting goods.

JUHI SUD
If I understand your question correctly, you would like to know whether zeroing should be integrated as an importer specific concept. Actually, the point is that zeroing cannot be an importer or exporter specific concept. The fact is that an anti-dumping duty is calculated for an exporter and is paid by an importer on import of the goods. That is clear. In the zeroing cases the panel was of the opinion the calculation of a dumping margin is an importer specific concept, whereas, the Appellate Body was of the opposite opinion that it is an exporter specific concept. I am not sure if that was where your question was coming in from. I would still reiterate that the panel said one thing and the Appellate Body said another thing: I would say that it is a matter of interpretation. If you want my personal opinion, I think it is an exporter specific concept, but that is just a personal opinion.

CARL BAUDENBACHER
Thank you all for this very interesting panel. I think at the end of the day one could say that there is clearly no doctrine of stare decisis, but there is something emerging which probably resembles the situation in certain civil law systems, as we have discussed, or also in the courts in Luxembourg.

What strikes me, is first of all the use of language, which is particularly important to the American government. They think that by avoiding certain expressions they can avoid certain principles to emerge. There is certainly something to that. I think the famous Austrian author Karl Kraus once said: *"Language is not the servant of our thoughts but the master"*. Obviously any panel or Appellate Body would have to avoid the use of the notion of precedent. I have seen that judges of the European Court in Luxembourg would speak frankly about their precedents when they write or when they speak. This would be avoided in Geneva and in particular in Washington, D.C. I also once had a discussion with Professor Sacerdotti, the former Chairman of the WTO Appellate Body. He did not even know that the choice of the notion of chairman is such a measure as well: The US government did not want the president of the Appellate Body to be called president; so, they called him chairman in order to downgrade him a little bit.

Over time the effect of all these measures will probably diminish. This is also my experience as a judge of the EFTA Court, which had to struggle in the early years against the claims of the governments that we steal their sovereignty. Over the years, judges become more self-confident and new judges do not even know about these old fights anymore. So, slowly, slowly, this will probably contribute to the development of some sort of a soft precedent system. Because at the end of the day, it is natural and human that if you have made a good experience with something in the past, you would rely on that. It is probably also in order to save energy. You cannot always start from scratch.

RACHEL BREWSTER

I would completely agree that there definitely seems to be this idea that institutions will naturally develop. I think it is naive to think that you can establish a standing body and think that it will act like an ad hoc arbitration panel, that it will not develop its own practices and that it will not develop its own ideas. I think that the United States certainly recognised that an Appellate Body was being formed and, in fact, the United States was a very big advocate of having a dispute settlement institution or understanding. I think early on, the US was much more excited than the European Communities about having a formal system of dispute settlement. The United States in particular, if I remember the negotiating agreements correctly, actually suggested initially the idea of an Appellate Body, which looks a lot like US Courts of Appeals.

I think that the US is trying to at least moderate the development of the Appellate Body and it is doing so through a couple of ways. One is this constant reiteration of the zeroing cases – which was so adequately and in such a nuanced way presented right now – that to some extent the US knows it is going to lose those cases. I do not think that they are even so much concerned about the idea that they are losing, but at this point it is a fight about the fact for them that each case stands on its own. The fact that the US was able to keep having panels agree with them saying, *"we are looking at the text, we think this is a permissible interpretation of the text and there is a specific provision within the anti-dumping agreements saying whenever there is multiple interpretations which everyone in the national government wants, they will be permitted to have it"*. The fact that they kept having panels agree with them made this a point that the United States continued to want to drive home to the Appellate Body. So, they are partly doing this through a litigation strategy.

The other thing that the United States is doing, is, that it is being very careful in who it appoints to or who it nominates to be the American representative to the Appellate Body. The European Community has just recently nominated a fabulous international trade professor, someone known for his jurisprudence and for his scholarly work; who does the United States appoint? They definitely do not appoint professors. They will never appoint a professor. I have no hope of ever being the US nominee to the WTO Appellate Body. Instead, they do not even appoint independent trade lawyers. They appoint long time civil servants.

CARL BAUDENBACHER
There are certain governments in Europe who follow exactly the same pattern when it comes to the ECJ and also to my court.

RACHEL BREWSTER
That is actually something I was not aware of. It is interesting that the United States is not the only one with this trick. But to the extent that they are trying to influence the Appellate Body from the inside, I think that they are dedicated to doing that. Of course, there is the third way, which is, will we ever end up complying with the WTO's opinions to the extent that the US says, that you can create a system of precedent. If we do not agree with it or we think it is an erroneous interpretation of the treaty, we simply will not comply.

AKIO SHIMIZU
I would like to add one thing about the Appellate Body with due respect to what Professor Brewster told us. The Appellate Body, from what I heard, meets from time to time to ensure its collegiality and they discuss their cases among the members. There might be more people making decisions for a particular case than just one chamber of three Appellate Body members. The Appellate Body has its own Secretariat with able lawyers as well, who might be helping the Appellate Body form its institutional memory also.

PARTICIPANT
Professor Baudenbacher said that something is emerging which he would like to call a rule of soft precedent law. So, let me be provocative and inject into the discussion a different notion which is the notion of customary international law. Could it be the case that consistent practice by the WTO tribunals leads to that sort of customary international law and that we are actually witnessing this process already?

RICHARD PLENDER
I am provoked by Professor Baudenbacher's comment to add some remarks on how very far the United States goes in opposing anything which resembles precedent in WTO tribunals. The anecdote that I have to account concerns one of my own reports to which the United States took great exception but for reasons that I am about to give, I am not embarrassed about the exception taken to it. The case was Antigua against the United States. It involved the broadcasting of internet gambling from Antigua to the United States. The issue that occupied both the panel and the Appellate Body most of the time was whether the United States by its positive list had committed itself to allowe access to gambling services. As the United States had committed itself to the provision of television services and the services in question were provided by means of television, neither we nor the Appellate Body had any difficulty in finding that the United States had made the relevant commitment and – although that occupies the greater part of the volume of the case – , it shows no relevant dispute. The United States argument to the contrary, I think, struck us and the Appellate Body as fanciful and one which caught a little surprise that so substantial a state would advance it. The next question was assuming that a commitment had been made, whether there was latitude for any relevant restriction. Now, the rules in GATT governing restrictions, follow word for word Article 36 of the old EC trea-

ty or rather, I should say, Article 36 of the old EC treaty follows GATT because the draftsman of Article 36 adopted the language directly from GATT. Restriction is necessary and has been necessary for the prevention of crime, the protection of the life of humans, animals or plants. The Court of Justice has said that the necessary means must be proportionate. That is to say, that a lesser restriction must not suffice. In our report we did not quote the European Court of Justice knowing that this might cause offence in Washington D.C.. We merely said that a measure in order to be necessary must not exceed that which is proportionate and that a measure is not necessary if a lesser measure will suffice. That statement taken in its abstract was not at all disadvantageous to the United States. Nevertheless, at the Appellate Body it was treated as though it was not short of blasphemous. The trade representative herself appeared to say that the language taken from the European Court was wholly inappropriate. Language used by a quasi federal court of an emerging super national state had nothing to do with international trade. The difference in function between the European Court and the WTO is not something that is entirely past our comprehension. We were concerned only to say that in order for a measure to be necessary, it must exceed that which could achieve similar ends by less drastic restrictions. I do think that was neither a shocking proposition nor one with which the United States would disagree. That the United States would take the matter so seriously as to oppose even an oblique and unidentified reference to another court shows the extremity of sensitivity that the United States has on the point and I am gratified to hear today that the word precedent is prohibited within the offices of the United States trade representative. That explains perhaps the vehemence with which the United States has dealt with that issue in that case.

MICHAEL WAIBEL
Thank you very much. Is there anyone on the panel who would like to offer brief concluding comments in response to these combined questions?

AKIO SHIMIZU
It is possible to say one thing about customary international law. No matter what the panels and the Appellate Body do, they are not exactly state practices. When the time comes for Member States to accept doctrinal precedents as state practices in the WTO, then you might be able to think about customary law. It might also be interesting to think of persistent objectors and if the concept of persistent objection is possible in the context of the WTO dispute settlement procedures.

MICHAEL WAIBEL
Thank you very much. I think the last few questions showed the political sensitivity of this discussion and the political economy behind dispute settlement in the WTO. With that, on behalf of the entire panel, I would like to thank Professor Carl Baudenbacher and Mr. Simon Planzer for this very rich conference and I would like to yield the floor to Professor Carl Baudenbacher to present some concluding comments on the last two days.

Closing Remarks

CARL BAUDENBACHER

Ladies and gentlemen, there is a yellow light for me as well. So, I will be rather brief. I think that we had a very fruitful gathering here in St.Gallen. Obviously, if you talk about the role of precedent, the common law must be the starting point because that is where this doctrine has been established. I have always been an admirer of the open and refined way English, for instance, or American courts would deal with precedent and also of the transparency which is thereby being created. But, there are at least four areas where this tradition does not exist. The countries living under the so-called civil law system, the field of international law, arbitration even to a larger extent and interestingly supranational law as it has emerged in the European Union and in my view also in the European Economic Area. Now, it is quite clear that values like legal security, stability and predictability are important values. That is why I have gotten the feeling that some sort of a precedent system is present in almost every legal order, even in arbitration. In particular, when it comes to public policy issues, I cannot see that commercial arbitrators would easily disregard the established practice of the Supreme Court of the country; at least where the award is to be enforced at the end of the day. There are certain failures in the systems which do not adhere to stare decisis. We have heard yesterday that compliance with higher court rulings is essentially based on extrajudicial factors such as the judge wanting to be promoted. I remember a marvellous article by Richard Posner under the title "What do judges maximise?". He answered himself, the same as everybody else, their utility. Then you may ask the question, what is a judge's utility? Posner says, prestige, power, influence and the chance to climb up the career ladder, but also leisure and to a certain extent moonlighting, he says. Now, in a system which does not adhere to stare decisis, there may be accidents. We heard how it might go in Switzerland that a lower court would avoid following the precedent of the Supreme Court knowing that the litigation value is too low in order for the decision to be challenged at the end of the day. We have also gotten the impression that the ECJ is less elaborate than the European Court of Human Rights. We heard a couple of reasons for that. There are certain fields where also the ECJ is quite open in overruling, but I think they can be counted on two hands at the end of the day. We have heard that the relationship between the ECJ and the European Court of Human Rights may change fundamentally now that the European Union is about to join the Convention. President Mahoney has explained to us that the people in the Union have a certain fear that the Human Rights Court may try to intrude into European Union law. On the other hand, we may use the technique of distinguishing in order to avoid following rulings of a higher court. I am myself familiar with the use of this technique because we are working under homogeneity rules which essentially bind us to follow or at least to take into account ECJ case law. A judge and former chamber president of the ECJ has acknowledged that we have some fantasy when it comes to that and he has called this kind of case law "creative homogeneity case law".

I have said in the discussion after the last panel that I think that also in international courts, and at the end of the day even in the WTO appellate system, there is some sort of a precedent system emerging. I remember, when I met Professor Shimizu for the first time, probably three or four years ago in Tokyo, he asked me the question: *"Do you have a system of precedent in your court?"* It has to do with power, that is quite clear. If you can rely on your own previous decisions, it gives you more legitimacy. In international law, legitimacy must also be acquired and defended against governments. I can tell you, when the EFTA Court started, we had a discussion on this. There were judges who said that we do not quote our own previous decisions. Those were the political appointees. Those were the ones close to the governments. And the ones who wanted to go for a deepening of integration said that we have to do that because it will enhance our legitimacy.

I have to thank many people here, in particular Simon Planzer. I asked him to sit here. He has contributed tremendously to the success of this conference. The speakers know that because he has been in continuous contact with them and I think he deserves a special applause for that.

Then, we had an excellent team here. I may mention Philipp Speitler, Frank Bremer, Felipe Perez-Pose, Michael Hofmann and Moritz Heidecker. A special thanks also goes to three ladies, Melanie Zemp, Patrizia Köbeli and Larissa Ronsiek, who have done a fabulous job in managing the back office of this conference. Finally, I would like to thank the University of Texas School of Law, which to a certain extent, I still consider to be my school as well. If I cut myself in the morning shaving, then I still bleed orange. Thanks to them for their support and their high presence here. As every year, we will publish the proceedings of this conference in a book and we hope to see you again in the upcoming year. I wish you all a safe trip home.

GLP
German Law Publishers
www.germanlawpublishers.com

DREAMING LAW
Comparative Legal Semiotics

by Bernhard Grossfeld
2010, 302 pages, € 148,–
German Law Publishers
ISBN 978-3-941389-05-2

Comparative lawyers have to deal with many questions: What is law at home and abroad, what are legal rules here and there? How can we compare the largely unknown?

The author answers as follows: Law is not fully explainable or understandable in scientific terms. It is part of a people's identity as an imagined community and stands for a common dream, e.g. an American dream or a German dream.

Geography and communications with signs form these dreams. Guided by Semiotics, the theory and study of signs and symbols, Grossfeld describes how the physical world and the networks based on particular signs (language, letters, numbers and pictures) interact with each other. They build our mental framework and influence the content of our thoughts – expressed in social behavior and interaction, some parts of which we call law.

In various chapters Grossfeld decodes the connections of religion, literature, poetry, music and mathematics with law. His perceptions are substantiated by many quotations. With this book comparative lawyers get precious insights and support for their work.

Please order at your convenient bookshop or go to www.germanlawpublishers.com

SWEET & MAXWELL  THOMSON REUTERS  BOORBERG

GLP
German Law Publishers
www.germanlawpublishers.com

THE EFTA COURT IN ACTION

Five lectures
written by Professor Dr. Carl Baudenbacher, President of the EFTA Court, Director of the Institute of European and International Business Law at the University of St. Gallen, Visiting Professor at the University of Iceland
2010, 180 pages, € 48,–
German Law Publishers
ISBN 978-3-941389-04-5

The book is based on lectures the author gave at the University of Iceland School of Law in 2009. Its aim is to explain the working and the case law of the EFTA Court in view of its embeddedness in the institutional framework of the Agreement on the European Economic Area. Although Europe is a special case with regard to the judicialisation of law, Baudenbacher's insight and his conclusions may contribute to a better understanding of the functioning of international courts in general.

INTERNATIONAL DISPUTE RESOLUTION

Volume 2
Dialogue Between Courts in Times of Globalization and Regionalization
edited by Professor Dr. Carl Baudenbacher
2010, 244 pages, € 98,–
German Law Publishers
ISBN 978-3-941389-06-9

The topic of the 2nd St. Gallen »International Dispute Resolution Conference« was »Judicial dialogue« from various perspectives. The conference featured outstanding speakers with rich experience in their respective fields. They shared their views on judicial dialogue from a wide array of professional backgrounds: as academics, counsels, judges or arbitrators.

DISPUTE RESOLUTION

edited by Professor Dr. Carl Baudenbacher
2009, 360 pages, € 98,–
German Law Publishers
ISBN 978-3-941389-03-8

The »International Dispute Settlement Conference«, which was held for the third time in the last few years, was hosted by the City of St. Gallen, which followed in the steps of Austin, TX, and Salzburg. Renowned experts from all over the world attended the International Dispute Settlement Conference to discuss and debate the newest developments in the field of Dispute Resolution. Dispute Resolution touches upon key aspects of law, politics and business, which alludes to its practical significance and its high grade of interdisciplinarity, a feature that the University of St. Gallen holds very dear.

Please order at your convenient bookshop or go to www.germanlawpublishers.com

SWEET & MAXWELL   THOMSON REUTERS   BOORBER